MOORING AT
THE MILLRACE

SUSAN RAU STOCKER

SUSAN RAU STOCKER

Printed Worldwide
First Printing 2023
First Edition 2023

ISBN:

979-8-218-27250-0

10 9 8 7 6 5 4 3 2 1

DEDICATION

Mooring at the Millrace is gratefully dedicated to all the "characters" you'll read about within these pages – the good, the bad, the wounded and the warriors. Each brought unique threads that created the quilt which was our family, our village, our community, our lives, woven from our ancestral heritage at this window of time that no longer exists, in this serene, sustaining place too few of us were privileged to know. Those were the days, my friends. Let me share them with you. We are all stronger, kinder, more tolerant for remembering, encountering, or re-visiting our Mooring at the Millrace.

"I remember the time I knew what happiness was.
Let the memory live again."

BARBRA STREISAND – "MEMORY"

Contents

PART ONE

MOORING AT THE MILLRACE

I made my big splash when I was two. I dashed across the street in front of our house in what previously had been the laconic village of Durham, Pennsylvania, population 75. Sadly, no one had a cell phone in those days, or the video would have gone viral. Apparently, after a small body starts rolling down a slick, grassy, fifty-foot slope, it picks up speed rapidly. I landed unceremoniously in the millrace at the bottom of the hill.

For the next three years, my mother didn't let me toddle off our property unless I was on a leash. She called it my "harness." Horse imagery was so much more dignified than dog imagery.

Okay, she was traumatized. I left her side. I ran into the road. And my rapid descent down the hill -- missing the huge oak tree by millimeters -- landed my two-foot-tall self in four feet of water.

She was even more traumatized, my always spick-and-span mother, because she didn't know how to swim and hated water.

Nevertheless, into that muddy-bottomed muck she jumped to fish me out. She was a noble mother.

She carried a screaming and inconsolable little girl up the hill. I scared myself at least as much as I scared her. She ran, dripping, muddy, and wet, across the street, up the steps in front of our house, into the house, up to the second story, and into the bathroom. Mud, muck, goop, gunk everywhere.

Two was definitely not my best year. I caught a virulent case of measles, causing a fever which spiked to 105 for five days in a row. Monsters and demons visited, which the whole village heard. I did not suffer such terror silently.

When the nightmares departed and the fever receded, my parents noticed something disturbing: before the unrelenting fever, I had clear blue eyes which looked straight at them and focused on them. Afterwards, they were left with a cross-eyed little girl. Both my mother and I hated the glasses I had to wear in an effort to straighten my vision. I protested confinement of any kind. I was already on a leash, for heaven's sake. Now glasses? She hated having to try to keep them on me!

Also, at two I had a run-in with a sparkler on the Fourth of July, but we'll get to that when we talk about Uncle Hollis.

Our home in Durham, built on a hill, had a beautiful five-foot-tall stone retaining wall in front of it to keep the house from tumbling into the millrace. I might have had a few problems learning to navigate that wall safely. I'm sure my parents regretted buying me a tricycle because I rode that little blue trike right over that five-foot wall, landing on the street and bashing the back of my head. I also rode it down the stone steps in front of the house, landing on the same street, but bashing the front of my head that time. My folks had Dr. Nadeau from nearby Riegelsville on retainer. Between my brother Skip's ear infections and my impetuosity, Dr. Nadeau made a lot of house calls for the two children of Miriam and Dave Rau.

Despite these dramatic, self-destructive events, the first five years of my life were lovely. Easy. Happy. Safe. Secure.

I was a wild child, exuberant and very fast on my feet. Glasses didn't slow me down; a leash/harness didn't slow me down. But when I was five, the eye doctor decided I needed surgery to correct the issue measles had created.

My parents took me to Wills Eye Hospital in Philadelphia. It was the premier hospital for eye surgery in the United States in 1951. In the far reaches of my memory, I can still hear myself screaming as they wheeled me down the hall to the operating room. I was screaming my little, terrified head off.

When the surgery was over, I was blindfolded in a ward where I could hear, but not see, other people. Every afternoon I was forced to drink castor oil. The highlight of the day was the chocolate cookie I got if I managed to swallow the slick, thick, oily fluid. I talked to— although I couldn't see through my bandaged eyes-- my mother and grandmother once in the two-week period. (It was a two-hour trip by car and train.) My parents were advised to come only once. "She'll never remember," the doctors and nurses assured them. Is there a difference between not remembering and never forgetting?

By the time I was released from two weeks of blindfolded horror, I was a new girl. No more shenanigans for me. I was not willing to let my mother out of my sight.

On the heels of this, just weeks later, I was sent to school. We had no kindergarten at Durham School, so at five I started in prime time: first grade. To get there, those of us from "town" walked. How my mother ever got me out the door is beyond me. I'm guessing she walked me down to Karen Melchior's house and Karen, my brave alter ego, walked me to school. Karen has always been a gifted talker, so she probably didn't notice I was the color of a Granny Smith apple and silent.

Our walk took us over Cook's Creek, between huge, fertile fields, past Limantour's beautiful stone house on the right, past Mack's house on the left, and into the half-moon driveway in front of the school. From Karen's house, it was probably a third of a mile. On a busy day there might have been one car on the road. I'm sure the walk home was my favorite part of the day.

As far as we knew growing up, the Limantour Family was simply the Limantours. In a 2006 issue of the *Durham Historical Society Newsletter*, the editor interviewed Clarice De Limantour who was 92 at the time and living in what we all thought of as the Limantour's house. Apparently, we Durham folk just shortened their name. In the article, she traces her family back to the Long's, whose names, Wm. and Jane, appear on the Durham Grist Mill with the date 1820. Ms. De Limantour says the date of 1688 had been cut into a stone in front of the family home in which she still lived. Passing that house every day on our way back and forth to school, we were completely oblivious to the fact that it was almost three hundred years old and belonged to people whose actual name we didn't know.

I was pretty much oblivious to everything else, too, except my daily, primary goal: live long enough to get home to my mother! My just-encountered first grade teacher, Miss Jackson, expected me to sit in a classroom for six or seven hours with my mother nowhere to be seen. I did it. I cried every day of first grade. Seriously and sadly, every day. I was still too traumatized to misbehave, so I sat silently, crying. Poor Miss Jackson. She probably quit teaching after that year. I know she never came back to Durham School. For both our sakes, she promoted me to second grade. Luckily, for her (and me), it was before the days of standardized tests.

So, my take-away from first grade was: sit still for prolonged periods of time and cry without making any noise. Enter Mrs. Ross. She wasn't about to let "a lazy, slow learner" like me get away without working. Somehow, in second grade, I learned to read. It wasn't pretty, but I submitted in subdued silence. I don't think I ever got to go out for recess.

To the best of my recollection, I only spoke one time in second grade. Mrs. Ross, not a beauty queen, had gotten her hair permed. I said to her, "You look like a poodle." It was a fact no one could or did dispute. She wrote a note home. There were no consequences, but I remember hearing my father laugh late into the night, my mother shushing him.

Now, I can't say which came first the chicken (my poodle remark) or the egg (Mrs. Ross' disrespect for hair in general). This I can say: fifty-nine years after we left her classroom, we were still talking about her hair issues. Gladys Koder remembered Mrs. Ross picking up more than one of our classmates by the hair when they didn't know the answer to a question. Many of us couldn't forget the time Ronnie Bodder was fooling around with his own hair, probably out of nervous anxiety because he didn't know an answer, and that so-called teacher put a barrette and a bow in his hair and made him wear both on the school bus ride home.

Third grade ushered in a new terror: Mrs. Keller, a woman of substance and girth. Mrs. Keller put construction paper collars around the mouths of any students who spoke. (Mrs. Ross punished us for not speaking; Mrs. Keller punished us if we did speak!) Some kids had to wear those collars almost every day. Sit beside someone who talked or needed help, and you were doomed. If you didn't answer the chit chat or the questions, you were likely to get shoved on the playground. Did you want that, or did you want to choose the color of construction paper for your horse collar?

Due to my training in silence, and my fear of anything and everything that moved, I only wore a Mrs. Keller collar once. She thought I was a quick study. Not really. Totally traumatized into submission was more like it. Mrs. Keller made us wear the collars on the way home, either on the bus, or, for "walkers," we had to keep them on in case she drove past us as she was leaving school. If we weren't wearing the collars and enduring public shame, we had to start over the next day with yesterday's collar back on. I remember we had a girl in our class who had suffered from polio, and, damn, if Mrs. Keller didn't make her wear a collar one day. I hated Mrs. Keller that day. I was only nine, but I knew that that was just plain wrong.

Then came fourth grade and Mr. Litzenberger. Things did not improve in fourth grade. For one thing, Mr. Litzenberger had a long memory. In Durham, Mr. Litzenberger was The Democrat, and my dad, Mr. Rau, was The Republican. That was the first, obvious problem. Then, Mr. Litzenberger had been my brother's teacher seven years before. That had not gone well for either of them. I don't know any details, only that when Mr. Litzenberger read off the names of the students and got to Susan Rau, he looked up, stared into my eyes, and I knew that he knew his name was not spoken in reverence around our kitchen table. He was my father's nemesis, and my father was his, and my brother had done nothing to ease the way for me.

Luckily, I mistakenly believed Mr. Litzenberger was harmless. It turns out Mr. Litzenberger strongly disliked boys and thwacked them on the head and even took them into his back room and used a belt on some of them. I found this out sixty-five years later from one of his victims. At the time, I was just glad my teacher wasn't Mrs. Litzenberger, who had a remarkable similarity in size and volume to Mrs. Keller. Perhaps I missed Mr. Litzenberger's abuse of the boys because this was the year a double tragedy came rushing in on our family. We had much bigger problems than Mr. Litzenberger.

DEATH COMES
IN THE NIGHT

The scene is imprinted on my mind because it is the only time in sixty-two years I ever saw my mother cry. Not when I got married —not either time, though she would have been justified – not when relatives lost their battles with diseases like uterine cancer and demons like Alzheimer's, and not when her dearly loved husband took his last breath. Only this time.

My bedroom was a little alcove between the steps and my parents' front room, and still I might have slept through the sobbing, but she stumbled up the last few steps. My dad caught her. And then she staggered through my bedroom, almost wailing.

My dad motioned my brother to talk to me. "Tell Susan you and she will be going to Aunt Agnes in the morning."

And then the black metal latch fastened their door, and I heard the weeping go on and on.

My brother, who was sixteen, sat on the floor by my bed and started telling me about all the things we'd do when we went to Aunt

Agnes' farm the next day. I have no idea what he said, but somehow his voice lulled me back to sleep.

In the morning, there was Aunt Agnes, efficiently packing a little suitcase for me and whisking me away with some prattle about my parents being busy and that I'd see my mom soon.

I stayed with Aunt Agnes and Uncle Hollis for a week or two. Their farm was like a second home. They told me that Grandad Hindenach died and my parents were straightening things out, whatever that meant. Finally, when I went back to my house in Durham, it was amid so much excitement I could hardly stand it. The renters on the other side of our duplex were moving out. We were moving to that side of the house, and Grandma Hindenach and Aunt Ruth were moving into our side of the house. I wondered if they were scared to live in the house without Grandad.

Grandad Hindenach had not been a "kid" person. He was a tall, fit man with white hair, whom I probably would have guessed to be as old as Rip Van Winkle or God. I don't remember him ever talking to me or teasing with me and certainly not playing with me. Once, though, when he came home from "market," and I awoke from a nap, he handed me a Hershey bar. I don't believe any words were exchanged.

I had no idea Grandad was a brilliant man, a gifted musician, or a person tortured all his life by depression. I had no idea why he died. I was not taken to the funeral. I think I probably stayed with Uncle Hollis at his farm and he let me shine eggplants or sort potatoes. Those were jobs within my nine-year-old skill set.

Soon my father and my mother's younger brother were working non-stop to get the Hindenach farm ready for sale. For a while, probably a couple weeks, my parents, brother, grandmother, aunt and I all lived in one side of the duplex so the side the Rau family would move into could be painted and repaired. I was surely the only one who loved those crowded conditions!

All I cared about was that Gram and Aunt Ruth were accessible twenty-four/seven. Two of my favorite humans in the same house. I think it was then that I took on the role of Little Mary Sunshine. Everyone but me was trying to deal with Grandad's death. Nothing like a clueless little girl wanting to chatter and play games to keep you from screaming out your pain. Life went on, and the details surrounding grandad's death were meticulously kept from me until I was thirty-five years old.

The Hindenach Farm had been a chicken and "truck" farm. Gram explained in one of her journals: "A truck farm, meaning a small farm where one raised vegetables and fruit crops, rather than acres of hay or grain." Gram remembered: "All summer long dad went to market three days a week with loads of produce." This was in addition to the chickens and eggs. Gram's amazing flowers were also a cash crop for the farmers' market in nearby Easton.

They were two college graduates, Grandad and Gram, two teachers who met at church and married on August 11, 1914. Since married women at that time were not permitted to teach, Gram was forced to choose between continuing her teaching career of six years or marrying Grandad. A year after they married, Grandad had "a nervous breakdown." It turned out, as I read Gram's diaries, this was his third episode. The doctors advised both families to pool their resources and help the newlyweds purchase a piece of property. Chicken farming wasn't as stressful as teaching, said the doctors, who, clearly, had never tried either.

To make ends meet, Grandad sold furniture in Easton, the closest "big" town. Grandad also played the organ at Durham Church, the only gig around. By default, he got all the weddings and funerals. Gram worked the farm and raised the four children. It was not easy, pleasant, or stress-free. Their intelligence and college educations had not prepared them for scratching in the dirt and killing chickens.

No one would have traded places with Gram concerning the reason she landed in the other side of our house. In fact, the Christmas before she died, at the age of ninety-six, I asked her what was the hardest thing she had ever gone through. "Grandad's death," she said softly but quickly. At that point I had known the secret for five years. Neither of us ever spoke of it. And, believe me, Gram and I talked about everything; I knew her monsters, and she knew mine. But she never talked to me about the biggest lump in her throat.

Gram left behind more than two dozen journals. In one, she wrote of her decision to quit teaching and marry Grandad: "I thought I was leaving the teaching in the hands of a brilliant young man. I had a rude awakening." I've often wondered how stoic she was when she married Grandad, or if the stoicism was learned because of the marriage. All I know is that by the time she relocated in Durham, she had a "game face" that gave away nothing. I was the fortunate recipient of as much softness as she could muster.

What a time we had. I understand now that I was Gram's reason to get out of bed every morning. When my mom left to go teach, she would shoo me over to Gram's, and Gram and I would play games until it was time for me to go to school. Only once were we so involved in a game that she forgot to watch the clock. She had to call our neighbor, Marie Marshall, to drive me to school that day. (Neither of my grandmothers ever drove a car.) We never again committed that "morning mishap," as she called it.

After school, I came home to Gram. She'd give me a snack, and then she'd sit in her green rocker by the kitchen window while I'd sit cross-legged on the nearest black vinyl kitchen chair, and she'd tell me stories. Endless stories.

Some of our favorite stories were about her four children and the pickles they got into. Aunt Ruth cut off my mother's curls one day when they were supposed to be napping. Uncle Lee got his finger sliced when my mother tried to wield an axe to split wood while he held the log. (He was showing people his scar at my mom's funeral!) There were stories about Gram's girlhood and her sister and brother. She was particularly close with her father and grandfather. We never had a quiz, but I was pretty clear on who was related to whom, where they lived, and which ones were of good character and which ones were simply characters.

Gram's favorite fodder for her tales, though, was clear and away the six years of her teaching, from 1908 until 1914. She remembered every detail. For three years she was assigned to Stout's School, the same school she attended as a girl. Here are some of Gram's girlhood memories as she wrote later in one of her journals:

I remember walking our mile and a half to school. I remember being taken on rainy days. Here again my grandfather got into the act. He liked those 'horse and buggy' trips. I remember the snow storms; drifts as high as a horse; no school until the neighborhood men got together and shoveled a path to drive through. I remember my father hitching two horses to the bob-sled, bundle us in warmly, and bells jingling take off for school, gathering up other children waiting along the way, knowing they could count on a ride.

Gram continues with her memories:

I started Stouts School when I was five [1894] and continued until I was fourteen. There were no rural high schools. The country superintendent gave a test each spring. The year I was fourteen I was ready for this. My grandfather took another girl and myself to Freemansburg for the examination. Grandfather waited for us all day long. Twenty-eight of us took the tests, and when the results were announced, my name was first. My, he was happy. I felt pretty good myself. This was my last trip with him. He died a few months later.

When Gram applied for teaching positions, she asked not to be placed in Stout's School where just a few years earlier she had been in class with some of the children still there. "I kept thinking, 'Man is never without honor save in his own country.' I was soon notified that a school had been assigned to me. It was Stout's. My father encouraged me by telling me, 'Of course, I could do it!'"

Early photo of Stout's School.

Gram, or "Miss Martha," as she was called, had been a natural. She taught in a one room school and taught every grade. She explained how, during planting season, the big boys would be "kept out" for the farm work. "I remember boys as tall as I was, and I'm sure stronger," she explained. She once counted up the number of languages her students spoke at home – six or seven, I'm pretty sure. Most were of Germanic origin. Slavic languages, for example, Polish and Yugoslavian, were also spoken, but she managed to communicate. She told me sometimes the students had to translate if she had a message for the parents, and she was never sure her exact message got through, especially if someone was being reprimanded.

One day she told me this story, which I later found recorded in a diary I had given her for Christmas in 1972. The incident took place in 1909:

I remember a girl who walked about a mile and a half to school, part way on a path through fields. One bitter, cold winter morning, rather scantily dressed for such weather, she waded snow drifts, came in crying, she was so cold. We helped her get her snowy clothes off, rubbed her frosted hands and feet to help warm her up. Just about three years ago, [1969] this girl, now a seventy-year-old widow, called me up. She said, 'Do you remember me? Do you remember the morning I came to school half-frozen?' It gives one a good feeling to be remembered like that after all these years.

Gram also remembered the boy who always came late because he hated arithmetic which started at 9:15 a.m.

I came to the conclusion that this was truancy, so I tried my own cure without saying a word to him. I considered each missed class a ¼ day of absence, so by the end of the month it added up to two or three absent days to put on his report card. Of course, his father wanted an explanation; after that, no more skipped arithmetic classes.

(I find Gram's "of course the father wanted an explanation" particularly interesting. When I was teaching high school from 1967-1969, I couldn't take for granted a parent's interest or involvement. Assuming parental concern is even less assured now in 2022—113 years later.)

Gram wrote about the beginning of a school day around 1909. She would have been twenty years old. (She finished high school at sixteen and graduated from college at nineteen.) Here she remembers opening exercises:

I remember, I think with pride, the opening exercises we had each day. When school was called to order at 9 a.m., all the children took their seats promptly (most of the time – we weren't perfect). They waited quietly to have a song announced. This first song was the hymn type, then followed a short Bible reading and prayer, after which we sang two more songs –Stephen Foster songs, patriotic songs, seasonal songs, ones such as Jingle Bells in winter. The children liked to choose these songs for the day. The older ones felt it a privilege to read the Bible verses; nobody worried whether this interfered with religious freedom. Are you getting the idea we spent too much time on 'frills'? This took fifteen minutes each morning and put us in a good frame of mind for the day's work.

(I love her use of the word "we" when she talks about her students. She and her class were a unit, a team!)

Then, to explain some of the changes she witnessed in her lifetime, she told this story:

One day a run-away horse hitched to a drag galloped off the road. The drag – a harrow type implement used for spreading manure-- swayed from side to side and hit a little girl as the horse dashed by. I still remember the little children coming, 'Miss Martha, Susan's hurt.' We got her into the building and I feared immediately her leg was broken. We took her to the nearest home, her aunt. This happened about 8:30 a.m. Compare this procedure with the way it would be done today, that's why I'm telling this. The aunt sent someone to tell her parents (walking). After her mother came, someone asked me to go to a telephone for a Riegelsville doctor. I walked (not too far) to the only telephone in the area. It was after one o'clock until the doctor turned up. He took one look at it, now swollen badly, and said, 'It's broken. Take her to Easton Hospital.' How? They scouted around the neighborhood for a wagon with a long enough body to put a couch in. They found someone to drive trusty horses, and it was about 4 p.m. until they took off.

As a child, I sat spellbound by the stories. She loved remembering, and I loved listening. Now, all these years later, her stories are nuanced with the changes in culture. Our America is not what it was one hundred years ago.

Gram and I were only about six weeks into our new routine when the second fatal trauma hit our family. Grandad was my mother's father and the Hindenach farm was a small, fifteen-acre, hard scrabble operation. My father's older sister, Agnes, had married Hollis Kline, and the Kline Farm was a one hundred and twenty-acre, state-of-the-art fruit and vegetable farm. Everyone who saw it admired it. Everything was as neat as a pin and as green and lush as the advertisements on the fertilizer packages. Uncle Hollis got top dollar for all of his fruit. He worked hard, and he played hard. He was both of good character and a character!

My dad and brother got up in the middle of the night each Friday and drove the three or four miles to the Kline farm to help load the truck for market. They sold every fruit that would grow in eastern Pennsylvania and vegetables like potatoes, cabbage, cauliflower, and eggplant. My brother, who was driving a tractor while most kids his age were still riding bicycles, once told me that many of their customers were Eastern European immigrants who resettled in Easton. They appreciated all that fresh, perfect produce.

When everything was sold, Uncle Hollis and his helpers made the return trip, unloaded the baskets and boxes, and got things ready for the next week. No money ever exchanged hands. My dad was never paid for his help on market day, nor was my brother. It was a family operation. Skip remembers he did get ten cents a bushel for picking potatoes. He said he used to try to pick ten bushels an hour so he could make a dollar an hour. The bonus was he got to drive the tractor, which was invaluable to a teenager's ego.

Here's one of my memories of Uncle Hollis. You'll see the beginning of a theme: he was always saving me from some disaster. I was allowed in the orchard one day, even though I was still too short to pick fruit, so I would have been no help. I'm guessing mom and Aunt Agnes went shopping. They didn't want to bother with me, so Uncle Hollis became the designated babysitter.

I got stung by a bee or a wasp. Uncle Hollis grabbed my arm and spit out a big wad of chewing tobacco, which he happened to have handy in his mouth. I watched the juice run down my arm and drip off my elbow. The wet, slimy tobacco landed right on that growing red welt. I was so surprised, I immediately stopped crying or screaming, whatever I had done to alert him, and I also immediately realized that the sting was entirely gone. I said something like, "It doesn't hurt anymore."

He nodded and dug in his pocket for more chew and quickly got it moistened and ready for the next crisis. I was too grateful to be disgusted by having been spat upon with stinky tobacco.

At the end of a day on the farm, Aunt Agnes reliably prepared a feast. (Aunt Agnes and my mom were alike in this one way: nothing they cooked ever flopped. EVER. I wish I was exaggerating, but I'm not. Nothing was dry or overcooked or burned or mushy. Very little was mixed together. We weren't casserole people. We had meat, potatoes, a vegetable or two, salad, bread and pie.) If Cousin Jackie was home, she let me help her make brownies, which we cooled on the back, stone step outside the kitchen. We all ate with gusto the freshest and best produce of the week and some meat bartered with a nearby farmer in exchange for fruits and vegetables. Then the card table came out and I was put to bed. I loved falling asleep hearing the adults laughing as they played pinochle and told stories.

My mother adored Uncle Hollis. She thought he was hilarious despite being far and away the most irreverent person she knew. She was also deeply indebted to him. When I was two, which, as you might recall, was a year I may have been a little accident prone, someone put a sparkler in my hand on the Fourth of July. I started twirling around so fast that the sash of my dress and the sparkler met in an unfortunate blaze. Uncle Hollis wrestled me to the ground and extinguished me before the blaze intensified. Other than Uncle Hollis, I don't think anyone else moved. Nobody could believe what had happened. I sort of remember him pulling me onto his lap to make sure he hadn't hurt me.

Seven years after that heroic save, Uncle Hollis started coughing and couldn't swallow or digest food. Two months later the doctors discovered that all the residue from the fertilizers, DDT for example, had collected in his lungs and intestinal tract. A 1946 ad proclaimed of DDT: "Let's Put It Everywhere." In 1947 ads assured, "DDT: So

Safe You Can Eat It." The city of San Antonio, Texas, sprayed the streets and the streams of San Antonio with DDT to protect children from polio.

Why would a Pennsylvania orchard keeper not use DDT to keep the bugs from his fruit trees? No one could prove it, but our family never doubted that the daily inhalation of DDT, which had made the farm a showplace and the fruit so spectacular, had killed him.

My father had no sooner organized and sold the Hindenach farm when he started on the Kline farm.

I stood with Gram on our front porch and watched an endless parade of cars pass through Durham on their way up the hill to the church cemetery. There wasn't even a tombstone on Grandad's grave, and already the dirt was turned over for Uncle Hollis. It must have been frightful for Gram to watch, but that stoic face of hers never gave any clue. My parents surely were devastated, not to mention mentally, physically and emotionally exhausted. They simply kept doing what needed to be done. At nine I remained clueless and sheltered.

It was years before my mom started telling me Uncle Hollis stories--and even more years before she started using his exact, colorful language when she told them. My mom had a spiritual struggle when Uncle Hollis died because someone, I never knew who, had intimated to her that being the non-church-going, irreverent person he was, he was not going to gain admittance into heaven.

My mom maintained that Uncle Hollis was one of the kindest and most morally upright people she had ever known, and she didn't think much of a heaven which wouldn't admit him. In fact, she didn't want to go to any heaven he wasn't going to be inhabiting. Apparently, it was someone at church who proclaimed this opinion because I don't think my mom was ever as enthusiastic about church after that.

Thirty-two years later, when my parents moved from the house in Durham to Westminster Village, the life care center in Allentown, we took down the last few bottles of moonshine Uncle Hollis had made and poured them down the sink. (That must have opened the drains!) That fabulous, perfect fruit, acre after acre of grapes, apples. apricots, cherries and quinces, had apparently made some mighty fine, strong drink.

Aunt Agnes would go on to be a widow for thirty-five years. This ate at my heart, and when I was in my thirties, I was in a discount store in Akron, Ohio and saw a plain, ordinary brown teddy bear about two feet tall and fluffy. I stood transfixed, looking at the teddy bear, and Aunt Agnes popped into my mind. Now buying a teddy bear for Aunt Agnes was among the riskiest things I probably ever did in my life. Aunt Agnes was a realist with not a bit of whimsy in her soul.

We have a picture of her opening the Christmas wrapping. She sat in shock. Then she shocked all of us by hugging the teddy bear. She loved that teddy bear. It was the only one she ever had. He sat on her bed every day for the rest of her life. When she died, my mom brought that teddy bear to me, and to this day, I love that teddy bear.

Aunt Agnes and her teddy bear.

THE AFTER-SHOCKS

Aunt Agnes never recovered from Hollis' death or the loss of their farm. Before her marriage, she had trained as a nurse and worked at St. Luke's Hospital in Bethlehem. After her husband's death, she went back to work as the high school nurse for Palisades School District. It was Aunt Agnes who taught hundreds of us to make "hospital corners" on our beds and tend to minor first aid emergencies like pros. She also instilled the fear of dirt and germs into us as completely as she could. "Cleanliness is next to Godliness" should have been etched over her doorway.

In addition to her nursing responsibilities for Palisades Schools, Agnes continued to cook and work and entertain and care for sick and ailing family members; she had known happiness and joy for almost twenty-five years, but that was ripped from her. Aunt Agnes' mother died when she was five, and she only recovered from that deep grief when Uncle Hollis, loud, boisterous, hard-working, ambitious and creative Uncle Hollis, grabbed her hand and taught her to laugh and dance.

Their daughter, Jackie, never recovered either. She was her dad's pride and joy. Aunt Agnes called the shots and Uncle Hollis winked behind her back and charmed both his wife and his daughter so completely that each knew she was his favorite. Jackie was in college when he died. While she had many successes and triumphs and adventures in her life, she never again had such joy as she had had as her daddy's little girl down on the farm. She never returned to live in Durham, rarely visited, and chose to endure her dad's absence by being absent herself. I saw her at my parents' fiftieth wedding anniversary. She had been the flower girl at their wedding; she may have been fifty-eight at that anniversary party. She looked seventy. One tragic event in the life of a family has such far-reaching effects.

Grandad Hindenach's death had much more subtle effects on the family. Gram always seemed to me to have been relieved that she was released from her marriage contract. She would have stayed married and continued to live the hardscrabble life, but she was freed from that and resettled in a lovely home where she never had to kill, de-feather, or process another chicken. All the heavy lifting was done by my father, and all the entertaining and cooking was done by my mother. Gram's oldest daughter, Ruth, paid the rent. Whatever fee was agreed on when they moved in, which I think might have been $250, was never altered in thirty years – talk about rent control.

Gram had time, finally, to pursue the things she loved. She read, sewed, wrote letters, and taught me – her one and only student -- and she grew her magnificent flowers. My dad dug up the dirt and brought home the incomparable horse manure for fertilizer. My mother helped her plant and clean up at the end of the season. Gram had all the joy of tending the gardens – in front of the house, beside the house, behind the house, a fabulous rose garden and a cutting garden, and the little patch behind her side of the house, and on and on. Everything was flowers: beautiful, living, joyful flowers. Gram was freed from growing what was necessary and able to enjoy growing what gave her pleasure.

Her sewing may have been as dear to her as the gardens. If she wasn't in the kitchen, or in her rocking chair at the kitchen window, reading, or doing what she called her "correspondence" at her desk in the living room – a desk which sits now in my living room -- she was upstairs, in what had been my bedroom alcove, at her sewing machine. She made every stitch of clothing I wore, and, trust me, I was not the trendiest, but I thought I was the best dressed kid in school. If you wore something Martha Leidich Hindenach created, you were a fortunate person. She could make anything – and she did. People came from miles around because they needed slipcovers, drapes, suit coats, wedding dresses, baptismal outfits and clothes for everyday or for special occasions.

(A note about Gram's writing desk: both my brother and I wanted it. He graciously said, "You take it. We are not going to be one of those families that fights over things." I felt a little guilty until I realized it was really poorly made. It would have driven him crazy because he is a master craftsman who creates exquisite pieces of woodworking. Its value to me was purely sentimental. I'm happy to have the raggedy old desk with drawers that don't slide smoothly and molding that comes off the panes of glass in the front. It went to the right person. But I've never forgotten my brother's generosity of spirit!)

If Gram wasn't sewing on her machine, she was doing her "hand work." And we're not talking cross stitch. PLEASE. Her embroidery was of the most intricate and detailed sophistication. I have three of her pieces hanging on my walls, and my brother and Molly, my sister-in-law, have again as many. One of theirs is a fabulous violin she stitched for Molly, who played the violin. Gram loved creating, and in Durham she was able to pursue her passions. She would never have meant to blossom from the adversity, she just did.

Things changed for each of Gram's four children, as well. Aunt Ruth, the oldest, lived with her mother all her life. She didn't set out to do that, either, I'm sure, but nothing she was ever offered seemed as good to her. My dad always said she was "too fussy." I think she inherited Grandad's "depression gene." Several times in her life she had car accidents which seemed curious but were never termed purposeful. Weekends, if there was nothing going on, she'd take to her bed with "a migraine." (My talent at being quiet came in handy here. I wasn't allowed to play the piano or make any noise, even in the other side of the house, when Aunt Ruth was in bed with a migraine.) She was never the least bit cranky with me, but she was certainly cranky with everyone else who lived there, especially my dad. She wanted my mother's attention, and so, reasonably, did my dad. It got snarly sometimes.

On the other hand, Aunt Ruth was bright and beautiful and ambitious and she became the CFO at a local hospital and worked there until retirement with great praise and a wonderful reputation. But I think she used every resource she had in her to get through the weeks. I never saw my aunt so happy as when she retired. She was an introvert who loved living alone for the last few years of her life, but she joined organizations my mom belonged to: the garden club, the reading group, and the quilting circle. I have her beautiful cross-stitched rose quilt on my guest bed. It will go to my granddaughter, Mikayla Rose, when she has a home of her own. Aunt Ruth was the last person to see my grandmother before she died, and that seems so appropriate. My mother was the last person to see Ruth before she died. I hope Miriam told Ruth she forgave her for cutting off her curls all those years before.

Gram's two sons not only left Durham, they settled on different sides of the United States. Like their father and mother, they were both brilliant. They made enormous salaries, owned extravagant homes, and raised healthy families. They never lost touch with the rest of us, and, in the end, had their own hardships to bear. They say if everyone throws their troubles into a circle and gets to choose which troubles to retrieve from the circle, we'd each take back our own.

My mom's life changed, too, when her mother and sister invaded her space. While always the caregiver of the family, all of a sudden, she heard, "Miriam?" on a regular basis. I never knew her not to answer patiently. If one word described my mother, it was patient. She was a first grade teacher, just as proof of what I say. Did I mention that all my life I never heard my mother raise her voice? In one of Gram's diaries, she talked about my mother not enjoying teaching in a one room school. According to Gram, my mother was unable to maintain discipline with the older children. Mom was always astonished I could teach high school and college. I was totally awed that she could teach first grade!

In retrospect, I see that when my mom reached the end of her rope, she sent me on "Miriam calls." Clueless, as I mentioned before, I was easily bribed. The bribe I remember best was that when we finished supper on our side of the house, my mother would say, sweetly, "I'll do the dishes if you want to go see how Gram and Aunt Ruth are doing." My mother, the consummate introvert, would gladly have done all the work in the world rather than have to communicate and converse when she had nothing left at the end of a day.

My mom's life also changed in a positive way when both the Hindenach and Kline farms were sold. My dad had been deeply involved in the operation of both, but especially the Kline farm. Now it was time for Miriam to pursue something she wanted. When she had attended Kutztown State Teachers' College, students could be awarded a teaching degree after two years of school with the understanding that the other two years would be finished over time. My mom, all these years later, had never had the opportunity to finish her degree. Now that my father wasn't tied up with the farm every weekend, mom enrolled in Saturday classes. She studied every Friday night for Saturday classes, so my previously unencumbered father found himself with a nine-year-old shadow every Friday night and every Saturday.

Daddy solved that problem: he took a job as custodian of Durham School. Friday nights we went together to clean the school. Every Saturday we mowed grass, or shoveled snow, or worked at something else at the school. No matter what he did, he had a buddy and a pal. I only remember one crisis from that time. One Saturday we were busy running errands, and he couldn't find a bathroom for me. By the time we got home, I was soaked and so was the front seat of my dad's truck.

LIFE IN DURHAM
CIRCA 1954

As time went by, my life changed by default, but my two best friends were still my two best friends. When I say Suzanne Beshore lived above me and Karen Melchior lived below me, you probably think I'm talking about a three-story apartment building. Right? Wrong. This is Durham, Pennsylvania.

So, the Rau property in Durham stood on a slope. Our back yard was probably at a 20-degree angle. Route 212, where our back yard ended and Suzanne lived, was definitely higher than our house. When you walked out our front door, you looked down the continuation of the slope and saw the general store and beside it the house Melchior's owned. To us girls, Suzanne was up, and Karen was down.

Now, before we go further into up and down, we need to talk a little bit about Karen. Not to get this straightened out right off the bat is to bring about ideas of West Virginia and in-breeding. Durham was a small, intimate community; maybe that small, but not that intimate.

So, Karen and I are cousins. Her dad, Tony Melchior, was my gram's nephew. Gram's sister, Mary Mae, was Tony's mother. Mae, as she was called, was married to Charlie, brother of Grandma Mary Rau, my dad's step-mother. So, I had two (living) grandmothers: Gram Hindenach (Karen's grandmother's sister) and Grandma Rau (Karen's grandfather's sister.) You don't have to keep this straight or even understand. Just remember that the one relationship was by marriage, not blood, as they say. Consequently, Mom, Gram's daughter, and my dad, Grandma Rau's step-son, were free to marry without being overly concerned about the mental and physical health of their children. Now, to get back to the main point, Karen and I are cousins.

Karen and I played together since we were old enough to play. Her parents, Tony and Lillian, and mine, Dave and Miriam, were avid card players and pinochle was again the game of choice. Tony and Lillian came "up" or Dave and Miriam went "down," but Karen and I were bi-directional. She and I had probably been playing most of the day and the place we played frequently was "on the street." We held parades. We had batons. There was no marching band behind us, but we strutted all over that little town, singing and laughing and high stepping and trying to twirl those slippery batons. Once Gram arrived in town, we even had uniforms – matching uniforms.

Karen Melchior and me playing at her house.

When we took a break from the band, it was to head back to the wild, wild west. We had little silver-colored toy guns, holsters, bandanas, and cowgirl hats. We'd hide behind rocks and trees then jump out to take a shot at the passing cars. Whoever was driving would, depending on how playful they were, wave, pretend we actually shot them, or ignore us completely. Our favorite was the guy who would always swerve the car a little and slip down in the seat as though we GOT HIM! Karen had brown hair, so she was Dale Evans. With my blonde hair, I got to be Annie Oakley. To this day we sometimes call each other Dale and Annie.

Our parents never had to wonder where we were; they could see us parading or keeping the peace. Tony, who was a pushover, would always let us grab a soda from the big red pop container on the porch of his store. All we had to do was drag ourselves into the store looking beat and tired, and he'd say, "Go ahead. Get a cold drink." The very thought restored our energy. We'd discuss the virtues of each flavor. I particularly liked the birch beer. Karen remembers always wanting a Coca-Cola. We'd open the bottles on the bottle opener on the side of that red monster, listen for the bottle cap to be swallowed into the abyss, then sit on the cement stoop and take a break to plan our next daring adventure.

Cook's Creek ran behind Melchior's store and house. Oh, the things you could imagine if you had a creek in which to play. A little way up the creek from Melchior's, there were two big, thick wire cables hanging about four or five feet over the water. The cables were strung parallel to each other and just far enough apart for us to walk the lower cable while hanging on to the upper one. The cables probably contained electric or power lines that were securely encased in what seemed to be sturdy metal of some kind. We felt like tightrope walkers in the circus, or perhaps the daredevil going over Niagara Falls, when we crossed the creek hanging on to those cables. We thought we were so brave. I don't remember any of us ever falling in.

For hours we walked in that frigid water, rock to rock, especially in the summer when we needed to cool off. We'd play a game where we'd take turns leading the adventure and choosing which rock to step on next. The rest of us, in case anyone joined us, had to follow the path. Karen and I only had one horrible experience that required Tony and his very real gun. Luckily, he heard us screaming our lungs out for him, and he came running. The cause of our terror was a huge black snake. (By "black" I'm remembering color; I have no idea what kind of snake it was.) I shudder to this day thinking of it slithering toward us. To my girlish eyes, it was very fat! Tony dispatched it into snake heaven. We probably got a soda that day, too. Maybe even a little penny candy from the beautiful old wood and glass candy case.

LouAnn, one of our gang, recently talked about the choices of candy in Tony and Lillian's enticing candy cabinet: Mallow Cups, Turkish Taffy, cigar bubble gum, wax lips and Necco Wafers – a pack of them lasted until lunch. LouAnn also remembers Black Jack Gum, clove gum, Tootsie Rolls in various sizes, candy cigarettes and Sugar Daddy. Karen actually thought of one more: watermelon slices. The delectable selection was amazing, and patient Lillian would stand behind the case and wait, for what probably seemed like forever, for each of us to decide how to spend our pennies.

Bike riding was another of our favorite activities, and we rode our bikes all over Durham and beyond. For years we had been content to ride close to home, but as we grew older we peddled farther and farther away, heading toward Riegelsville or Springtown or "up the hill" in the direction of Easton. Not only did we venture farther from home as we got older, especially as we grew into our teens, but we became more daring in the way we rode. The hill between Durham School and Durham Church was really steep and curvy. Somehow, we got the idea – not a good or safe idea –that we should walk our bikes up the hill (the hill being too steep to ride very far up), then coast down that steep and curvy road, picking up speed as we rolled. Yup. Almost all of us crashed at the corner of Mack's house. Suzanne remembers her crash.

I don't remember my crash because I didn't crash. I never had the energy to make it all the way to the top of the hill! I'd stop at

Antoine's driveway, which was about a third of the way up, and sit and daydream until I heard the brave and daring approaching. After they whizzed by, I'd climb onto my bike and slowly follow after. (Physical daring started and ended for me with the cables over Cook's Creek.) Nobody ever got seriously hurt, but there sure were scratches, scrapes, and bloody clothes to explain.

In addition to zooming down from the top of the steep daredevil hill, Karen remembers we started riding further away from Durham. At Mack's house on the corner, right below the school, there was a dirt road which led for a couple miles into Springtown. We pedaled past Ulmer's farm, Gilbert's homestead, and a few scary, deserted properties. Since it was two miles to Springtown on Route 212, this trip was probably about three miles on a winding, hilly dirt road.

That dirt road ended opposite Carol Chaser's driveway, and whoever was around when inspiration struck would join the caravan. I remember one time when we took this dusty trail, we were invited into Carol's house to see their new Scandinavian furniture. That was exciting. We didn't even know where Scandinavian furniture was from, or what it looked like, or that something with such light-colored wood and sleek design even existed. We were living in homes with heavy maple or walnut furniture which had been passed down for generations. New? Scandinavian? Wow. Radical! That was worth the ride. Plus, I remember being given mugs of ice water before we started back to Durham. We only had glasses at my house – nothing as nifty as "mugs."

Outdoor sleepovers seemed always to take place in Karen's backyard. Part of the reason for that may have been that she had a dog. Her collie, Queenie, was no doubt the guard dog for the scary idea of sleeping outside.

Suzanne remembers that she and LouAnn took a metal cement mixing trough, climbed in, and poled down Cook's Creek. Karen remembers that she and LouAnn used to call each other on the phone, making sure each of them was home, and then quickly hanging up and dashing to the doors of their houses to commence hollering to each other to have a conversation.

LouAnn remembers she and Carol sitting on the bridge one morning after a sleepover and seeing Grandma Boyer walking toward them. "We decided to be impertinent brats and lift our hands and say, 'How!' to her. Granny Boyer's response was to reach under her shawl and pull out her brass earphone and screech out, 'AY,' to us. We were so frightened, we jumped off the bridge and ran."

And we remember all this some sixty years later.

While Karen was my outdoor adventuring friend, Suzanne and I played in my back yard, between our houses, or in my house. Suzanne was a beautiful, petite girlie girl, and we had a wider range of imaginative scenarios we'd undertake. Once again, all we had to do was mention "who" we were pretending to be, and Gram would produce the appropriate outfits from leftover materials she had on hand. In my closet to this day is my white nurses' uniform with a small faded red cross stitched on the front pocket. It might be a child's size eight.

One of the things Suzanne and I did was much more serious and required our shared strength. She decided she'd like to try learning the cello. Since we walked to school every morning, the cello had to be carried on music day. I swear sometimes we'd stop every ten feet and trade who was lugging that cello and who was carrying our books or lunches. A cello is very heavy for elementary school girls to carry.

The walk to school was an historical journey, but we took all the history for granted. Suzanne lived across Route 212, opposite the hills in which iron ore had been discovered. The mined ore was taken to the Revolutionary War era furnace across from the mill. Shot, cannonballs and shells were cast there for several wars, including The Revolutionary War. But the Furnace was in use before that; it bears a carving into its keystone which says 1727.

Between the Furnace and Old Furnace Road (which runs in front of my house) are some fascinating steps. They are stones placed in a steep and uneven pattern without a railing of any sort. Up and down them we climbed like little mountain goats. Then we walked around the mill and met the road which crossed the bridge over Cook's Creek. To us it was just part of our walk to school.

We didn't need to carry our lunches since a hot lunch was served at Durham School. Unfortunately, Mrs. Fox, the school cook, was a stickler about eating everything on your plate. Suzanne didn't eat much, and I was a fuss-budget, so this was a problem we shared. If you didn't finish everything on your plate, you couldn't participate in recess, whether it was inside (bad or cold weather) or outside. (The playground equipment for about one hundred children consisted of four swings, two see-saws, one sliding board and a merry-go-round.

None of us girls ever went on the merry-go-round because the boys were too fast and rowdy!)

Suzanne lived in Durham for only a few years, but she and I were friends all through school, although never again so conveniently. We are in touch to this day, as are Karen and LouAnn and I. Amazingly, in a town of seventy-five people, there were eight of us who were all the same age. We were the baby boomers – the very first of those born after World War II. Five girls and three boys lived in "downtown" Durham. The boys weren't as bonded as we girls were, but we all had a lot of fun.

In the summer we girls "owned" the millrace. Cook's Creek had been partially diverted to carry water for grinding to Riegel's feed mill, located in the center of town and across from Melchior's store. The runoff from the millrace flowed between Riegel's house on the right and Kunkle's on the left, then behind Melchior's house and back into the main creek. Where the creek was dammed, someone had built a cement wall and attached a ladder for climbing into and out of the water. The section in which we could swim was about five feet deep, with an incredibly thick, muddy bottom. That "pool" might have been, at most, twenty or thirty feet long and, maybe, six to eight feet wide.

The most excitement we had at the "race," as we called it, was when Mrs. Kunkle would come and swim with us. She was from Australia, a "war bride," and by far the most elegant and interesting person any of us knew. She wore a bathing cap, the height of fashion, we thought, and she did the Australian crawl with such grace we'd all just watch open-mouthed. She also knew how to do a sleek sidestroke. The water just parted for her. (All we knew was the doggie paddle.) Mrs. Kunkle was sweet and kind to us, too. I remember she would bring out cookies for us sometimes. Maybe the cookies were intended to keep us busy and out of the water so she had room to swim.

When we girls weren't in the water, we were having contests. We'd make anything and everything into a contest, but what I remember most, because I never won, was that we'd judge who had the prettiest hands or feet. That darnn LouAnn Anderson always won hands. I think Judy Eliason won feet – or it might have been Karen. Wasn't me. Suzanne says we sometimes extended the possibilities of excellence. She remembers it was decided I had the prettiest lips, Karen had the prettiest eyes, and LouAnn had the prettiest hair. We were all unfailingly kind to each other, so I imagine each of us had our moments in the sun! (It's fascinating that none of us can remember winning anything ourselves, only what the others "won.")

Our other big summer pastime took place in Limantour's field, which was just across the bridge over Cook's Creek. This activity included more than the eight of us who were the same age. The older kids materialized for this happening: Baseball. Two of the older guys would be captains, and it took them forever to choose their teams. I can tell you for a fact that I was always the last one chosen, always sent to the outer outfield, and that no rule existed that said everyone had to be allowed to bat. I know this because in all the years we played baseball, I never so much as held a bat in my hands, unless someone, like my big brother, assigned me to carry a bat home.

In winter, that hill where Karen and I led our imaginary band and shot the invisible bad guys became the sledding hill. Anyone and everyone who had a sled or a cookie sheet or anything that would slide showed up for those snowy evenings. The gathering was never planned. We all just came out like the stars when dusk settled in.

Someone was assigned to stay at the top of the hill and scream if a car came. Obviously, some helicopter mother demanded this, although it was totally unnecessary. First, it was pitch black in Durham, Pennsylvania, on a winter night. There was one street light in the whole town, and it was turned on and off with a switch in our dining room. (My dad paid the electric bill for that light for sixty years.) We could see if a car was coming.

Second, there was snow on the ground and no car was coming at any dangerous rate of speed. Third, on a good day, like a sunny day when there was an activity at the church at the top of the hill, there might have been a couple cars an hour. In the summer when we sat on our front porch, we could be out there all evening and see three cars, tops. Also, we knew who was in the three cars and could have guessed pretty accurately where they were going. Durham was not full of surprises.

But we good naturedly went along with a watch-person, and if he or she screamed "car," we all ran our sleds into the nearest snowdrift and waited until the car had crawled by or slid down the hill before we resumed our trip. Having said there were no surprises in Durham, I have to admit there was one: after we coasted down that hill a good number of times, and, brother, you had a great ride if you got as far as Melchior's house, Mrs. Marshall would call us to her house for hot chocolate.

Now the surprise was not that some mother or other would make us hot chocolate. The astonishment (surprise) was that it was Mrs. Marshall! She was not the motherliest of the mothers, to put it mildly. (She summoned her son with a loud, shrill whistle which sounded like boot camp! When we were playing some game or other and heard the whistle, we'd all look away while Billy ran home.) But Mrs. Marshall was the hot chocolate lady. I have no idea why she felt moved to invite, repeatedly, twelve or fifteen cold, wet kids into her house to use her bathroom and drink hot chocolate. It was a good lesson for us kids not to think we had everyone figured out and put in a box. People can surprise you.

Before Marshall's lived in the house next to us, Stemler's lived there for many years. Stemler's also owned and operated Weldrite, a welding shop, which was located on 212 behind and "above" our (the Stemler/Marshall house and the Rau) houses. Between our houses was a sturdy wooden fence for climbing and sitting and talking. Ronnie Stemler, (one of the three boys our age,) and I were on that fence one day, hanging out, we might have been seven or eight, when a log went flying from above the welding shop where some trees were being dynamited. This flying missile sped at least a quarter of a mile, shot between an opening of no more than six or eight feet which separated our homes, ruffled Ronnie's and my hair, and landed not three feet from where we were sitting. My brother says he still remembers the divot in the front yard. That log went into the ground with serious force. Some angel was watching out for the two kids on the fence. That could easily have been a double tragedy.

Marty Stemler, who was a year or two older than the eight of us, was the person who corrected me when I said, recently, that Mr. Litzenberger was harmless. "Not to the boys, he wasn't. He did not like boys." Marty married my friend, Suzanne, which is how I happened upon his expertise. So, I asked him about the incident with the flying log. He said a workman had used fertilizer instead of dynamite to get some stumps out of the ground across the street from his dad's shop. He, too, remembered the amazing trajectory of the flying log.

The Stemler's moved soon after that excitement! They restored and expanded a colonial era home at the edge of town. This was a whopping six houses away, right on the corner where 212 intersected with Durham Road, which brought one or two people an hour into Durham. If you went straight in front of our house, you had veered off of Durham Road which went up the hill to the church. The road in front of our house, later named Old Furnace Road (because it ran over the original cave and furnace), took you past about eight houses and curved back up to 212.

I suppose you could say rudely that Durham was nothing more than a needless detour. If, however, instead of going past our house you went down the hill to Riegel's Feed and Grain and Melchior's General Store, crossed Cook's Creek, passed the Limantour's field, our baseball field, and the Limantour's beautiful stone house on the right, Mack's house and Durham School on the left, and went up the hill, you arrived at Durham Church. Travel another mile or two and you'd pass both Gram's childhood home, on the left, and, a mile later, turn right onto the road that ran between the two sections of the Hindenach Farm.

The house in which Gram grew up is located on what is today called Durham Road, but in her growing up days, it was known as Old Philadelphia Road.

My mother, then, until our folks moved into the life care center in Allentown, spent the first 76 years of her life in about five square miles. Our dad spent the first five years of his life in Bethlehem. Once his widowed dad married Mary Melchior, our dad lived less than two miles west on Route 212. Consequently, he also spent 76 years of his life in a similar five square mile radius. Their ashes now rest in Durham cemetery. Every time we'd get after our dad about working so hard, Daddy would say, "I have all eternity to lay down."

MR. DURHAM,
THE MAYOR

If our dad ever had a mistress, it was the town of Durham.
Durham lies in the northernmost part of Bucks County, a
county the writers James Michener and Pearl Buck made
famous. If Bucks County could be compared to a glitzy, elegant
house, which it certainly can with its history and arts, stone homes
and covered bridges, then Durham comprised the sturdy concrete
basement and foundation of that glitz and glitter. There was nothing
about the Durham I grew up in that could remotely have been called
"cultural." What we had was "community."

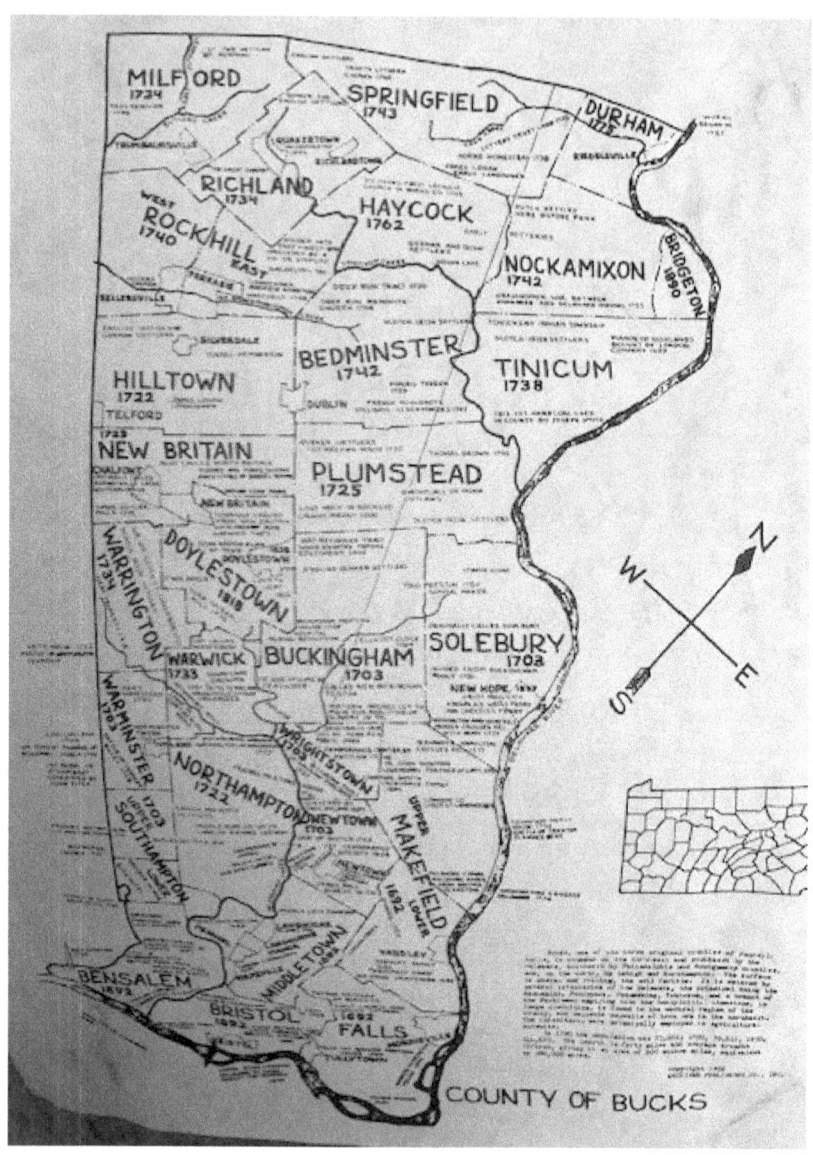

Bucks County, 1956.

When I lived in Durham from 1946 to 1963, there were more cows than people and more dirt roads than paved roads. To say that life in Durham was safe is a simple truth. Just recently my youngest son, Nick, was telling his children how much fun he and his brothers had when we visited Grandma and Grandad. The three boys would set out in the morning along the creek and when they got hungry, they'd come back. In the afternoon they'd take bats and balls and walk over to the ballfield at Durham School – a ballfield their grandfather had lobbied to have built and worked to maintain. They'd play there until supper time, free to explore and enjoy new adventures in all that open space. In Akron, Ohio, where we lived, I needed to know where they were at all times; in Durham, I knew that wherever they were, they were safe.

Not everyone knew everyone else in Durham, but there was one guy who did know everybody: Dave Rau, the township supervisor. Every few years, when he ran for office, my dad went door-to-door to see if people had any concerns about the management of the township and to ask for people's votes. Most of the time he ran unopposed, but that didn't alter his campaign strategy. He was not a man who took anything for granted. And, if something was the right thing to do, it was the right thing to do under any and all circumstances.

David Meffan Rau, named after his maternal grandfather, David Meffan, was a concrete-thinker and a rule-follower. In fact, he was such a rule-follower that once, when a young cop in Leithsville, Pennsylvania, gave him a speeding ticket, my dad called his neighbor and friend, Al Chaser, a county sheriff, to question how the young police officer decided he was speeding and to ask if there was anything to be done but pay the ticket. When told about the speeding ticket, Sheriff Chaser burst out laughing.

Dave Rau had never broken a law in his life, not a big law, not a little law, not a law where he might get caught, and not a law where it was totally unlikely that he would be found out. If you ever watched him mow grass, you'd see that not a corner was cut, not a blade was missed, and not a line wavered from straight and true.

Sheriff Chaser called the Leithsville cop and explained in no uncertain terms that he had targeted the wrong guy this time. Dave Rau had never gone over ANY speed limit and there were thirty people who would show up in court, put their hands on a Bible, and say so. Most of the thirty people could testify to this because they had been forced to follow him over the country roads – sometimes he'd have a whole caravan piled up behind him. The speeding ticket disappeared.

Such was the reputation of Dave Rau, and in the fifty-four years I knew him, he never veered from his center, tried and true.

My dad's mother, Charlotte Meffan Rau, and her baby both died during childbirth when my dad was two. His mother, called Lottie, was the fourth of seven girls born to David and Elizabeth Meffan in Bethlehem, Pennsylvania. Lottie's six sisters gathered closely to assuage their sorrow by caring for Lottie's beautiful little blonde boy with the sparkling blue eyes and sunny disposition. Dave's older sister, Agnes, was five when their mother died. Her death hit the little girl her much harder and left a devastating, lifelong impact. David was soothed, Agnes was not.

The June 8, 1913 Bulletin of First Presbyterian Church in Bethlehem, included this announcement:

We extend our tenderest sympathy as a church to Mr. Floyd W. Rau, in his trying bereavement over the loss of his wife, Charlotte Meffan Rau, who entered into the heavenly rest on May the thirty-first, and also to the relatives of Mrs. Rau, who was a member of our congregation. We pray that the Comforter may sooth their sorrow, and guide and protect his motherless children.

Just the year before, the June 16, 1912 bulletin announced the joyous occasion of the baptism of David Meffan Rau, son of Mr. and Mrs. Floyd Rau. And on October 22, 1906, a mere six years before the baptism of their second child, Lottie Meffan received a leather postcard from Floyd Rau, the only remaining evidence that they had courted. This postcard showed a picture of a Native American on the left and an Irishman on the right with this script: "The Indian with his pipe of peace has slowly passed away, but the Irishman with his piece of pipe has come prepared to stay." Lottie's suitor signed the postcard "F.W.R." Apparently, Floyd's courting correspondence met with Lottie's approval since they soon married. Lottie kept that leather postcard, and eventually it came into my father's possession. He, then, kept it all his life. One hundred and fourteen years later, it is tucked into my Bible.

Lottie Meffan Rau's leather postcard, 1906.

The proverbial step-mother arrived on the scene three years after Lottie's death, and soon a second sister was born. Neither Dave's older sister, Agnes, nor his younger sister, Katharyn, could abide the step-mother/mother. Animosity, control battles, shouting matches, and a lot of "silent treatment" ensued among the three females. Dave learned some disarming charm, some distracting humor, and various peace-making skills. The major recipient of this well-honed charm was Miriam, the quiet, little blonde five years younger than he. They saw each other every Sunday, since Dave's step-grandfather was the minister and Miriam's father the organist of the church at the top of the hill in Durham. They smiled at each other. For years. But Dave was patient and willing to wait for her to grow up. They began dating when Miriam started college at Kutztown. In fact, the naughtiest thing she ever did in her life, she did to him. He drove more than an hour one night to take her out on a date. Later, while he started his drive home, she and her roommate went back out with two fraternity boys. Fraternity boys, no less! She confessed. He forgave. He did tease her all their lives about preferring redheads. She just laughed. She knew whom he had chosen.

My dad was born under the sign of Capricorn and fit the stereotype. Capricorns are supposed to be good with money. He had a unique double method for handling money. First, he worked. He had his day job as an accountant at Bethlehem Steel, and he took every other job he could find. He was, of course, the custodian at Durham School, cleaning the halls, desks and toilets all year long. Spring, summer, and fall, he kept the school grounds and ball fields meticulously neat. All winter the snow was shoveled and plowed.

My dad was also the accountant for a car dealership in Springtown, a small village two miles from Durham. My brother remembers our dad sold cars there sometimes, too. He worked on both family farms, kept the township books, and was instrumental in turning the township books from red to black. He cared for the homes of people who owned "summer places" in Durham Township. He kept a big ring of keys in the glove compartment of his blue '54 Chevy truck. People called from New York City, or wherever their "other" house was, if they thought they had forgotten to turn off the heat, or if they were expecting a repair person. When those calls came, my dad would sort through his keys and handle the business for them. No charge, of course. In his mind it came under the heading of being a good neighbor.

The volunteer lists and the charities to which he pledged were as numerous as the jobs he held. He helped found a Lion's Club in Springtown and went to meetings every month until the last three months of his life. He served for twenty-eight years on the Palisades School Board, including many years on the Bucks County School Board. And every year he had a picture of a child from a different country on his desk. He sent money to an organization monthly to feed and clothe that child and the charity sent him a picture.

But, step one in Dave Rau's money management system was: WORK.

The second part of his money brilliance was deceptively simple: he kept track of every penny. He also, literally, saved every penny he had in a big (empty) wine jug. (Actually, it might have been one of Uncle Hollis' moonshine jugs.) He'd fill the jug, cash in the pennies, put the money in their bank account, and start over.

Every time his wife returned from shopping, she handed him the receipt or receipts. All he ever said was, "Thank you." He didn't care how much she spent or what she spent it on. Her spending was never criticized. (He could always get another job.) But he knew where every cent they earned came from and where every cent they spent went.

The stories about him are as endless as the stories he told after every family dinner. He was once written up in the newspaper because when some schlep dumped a trash bag full of dirty diapers along the road, it was Dave Rau who stopped his blue truck, got out a trash bag, which, of course he had in the back of his truck, and cleaned up the smelly mess. A reporter from the Doylestown

Intelligencer happened to be passing by and caught him red-handed doing the clean-up!

David Meffan Rau was born more than a hundred years ago in Bethlehem, Pennsylvania, and died in neighboring Allentown. He lived most of his life in his beloved village of Durham. As an accountant for "the Steel," he was no doubt well pleased that he was born in 1911 and died in 1999 at the age of 88. Nice, neat numbers. He would have liked that.

Two other stories beg to be told about the man they called, "Mr. Mayor." That man did love his Durham. I believe it was the early 1960's that word came to Floyd Riegel, the mill owner and postmaster, that the government would be shutting down the post office because it was no longer profitable. This was alarming on many fronts because without a post office, Durham would cease to be a town. I don't know how it all worked, but I remember the upset that Durham might be stricken from the maps. Durham could no longer be Durham without a post office.

I don't imagine my father thought about it very long or hard before he walked into the post office and bought a hundred dollars' worth of stamps. He took the stamps to Bethlehem Steel and told the fifty or so fellows with whom he worked that he'd appreciate if they'd come to him if they needed stamps. They, of course did, or at least enough of them did. This went on for years. Every time my dad was about to run out of stamps, back he'd go to see Floydie, as he was called, and replenish his stamp supply.

I know in my bones that Dave Rau single-handedly saved the post office and the town of Durham which dated back to at least

1727. I don't know that anyone other than he and Floyd realized it. I don't suppose either of them cared. Naturally, he never made a cent on this stamp-providing-business. He merely preserved the town he loved, and Durham, Pennsylvania, is on the maps today because it hit the mark of being two-hundred and fifty years old. Durham is now an historic landmark with its own Durham Historical Society. Durham also boasts the second oldest post office in the United States – second only to Philadelphia.

The other story sums up the man, as well. A member of the church who had access to the finances of the church, got in a hard place and "borrowed" some church funds. My dad, with his accounting background, thought something was going on that did not reflect an accurate picture of church finances. He investigated. He discovered the missing funds and deduced who had appropriated them.

He went to the home of the man who had "borrowed" the money from the church with exactly that amount of money in his pocket. He sat down with the man he knew well, pulled the money from his pocket, and told the man to put the money back in the church coffers. Nothing would be said, my dad told this man. The problem would simply disappear before anyone else ever knew of it. My dad never told a soul, except, I bet, my mom, what had happened or what he had done to repair the damage. I have no idea if the money was repaid, but I imagine so. Someone who was also at that kitchen table told me fifty years later what my dad had done.

I know I said "two" stories, but I forgot about The Purple Gang! The Purple Gang from Detroit was a notorious organized crime gang in the 1920s and 1930s. Also known as The Sugar House Gang, they are believed to be responsible for 500 unsolved murders. Murder, extortion, theft, armed robbery, kidnapping, gambling and bootlegging were their prized past times. Apparently, things got a little heated in Michigan, so they slid south to Pennsylvania and "hit" a few banks there. At one, they pistol whipped a young man working at the bank. They were not quite quick enough, however, and whoever was in on this job got nabbed by the police. "It was very difficult to get a statement from witnesses," the information on the gang says. Yes. These were not forgiving fellows.

Anyhow, since this is a story about Dave Rau, you can surmise that he, in his short career as a bank employee, was pistol whipped and asked if he would identify and testify against the gang. Yup. If it's the right thing to do, Dave Rau did it. Some of the Purple Gang landed in jail. He, wisely, quit the bank, took a job at Bethlehem Steel, and the rest is history.

THE DUST SETTLED
IN DURHAM

Gram and Grandad's farm was cleaned up, organized, and sold, and the house in Durham painted and made ready. Aunt Ruth went back to her job at Easton Hospital, and my parents returned to their work, my dad to the accounting department at Bethlehem Steel and my mother to her second-grade classroom at Springfield Elementary School. Unfortunately, to his way of thinking, my brother never got to miss any days at Palisades High School. And Gram and I started the relationship which now, in retrospect, I see enriched my life immeasurably and, maybe, helped save hers. We were inseparable.

Aunt Ruth never married, so I was as much of a daughter (to her) as she would ever have. She spoiled me rotten. Gram spoiled me in entirely different ways. Both treated me like a little adult, listening to my girlish chatter as though it was worthy and showering me with attention.

After the house was renovated and the Rau family of four moved to the larger side, the Hindenach family of two began acclimating to life in Durham. A new furnace was installed in the basement, a unit big enough to heat both sides of the house. This necessitated knocking out a doorway between the two basements, which became the inside route for traveling between the two sides of the house.

This cellar was my enemy. It was dark and shadowy with a cement floor and two open coal chutes, one along the steps going down to the cellar from "our" side, and one along the steps going up to "Gram's" side. I desperately wanted to get to Gram, but I had to pass those two spooky, scary, dark tunnels that curved up to the old openings from which the coal had been dumped into the basement to keep the fires burning.

As a little girl, I became fast and loud. I'm sure I started calling for Gram the moment I left the doorway on our side and began running down the steps, across our basement floor, up the one step joining the two basements, across her basement floor and flying up her steps, past the second coal chute, tearing open the door on her side and landing loudly and out-of-breath in Gram's kitchen. It was a feat I got quite good at.

Gram and me by one of my clients.

I remember two years later when I had mumps, and Gram would make the trip through the basement with my lunch and sit on the step at the top of our stairs and talk to me for a few minutes before she would go back down the steps and call to me to open the door and get my lunch. She had never had mumps, and all the adults were so worried I'd break the rules and try to see her. I never did.

Soon after "switching sides" of the house, my cousin, Jackie, who was at West Chester State Teachers' College, where my brother would also go, found a bedraggled gray kitten. She couldn't keep it in her dorm, so she made a present of the kitten to her young, unsuspecting cousin – me – and I had a wonderful, new best friend. Amazingly, my neurotically clean mother allowed me to keep the skinny little kitten, and she fattened up under my watchful eye. But I do remember a time she wouldn't eat. My father came home to find me sitting on the back sidewalk beside the cat food dish trying to coax my new best friend, who I named Gretchen, into having a bite. We were at a standoff when he appeared.

"Susan," he said, "She's a cat. She'll eat when she's hungry. Come on inside. We'll let nature take its course."

My new best friend was allowed to sleep in my bed and wander around the house at will; my mom was always amazed that Gretchen would glide in and out of the dishes and knick-knacks and never break or move any of them. She charmed my mother because during the years mom taught at Durham School, anyone who was in the house would swear that cat knew the sound of Mom's car and she would be sitting, waiting for her to walk in the door.

My mom grew up on a chicken farm where all the animals lived outside. She gave me a different opportunity. Gretchen and I were "tight," and I hated hearing, when I was in college, that she had an ill-fated crossing of 212 and wouldn't be waiting for me when I came home the next time.

BUSED TO SCHOOL
IN 1955

Durham School had only four rooms, first through fourth grade, For middle school,-fifth and sixth grade, we went to Springfield Elementary School. This necessitated a bus ride.

Tony, the general store owner and Karen's dad, was either elected, chosen, or offered, to take responsibility for driving the bus. This may have happened because Tony had a strangely big, empty, spooky building on the back of his property behind the store. I don't know how he ever imagined a school bus would fit in one of the sections of that building. Did he measure? Did he eyeball it? How did he ever borrow or steal a school bus to try it out? It was incredible that that big yellow school bus fit in that rickety old building, but fit it did.

To get the bus in the building, Tony had to start on the street and back down the narrow driveway between his house and store. Then, he had to back over a bridge which had no sides. Sides on the bridge would have prevented the bus tires from sliding and tilting the bus into the mill race, but there were no sides on that bridge. Yet, somehow, Tony always safely crossed the bridge – backwards and forwards, even on snow and ice.

After crossing the bridge, Tony's next challenge was positioning the bus in front of the opening of the building and backing in. The bus fit as if the building was designed for it with not more than a foot of empty space on either side or the top of the bus. That was one impressive feat of driving that man accomplished every day to house the bus that delivered us back and forth to school.

For the next eight years of our lives, two years of middle school and six years of high school, we walked down to the back of Tony's driveway at 6:50 in the morning. In winter, the bus had been pulled out of its envelope by about six feet and the heater turned on by the time we all climbed in. Tony would bounce down into the driver's seat and call out, "Everybody here?" If someone was missing, one of us would have been contacted so the bus didn't "wait" for us. Then ten or twelve of us would settle in for the hour-long ride to school, picking up a lot of other kids along the way.

I don't remember the ride to middle school, but I could recite the entire high school bus route, who we stopped for when and where. It was really a beautiful ride over the Pennsylvania hills and beside the Delaware River. When I was in seventh and eighth grade, however, there were some scary older boys who got on that bus. Some of them had beards and sideburns and moustaches! I always made sure to sit close to Tony. I didn't want to spend an hour being harassed, but that was just me being a tootsie. There was no funny business on any of our buses; no one was ever kicked off the bus. Our parents would have killed us if we had misbehaved. Also, we knew kids who were forced to drop out and go to work or stay home and help on the farm. We didn't have to be very smart to know attending school was the better option.

Plus, you could study anything and everything at Palisades High School from agriculture to shop to woodworking to automotive repair and more. Girls got good jobs right out of high school if they did well in business classes and mastered shorthand and typing. The majority of kids who went to Palisades with me were not going to be fortunate enough to go on to college.

DURHAM LUTHERAN REFORMED CHURCH

Durham Church, Durham Pennsylvania.

Besides going to school together, most of us kids who lived in Durham had one other major, shared activity: church. Every other week either the Lutheran or the Reformed congregation claimed the use of the sanctuary for church. But every week, all of us had Sunday School together before church. We'd meet in the sanctuary, hear announcements, and sing a few hymns, which Tony's wife, Lillian, played with gusto on the piano. My dad led the singing. Then various age kids went to different classes while the adults stayed in the sanctuary. Gram or my dad prepared the adult Sunday School lesson every week.

Gram's lessons were historical and precise, heady and meticulously researched. She began to plan them the moment she finished the previous lesson two weeks before. In comparison, my dad was a Saturday afternoon preparer. This got a little tricky during baseball season when he liked to listen to the Saturday afternoon game on the radio. It also resulted in a Sunday School lesson I bet no one ever forgot. I think the baseball player's name was Jesus Alou, pronounced, "hay-soos," but spelled Jesus. I'm positive about the name of the Sunday School lesson: "Jesus is stuck on third, waiting for you to bat him home." It doesn't take a genius to know what happened in the ballgame to give my dad such a memorable lesson title.

For Sunday School, all of the high school kids (7th through 12th grade) were stuffed into a small room beside the sanctuary. The room was probably designed for brides to get dressed or ministers to don their robes but all of us baby boomers managed to squeeze in. (We didn't know we were baby boomers. We just knew there were a disproportionate number of kids our age in Durham, Pennsylvania.)

Vera Riegel, wife of Floyd, the postmaster and owner of Riegel's Feed and Grain, was our teacher. By day she had become Mrs. Keller's replacement, since Mrs. Keller mercifully retired and took her horse collars with her. Mrs. Riegel taught third grade at Durham School, but all of us knew what she really enjoyed teaching was our Sunday School class. She was full of energy and enthusiasm and had a real gift for stimulating discussion; most of us had a real gift for discussing, so it was a match made in heaven.

Looking back, our Sunday School classes were like a six-year study of ethics. What was appropriate moral behavior? What was ethical? What were our responsibilities as students and citizens? She inspired us to become involved and thoughtful. I'm sure everyone who sat in that stuffy little room was a better person thanks to the time spent in Vera Riegel's Sunday School class.

However, church every other Sunday and Sunday School every Sunday were a mere pittance of the activity and togetherness we enjoyed at Durham Lutheran Reformed Church. (Don't you wonder what the Lutherans did to get their name first in the formal name of the Church? I hope it was nothing Martin Luther would have objected to!)

I found evidence that early on some Presbyterians were part of the shared church space, too, but they wandered off on their own before I was aware of that. (Growing up I didn't even know any Presbyterians or realize my father's mother's family were all Presbyterians. Years later, in Akron, I became one!)

The name of the church changed again since then. Now it's Evangelical Lutheran Church of Durham. Apparently, whatever the Lutherans did, they undid. Now they're second. Nonetheless, all any of us ever called the church was Durham Church.

Our church was also our town restaurant – it was where you went in Durham if you went out for a meal. It was the only option. We didn't eat at each other's houses. Families ate together, but friends didn't have meals together the way friends do now. Our parents were depression era children; we were World War II babies. People helped each other when needed, but for the most part everyone was in a saving mentality, not a frivolous "eat, drink, and be merry" mood. Life had been "serious" for most of the twentieth century.

Our church was the community center, too. It was the town meeting hall. It was the amusement park. It was the picnic pavilion. It was the hall used for anniversary celebrations, birthday parties, wedding showers, and family reunions. It was where you were married and where your funeral was held. Durham Lutheran Reformed Church was pretty much where you started out in Durham and met the town folk when you were baptized. It was definitely where family and friends said goodbye to you as you moved on to the adjacent cemetery.

Durham Church cemetery. (photo: Martin Stemler, 2013)

I don't know about the other kids, we never talked about it, but I never went to a funeral there until Aunt Ruth died in 1989. I guess my parents thought kids would have enough sadness in their lives without being subjected to funerals. Plus, funerals made my mom angry. She'd come home from a funeral tight-lipped, and eventually she'd start telling me that so-and-so, whomever it was, had always treated the dearly departed poorly, yet now so-and-so was at the funeral, weeping and wailing.

My mother detested hypocrisy. Actually, in our family, there was a fine line between being polite, which was insisted upon, and being a hypocrite, which was considered despicable. Knowing where the line ran was something you wanted to figure out early – zero tolerance for missing that mark.

Spared the heavy end-of-life events, church was pretty much a fun place for all of us. The absolute most fun was Christmas caroling.

Every year we young folks put on a Christmas Eve Pageant. When that concluded and the sanctuary was cleaned up, we headed for the cars. There must have been a Christmas Eve when we didn't have snow, but I don't remember one. Off we'd go, Lillian Melchior in the lead, destined for the first house out of probably five or six where someone was shut-in, elderly, or ill, or we just thought they needed some Christmas cheer.

We'd pile out of the cars, maybe twenty-five of us altogether, gather round, and Lillian would name a Christmas carol and raise her hands. She'd hit a note, and we'd all join in. At every stop we'd sing a different assortment of maybe three or four carols, but we always ended with Silent Night. By the last house, we were sounding like a well-practiced chorus.

People would wave out their doors or windows and thank us for coming, but no matter what joy they might have gotten from our little concert, no one enjoyed it more than we did. Back in the cars we'd go, laughing about who fell in the snow, whose voice cracked at a noticeable place in which carol, who sang the wrong words, and other bloopers we found hilariously funny.

But then came the best part of Christmas caroling: our visit to Gertie Koch's house. The route was always planned so the last house at which we sang was not too far from the Koch farm. Now, we ate Gertie's cooking other times during the year because eating was one of our main bonding activities. Almost any church occasion included a meal. But Christmas Eve, Gertie prepared and provided the entire meal. For many of the chorus, Gertie's Christmas extravaganza outdid Christmas dinner at their home. (Not for me. I haven't talked about Miriam's cooking, yet. However, Miriam was a very health-conscious cook, whereas taste, not nutrition, was clearly Gertie's only concern.)

At about nine-thirty or ten o'clock on Christmas Eve we spilled out of the cars and tromped into the Koch dining room which contained a magazine-worthy smorgasbord of meats (from local livestock, of course, or perhaps even venison from a lucky hunter), potatoes (freshly mashed), noodles (made from scratch), home frozen vegetables and breads and rolls (all made that day) and butter from the Koch cows. Desserts required their own separate table.

It never occurred to me until now that the Koch's probably had left-overs for Christmas dinner. Not necessarily, though. More likely, Gertie got up at 4 a.m. and started over on another feast.

And we laughed. I'm surprised that any of us could sleep after the rich food, wickedly sweet desserts, and all the conviviality and good humor. We went to bed smiling. The Kochs didn't really have a cameo role any other time of year, didn't teach or usher or stand out from other parishioners, but Gertie more than made up for it on Christmas Eve every year.

Coming in a distant second, only because Gertie set such a high bar, was the Easter sunrise breakfast. For this we had John and Mildred Frankenfield to thank. They were the leaders of our youth group which met one Monday evening a month (my brother remembered that!) and planned all sorts of service projects, which, in retrospect, served us as much or more than anybody else. Of all the things we did, though, I think Easter breakfast was the only time we kids tried feeding others. We lived in a Pennsylvania Dutch farming community with some of the best cooks in the state. Nobody wanted our youthful, unpolished culinary efforts. Easter Sunday morning was the exception.

No ham in the world compared to the gigantic ham Mildred and John cooked in their roaster. It took John hours to carve, it was so big. And, dear heaven, if you want a delicious piece of meat, cook something big. Same with coffee. We made coffee in massive urns in that church kitchen and everyone raved about the delicious coffee. We also managed to serve dozens of scrambled eggs. I'm sure we were generous with the butter which made them scrumptious. Each of us brought bread and rolls from home. It was a wonderful meal.

We sat at large tables covered in white paper with china plates and real silverware. No plastic for Easter morning. Serving plates heaped with food lined the middle of the tables. Reverend Bieber offered a prayer, we'd have a few minutes of noise while everyone jostled for food, and then silence would reign. Gradually people would start talking and laughing, sharing their plans for the day, although in those days most people were headed to grandma's after the church service.

While Christmas Eve and Easter Morning were the two big events, they were far from the only ones. There wasn't a month when we didn't have a church dinner for some occasion. Summer picnics were great fun. Up came the long tables from the basement, covered with that endless white paper, and picnic baskets claimed whose spaces were whose. There was invariably some theme or reason to get together. I remember a lot of chicken suppers with a staggering variety of dishes to share. Anyone who couldn't find something they liked to eat at those suppers was not Pennsylvania Dutch.

A note about the term I use so much: Pennsylvania Dutch. Durham is not actually in Pennsylvania Dutch country, which is west of Durham, around Lancaster. Pennsylvania Dutch, as we're called, is a version of "Deutsch," meaning those of German origin, like my ancestors: Rau, Hindenach, Leidich, Lambert, Beidleman. Pennsylvania Deutsch is defined as a dialect of High German spoken in parts of Pennsylvania chiefly by descendants of 17th and 18th century Protestant immigrants from the Rhineland.

From the Hindenach side of my family, for example, we have Elias Beidleman who was born in Palantinate, Germany, September 17, 1707 and "sailed to America on the 'Thistle' in September 1730." Nicholas Hess, another Hindenach ancestor, sailed to America in 1741. These facts come from Aunt Kitty's son, John-Pierre Hannam, who traced my mom's genealogy back nine generations. I'd love to spend an afternoon in Durham Cemetery with that record in my hands!

The Pennsylvania Dutch practice many different religions: Amish, Mennonite, Moravian, Lutheran, and German Reformed, are examples. The umbrella similarities include the Germanic mother tongue, a proclivity for farming, cleanliness, simplicity of style, thriftiness, and plentiful, quality, home grown food. We are not known as "light eaters." When my husband and I went to Berlin in 1970 we got so weighed down by the heavy German food that on our last night there we went to a Japanese restaurant. The Morning Call

(Allentown, Pennsylvania) published a weekly newspaper column, written in Pennsylvania Dutch, which, as far as I could tell, was pretty much German with a few liberties. Every week Gram would sit down and translate that column "to keep sharp" on her language skills. (*For additional information see:*

https://richardmammana.wordpress.com/2022/04/03/s-pennsylvaanisch-deitsch-eck/)

Mostly, I'd say Pennsylvania Dutch is a cultural label which simply means that we may be identified by those features I mentioned. Others, like the Irish, French, British or Italian immigrants seemed to have identifying similarities, too, which they packed up and brought across the Atlantic with them.

Back to food: we had no spaghetti or pasta other than egg noodles. We Germanic types didn't sauce our tomatoes. If it was summer, they were sliced cold, with a sprinkle of sugar, or fried in a flour crust. In the winter they were stewed and served on mashed potatoes. Homemade noodles were aplenty; breads and rolls and muffins were available in dozens of varieties. Corn on the cob and fresh green beans sat beside the coleslaw and the sauerkraut. Piccalilli, a relish everyone made differently, consisted of lima beans, corn, carrots and other vegetables left in the summer garden and mixed with an oil and vinegar dressing. Our coleslaw was dressed in mayonnaise and vinegar. Oh, and good heaven, the quantity and variety of pickles! What a feast!

Supper was often followed by singing, music, or just "fellowship" as people sat around to "kibitz." Sometimes the meal might have followed a meeting or a church service celebrating something ecumenical or familial, if a family was commemorating an occasion. The Lutherans and the Reformed folks, who apparently couldn't agree on how to pray or preach, didn't seem to have any problem eating together.

The Church Picnic, though, was the top dog celebration every summer. For this the Quakertown Community Band came to play which was a very big deal! (Again, thanks to my brother, the musician and music teacher, for this memory!) We ate first. Of course. Then the band played while we tried to recover from feasting. After that we were ready for the games to begin.

Behind the church parking lot sat a low building divided into about six separate "stalls" where horses were stabled back in the days when folks came to church in their horse-drawn buggies. Now, in the days of cars, this raggedy old building sat empty until once or twice a year when it was called into use. On rainy picnic days, the stalls kept us dry while we ate our suppers. Families took up entire tables. Most of us were related to each other through marriages either recent or going back generations. All of us knew and loved (or kindly tolerated) each other.

Stables at Durham Church. (photo: Martin Stemler, 2013)

After the meal and band concert, while the older folks sat around and talked, we kids were sent to play games at the carnival segment of the church picnic. I remember "fishing." For a penny, or maybe a nickel, each child was handed a fishing pole and behind the curtain in front of us something magical and wonderful was attached to the hook on the end of the line. (For safety, the hook was actually a clothes pin.) What treasures we caught: coloring books or little dolls or dump trucks. Somehow the treasure always matched the age and gender of the child.

We wandered from one stall to another and tried our hand at each of the games. One game had a small swimming pool (probably a metal watering trough from some temporarily thirsty pig) with things a child might like bobbing in it. Another game was a bottle toss, where you had to get a ring over the top of a bottle. Everyone received a prize no matter the age or skill level of the participant. We all left, smiling, with surprises in our hands.

Another of the favorite celebrations, at least my favorite, was Harvest Home Sunday. I remember clearly that the Church was never more beautifully decorated than it was on this fall Sunday. The growing season was over, crops were gathered, and the women had preserved, canned, and pickled everything that didn't escape their eager hands. Then, on this Sunday, they brought their offerings and laid them around the chancel of the church.

When the service was over, this bounty would go to the needy. Either old folks' homes, children's homes or food pantries would be gifted with beautiful big canning jars full of vegetables, fruit, pie filling, piccalilli, pickles, everything pickled known to man, including pickled meats, pickled beans and surely pickled "sweet meats." (Don't ask!) These were displayed on bales of hay and the church looked like a picture in a gourmet food magazine. We all left church on Harvest Home Sunday with stomachs growling. The bounty was as overflowing as was the generosity of the people who worshipped there.

One remarkable difference between the generation when I was a child and the generation when I had children of my own was church attendance. When I was a child in Durham, church attendance was non-negotiable. This was true for all of my friends and everyone in Vera Riegel's Sunday School class. We were all there every Sunday. But fascinatingly, it wasn't a battle and we weren't "forced" or "bribed" or "threatened." I wanted to go to Sunday School, and I never heard anyone else complain.

Part of the "privilege" of church attendance was what the options were if we stayed home. (We wouldn't be watching television, which most of us didn't even have yet, much less playing on Xbox or talking or texting on our phones. The only phones around were hanging on the kitchen wall and used mostly for emergencies since we couldn't "tie up" the party line.) Farm kids had chores. Endless chores. I wasn't one of them, but many of the kids in church were. For those of us from "town" the choices were reading or starting to fix Sunday dinner which might have included peeling potatoes or apples and/or setting a big table.

The most horrible consequence of not going to church was missing Sunday dinner if it was at Grandma's because, believe me, no one was going to come back and get you. You went with the boat, or you were left on shore. I don't know about other kids, but it never occurred to me that there was anything better to do than be part of what everyone else in Durham was doing, whether it was baseball, sledding or church.

THE RAINS CAME DOWN

In 1955 two hurricanes, Connie and Diane, arrived on each other's heels. They caused one of the worst floods in history for the Delaware River, the river which divides Pennsylvania and New Jersey. Two miles from the river, in Durham, the Riegel's and the Kunkle's properties flooded from spillover from the millrace, which couldn't drain fast enough. The Melchior's house looked like a houseboat, totally surrounded by water from Cook's Creek. Karen remembers her family's relief when the water leveled off a half inch below their living room floor. Tony's basements under both the house and store were swamped. The Riegel, Kunkle, and Melchior families took the major hit in Durham.

No one could get from Durham up the hill to the school or the church – or down into Durham -- because the bridge was flooded. That old stone bridge, built in 1925, didn't collapse, though. The flood waters receded, and the bridge was littered with things no one wanted to identify, but it stood tough.

Along the Delaware River, it was a different, devastating story. Two hundred people lost their lives in that flood, and the destruction to property and livestock was catastrophic. Freddie Trauger owned the loveliest, most fertile farm land anywhere around. It was a wide strip of rich soil between the Delaware River and the canal which ran along the river. At most places the canal flowed directly beside the river, with the road, Route 611, winding immediately beside the canal. But Trauger's Farm was an exception to that. A wide strip of land had somehow formed or remained between the river and the canal. The ensuing farm was a wide island a couple miles long; Freddie Trauger had a goldmine in that rich farmland.

Freddie grew mostly corn, but since crops were seasonal, he also raised chickens. Lots of chickens. I'll say thousands of chickens. Not trying to be a wise guy here, but chickens can't swim for long. Freddie Trauger lost the late plantings of his beautiful, golden corn, but more disastrously, he lost all of his chickens to The Flood of 1955.

As the Durham Historical Society Newsletter said in a story about The Flood, "The river and the Delaware Canal merged in the fields at Trauger's farm." Mary Shafer, an author who lives in nearby Ferndale, wrote about the "deadly flood of 1955" in a book entitled *Devastation on the Delaware*.

I don't know who else helped the Traugers, but I know my dad did, for more than one day. In addition to being a financial disaster, the flood caused a massive mess. Luckily one of the other men who had come to help brought a supply of cigarettes. Now, my dad was not a smoker, so we never knew, when he came home looking green, if it was from the stench of dead chickens or the cigarettes he had to smoke all day to deal with the dead chickens. By the time we sat down for supper, he was in no mood to talk about anything that had transpired that day. I believe when he thought back over his life, he would admit that helping Freddie Trauger was one of the most difficult and miserable good deeds he had ever performed.

But all along the Delaware and all along the creeks that fed into the Delaware there were bridges destroyed, homes collapsed, and mud, silt and the wettest, messiest goop left stranded in the most unexpected places. Gardens were ruined, and basements were damp and smelly. I doubt if anyone named their daughters Connie or Diane for a few years.

TELEVISION

The first thing you noticed when you looked at the small black box which was the television were the tiny white dots all across the screen. We called this "snow." I remember squinting like crazy to try to see the blurry picture on the little screen. Years later, while driving through a whiteout, I realized, "This is just like that first television set we had." The cabinet housing the television was as big as a desk and the TV screen was as small as a computer – somewhere between 9 and 17 inches. (I looked it up. I didn't know the measurements – just that the screen was small and you had to sit close to see much of anything!)

Having to sit close to the television, probably within two feet, was a constant source of "difficulty" between my mother and me. "Susan, move back from the television," she would say repeatedly. The parental suspicion was that sitting close to whatever electricity was behind that small panel of glass was probably not good for kids and, in particular, would harm their eyes. Because my eyes had already taken a childhood beating, my mother was on high alert to preserve whatever could be preserved. So, I would dutifully move back whenever told to and then, unknowingly, since I couldn't make out what was happening under the snow, I'd inch forward. "Susan, move back."

We were not the first people in Durham to buy a television set, not by a long shot. My parents were more the type to watch others experiment with new-fangled inventions until the invention had proven reliable and worth the money, then they'd join in purchasing.

Gram and Grandad Hindenach even had a television before we did. Remember, Grandad worked at a furniture store, and I think the store sold this latest addition for the family living room. Sunday evenings we'd drive to their house for supper and TV – a change from the former visit for lunch after church -- so we could watch *Meet the Press* and *Ed Sullivan*. The advent of television might have changed the time of day we visited the grandparents, but not the fact that their house was still where we could be found every Sunday.

My brother, the skunk, was allowed to bike to neighbor Arthur Frey's during the week and watch Frontier Playhouse, which hosted a variety of cowboy shows. I shouldn't have been resentful because I imagine his lobbying for a television set of our own was instrumental in our getting one.

Speaking of cowboy shows, Karen and I were glued to the sets when Roy Rogers and Dale Evans or Annie Oakley were on. We had to watch so we knew how to keep the streets of Durham safe from the bad guys and to pick up hints on how to twirl those six-shooters of ours. Even today, as in our childhood, Karen and I will joyfully sing, "Happy trails to you, until we meet again; happy trails to you, keep smiling until then!"

Between the snow on the TV screens and the rather predictable plots on all the shows, television required a lot of imagination in those days. There was no sex, no blood, no gore, no terror or trauma from watching a television show in the 1950's. The criminals were usually rehabilitated before the show was over, and the heroes rarely ever lost their hats. Most often, the criminal was just a desperate community member down on his luck. The town would help out, and all would be forgiven. Seriously. That was the television plot most frequently used.

Quick flash to 2022: The place where I go here in rural Johnston County, North Carolina to get my car fixed or my oil changed has a small waiting room with a very large television that is constantly re-running old black and white westerns. While waiting for my car, I am reminded of the predictable story lines and how "clean" the language was on those early shows. Compared to today, they were so innocent and uplifting.

Other programs were on television in the 1950's besides the generous supply of westerns, but Karen and I weren't interested in the variety shows, the quiz shows, or the comedies. We loved the cowboys and cowgirls! As children, there were only certain hours we got to choose the channel or the show. If there was an adult, or even a big brother (in my case, big sister in Karen's case) in the room, we were out of luck. That's just the way it was. The pecking order was firmly in place and favored age. I remember watching westerns on Saturday mornings when, mercifully, everyone older must have been busy.

JAKE WAMPFLER

In addition to Tony Melchior, the genius at backing a school bus into a tight space, Durham was home to another extraordinary school bus driver who was famous for a number of reasons. Jake Wampfler lived along Route 212, about halfway, or a mile, between Durham and the Delaware River in a stone house which should have been pretty but wasn't. I found it somewhat intimidating and foreboding. My granddaughter would today label it "sketchy."

Apparently, the house did not reflect the man, though, except perhaps to reveal that he was too busy being creative and entrepreneurial to worry about the upkeep of his home and yard. Jake was an inventor and held a number of patents; he saw a need, and did something about it.

During World War II, gasoline was strictly rationed. A number of men from Durham and the surrounding area worked at Bethlehem Steel. Unfortunately, the drive to Bethlehem five or six days a week required more gas for the commute than was allotted to each man by the gas ration. Jake concluded he should procure a bus because if you had a bus, and were transporting a number of people, you were permitted a larger gas ration. So, Jake put out the news – by word of mouth, of course. No internet or cell phone existed, just people who talked to each other. He devised a route whereby he picked up a goodly number of Steel employees in the morning and delivered them back home at night.

It would be interesting to know what Jake charged for his bus service. Dave Rau was one of his loyal riders. One reason many of the men wanted to participate was, of course, to conserve gasoline and help the war effort. A second reason may have been equally compelling: many of Jake's riders took voluntary civilian air defense shifts during the night and went down to the river to stop traffic and keep a watch on the skies. It was challenging to stay alert driving back and forth to Bethlehem when these men had been up walking along the river all night. Riding Jake's bus to and from the Steel allowed for napping.

With no unified radar for air defense, civilian aircraft spotters were stationed at observation points so they could look for and report nightly air traffic. Another part of the job was making sure that no cars were driving along the river road with lights on since a blackout was enforced. "They also serve who stand and observe," was the slogan that recruited them for duty. My dad, like so many others, was on the schedule and did his part.

All this watchfulness was necessary because Bethlehem Steel was so crucial to the war effort. Bethlehem and the surrounding area were believed to be possible and probable bombing sites. Bethlehem Steel employed 300,000 workers during World War II and manufactured 1,121 ships, making almost every part of the ship, as well as armor, ordnance, guns and munitions. To have destroyed Bethlehem Steel would have been to cripple the navy and the United States forces. The USS Missouri, the USS Lexington, the USS Massachusetts, and the USS Hancock were among the more famous of Bethlehem Steel's contributions. (*For additional information see:*

https://ei.lehigh.edu/envirosci/watershed/history/industry/steel.html)

Dave Rau, rule-follower and patriot extraordinaire, would definitely have gone into military service, but he would never have been accepted. When he was eighteen, he was picking apples high in a tree and fell, landing in a cement culvert. He broke his back and spent half a year in St. Luke's Hospital under the care of a nurse named Olive Pickle. Yes, truly, Olive somebody-or-other married Mr. Pickle. What were the chances?

No matter her name, my father would have canonized her if possible. The treatment for a broken back in 1929 was rather primitive. They straightened him out, rearranged those bones, and strapped him to a solid surface. Every twelve hours he was flipped over. Twelve hours looking at the ceiling; twelve hours looking at the floor. For six months! Unable to do anything about that, and unable to unstrap him, Olive took kind and gentle care of the man with the broken back.

If you saw Dave Rau, you would say, "There is a man with the best posture I have ever seen." That man's back was ramrod straight. So, my dad stood, very straight, indeed, and observed, as his part in the war effort, and let Jake Wampfler chauffeur him back and forth to Bethlehem, no doubt sneaking in a nap both directions.

My father was legendary for his napping skills, perhaps learned on Jake's bus and perfected throughout life. He demonstrated this skill once when he was playing cards with my three little boys. The youngest had just learned to shuffle and deal and was doing both - this was not a quick process at that time. Finally, after everyone was dealt their cards and picked them up, the boys turned to look at their grandfather, who was not gathering in his cards. Sound asleep.

Another example of my dad's napping "skills" could have had disastrous consequences. He actually fell asleep on Interstate 80 driving to Ohio to see us. While crossing over a bridge, the car swerved into the low curb on the side of the bridge. The jolt awakened him, and he was able to get the car under control. He pulled over to the berm of the road. A trucker saw what happened and stopped to help. It was that kind soul who changed the flat tire which was mercifully the only result of that quick nap. The trucker almost made my dad cry because he refused money for his kindness.

As a result of the near disaster on Route 80, my mother put her crossword puzzle book away and began a campaign of chattering to her sleep-prone husband. For the rest of their lives, she never again took her eyes off her husband when he was driving. She also amassed a fine supply of candies and mints to keep him a little revved up. Unfortunately, my mom's stay-awake campaign wasn't 100% effective because there was another time Dave Rau's ability to fall asleep at the drop of a hat could have been tragic. My parents had picked up Molly's mom, Esther, in Bethlehem and the three of them were heading to Massachusetts for Skip and Molly's daughter Gretchen's graduation. Mom was turned in the seat, talking to Esther, when Dad nodded off. The car veered toward the side of the road. Mom hollered, and once again Dad was able to correct quickly enough to have kept from wiping out the entire supply of living grandparents. He noted in his 1995 calendar: "Bad accident. I feel asleep and ran off road and right back on. I sure was embarrassed. Thank God all ended well."

Now, back to Jake Wampfler's claim to fame: he saw the need for steps to be attached to the rear exit of all school buses. In an emergency, when the rear door was required for a quick escape, the distance to jump was dangerously far for younger children to land safely.

We all understood that Jake held the patent on this invention of his, which did appear on every bus we saw after that. When I looked it up recently, on Google, I found one picture of a Jake Wampfler taken in 1929 in nearby Tinicum, Bucks County, behind a plow. There was no mention of rear exit steps for school buses. That's kind of sad. Jake's simple but necessary invention has probably been so updated and revolutionized that now a button releases plastic steps which clean themselves before sliding back into the belly of the bus. Sorry, Jake. I remember what you did. We were all really proud of you!

OUR MOTHER'S COOKING

One thing on which my brother and I totally agree is that our mother wasn't just a good cook, she was a perfect cook.

Everything she cooked tasted like itself. The green beans weren't hidden in bacon and onion or drowned in cream of mushroom soup. The green beans were green beans, simmered to the exact moment when they were tender but still a little springy on your tongue. If you don't like any given vegetable, it's because you never tasted it as prepared by Miriam Rau, who had picked it fresh from her garden that morning.

Her mother, my dear Gram, was a woman who *had* to cook. Miriam Rau was a woman who *lived* to cook. The only kitchen disaster she ever endured was right after she cleaned our oven.

Cleaning the oven in days gone by was not a matter of setting a timer and enduring the smell while all the crusty residue in the oven baked off the sides and deposited a pile of ashes on the floor of the oven. No. Cleaning the oven was an ordeal not many housewives undertook. (It was easier to buy a new oven!) To begin, one removed the racks from the oven and battled with them separately. Then the entire oven was sprayed with a foul-smelling concoction misnamed Easy Off. There was nothing easy about the off.

Adding to the grief of the project was the physical impossibility of twisting and contorting oneself so the back, top and sides of the oven could be reached. This required knees on the kitchen floor and body mostly inside the oven. The necessity for this contortion was that Easy Off might loosen grime on the oven walls and top, but it surely did not remove it. That required scrubbing. Steel wool pads could be used but risked permanent scratches on the oven's surface. Actual elbow grease was the safest bet. Lots of elbow grease.

We're talking about, if you were focused and practiced, a two-hour ordeal. And then came the stretching out and trying to stand up straight because you still had the two racks to scrub. A headache was common. The smell was strong and not pleasant, to say the least. Despite the best efforts of the person cleaning, (it was always a woman, but I'm trying not to be sexist,) the floor always ended up a mess as did the adjacent counters and sink, where the racks had been soaking in a vain attempt to loosen burned on grime.

So, I was about ten, and I think it was right before the impending disaster when I had the misfortune to ask my mother what the horrible smell was. She explained that she had just cleaned the oven, and that the odor would soon be replaced by the lovely aroma of baking potatoes, which we Pennsylvania Dutch think is probably the welcoming smell at the Gates of Heaven. If you believe the Irish like potatoes, you haven't met the Pennsylvania Dutch.

It was at about that lovely, quiet moment, my mother triumphant and in control, that we heard the boom of an explosion come from inside the oven. My mother said a word I had never heard in our house: "DAMN!" In her exhaustion, she had forgotten to prick one of the potatoes. That one potato with the tight skin and no air vents, exploded all over, and I mean all over, her clean oven. Who knew a potato could disintegrate into that many small, sticky, starchy pieces? And those pieces covered, like a first snowfall, her immaculate, sparkling clean oven.

I muttered something about homework and escaped to my bedroom.

Other than that, my mother had a flawless record in the kitchen (It lasted all her life. Amazing.) Her pies crusts were browned to perfection, her meat never came out dry, her hand-mashed potatoes were never lumpy, and here's the most amazing feat of all: her fruit salad.

My children, three thankless boys, were ridiculously fussy eaters at home. Nothing suited them, and nothing I made was eaten by more than one of the three. But let us go to Grandma's, and the story stood on its head. I would just look at them in disgust as they would fawn all over her cooking. Oh, Grandma, this meat (which they didn't know the name of because back in Akron they wouldn't try it) is SO good.

Well, those same three boys, who would never touch a piece of fruit, especially not a grapefruit or an orange, LOVED her fruit salad. Do you know what that woman did? She spent hours cutting the fruit into individual sections and then squeezing the juice over the sections. (It would take me thirty minutes to section one orange. I know, because, one day, feeling delusional, I tried.) My mother probably cut up and sectioned a dozen oranges and a dozen grapefruit. When the boys ate it all, she effortlessly cut up more.

But here's the rub. This is what really fries me. Never, and I mean never, because they looked, never did my boys find ONE seed in the dag-blasted fruit salad. Not one. No lumps in the mashed potatoes. No over-baked or under baked pastry, no tough, stringy roast beef, no rare hamburgers, unless requested by a guest, nothing, not one simple solitary thing that wasn't cooked perfectly.

My mother set an unachievable standard!

But it gets even worse or better, depending on who is telling the story, and depending on whether you're expected, as Miriam Rau's daughter, for example, to have inherited this skill and meet the standard she's set, or whether you can just sit back and enjoy the delicious results.

Once, when my brother Skip was teaching music in Vermont, he brought his jazz band back to our high school for a concert. He and his former high school music teacher, Bob Homonay, had become good friends, and this was a long-overdue reunion, so their bands could play together. The concert was scheduled for February, and my brother planned to treat his band to supper before the concert. It snowed. That didn't bother those going to the concert - they lived in eastern Pennsylvania and were used to February snows. But unexpectedly, the restaurant my brother had chosen to take the band closed.

What else could he do – he called his mother. "Come here," she invited. So, Skip showed up a short time later with seventeen hungry teenagers. My mother fed them hamburgers, French fries, side dishes of all sorts and cherry pie. Not only did she have enough food for eighteen spur-of-the-moment guests, she fed them all the same thing. Now, I could feed a few people if they showed up on my doorstep, but they certainly wouldn't be eating the same thing--as though I had intuitively known a crowd was coming by for supper in the middle of a blizzard.

And speaking of cherry pie. My mother was famous three counties away for the lightest, flakiest pie crust known to man (or woman or child). I really don't remember my mom ever serving anything other than pie for dessert, because any guest who didn't get her pie would think Mom was angry or holding a grudge. "What's Miriam got against me that she didn't make pie for me?" Even after the spaghetti dinners that our dad and the guys from work had, when my mom hosted them, pie was required. The Maiorello's always brought the spaghetti sauce, of course. Why trust a German Rau with pasta sauce when there was an Italian Maiorello available?

But there is a strange story about her cherry pie. Remember the no seeds in the fruit salad? Well, no one ever found a pit in the cherry pie, either. Except our dad. He found a pit in every cherry pie she ever made for over 60 years. Uncanny. Inexplicable. True. It got to the point where he never said anything, but we always checked his plate after the dessert course. There it was. One single, solitary pit. And nobody ever got one but him. You could mix up the plates and not give him the one my mom said was for him. It never mattered. We tried everything. We thought for a while he was just playing a trick on us and carried a cherry pit in his pocket, but we watched him like hawks and could never detect any foul play.

If you were sick, Mom whipped up a little homemade chicken noodle soup. When I had my wisdom teeth extracted, she made me a baked potato every night for a week. When I had my first job at Easton Hospital and had to leave home at 6:20 every morning to get to work on time, she woke me up and then went down stairs and cooked fresh green beans and sliced fresh strawberries – my choice of menu – for two months.

She and our dad once babysat Skip and Molly's Dalmatian, Felicity. Felicity took sick under our parents' care, and they rushed her to the vet who suggested chicken broth. My mother got out a chicken and made the dog fresh chicken broth. Of course, Felicity recovered. Any self-respecting human, or animal, would have recovered with that level of care. (And you know what Felicity did two years later? She bit a child and had to be put down. My mother was not happy!)

Since Mom paid attention to every detail, she remembered what each child in the family liked and those favorites magically appeared. She always had just the right thing for each of my boys – gum in the drawer for Andy, doughnuts in the bread drawer for Eddie, and red licorice waiting for Nick. One Christmas Nick and Gretchen, the two youngest of five grandkids, each got their own can of black olives so they wouldn't have to share with anyone. Mom's thoughtfulness and planning accentuated her amazing ability as the best cook any of us have ever known or will ever know.

My brother and I have both tried unsuccessfully to replicate her peach cream pie – the loveliest texture and taste any tongue ever experienced. We have the recipe in her hand writing! We do suspect, however, that it might have been that the peaches were from Uncle Hollis' orchard which made the pie irreplicable.

It was no coincidence, either, that my father always said the same thing when he rose from his chair at the dining room table. I might add, before I state his remark, that his step-mother was a woman not known for her cooking. (More about that next.) Every time my dad left the table where his wife had prepared food, he said, "Miriam, thank you. That was a wonderful meal." Whether it was potato soup for a Sunday night supper or a sandwich when he came home between jobs--and he arrived at 12 noon sharp--he never failed to thank her and tell her how much he enjoyed and appreciated her cooking. I wonder how big a part of her attention to detail was because her husband never took her for granted – in 64 years -- and never missed an opportunity to tell her how grateful he was.

GRANDMA RAU

On the other end of the cooking spectrum was Grandma Rau. Grandma Rau's parents were Reverend Charles Oliver Melchior, beloved pastor extraordinaire of the Durham Lutheran congregation, and his wife, Anna, Grandma Melchior, described as 'saintly' by all who knew her. My dad was sixteen and sitting alone with her, holding her hand, when she died.

Grandma Rau.

Grandma and Grandpa Melchior had four children. Two of the three boys went off to college on scholarships and then taught at Syracuse or MIT or some other prestigious university. They were very much "head people." The parents and third son were definitely "heart people." The third son was Charlie about whom we will speak later. Charlie deserves his own cameo appearance here.

But the fourth child, Mary Montfort Melchior, known to me as Grandma Rau, was another "head person" -- definitely a woman ahead of her time. Today she would have been an editor at a newspaper or a librarian, but I don't believe she had or took the opportunity for professional education. Grandma and Grandpa Melchior were impoverished. As a pastor of a small country church, he earned a pittance of a salary. When he officiated at a wedding or funeral, he was most often paid on the barter system: some tasks would be completed at his home, or on his land, or he'd be given a pig or a fruit tree – or whatever "extra" the family had that they thought "the preacher" might want or need. So, I suspect there was no money for Grandma Rau to be sent to college, but I do think she attended business school.

Grandma Rau loved to write in a journalistic style and was a good typist. (I remember her black typewriter – a Smith-Corona.) She also loved to talk on the phone and was a crafty investigative reporter. Unfortunately, how she used these skills was a source of aggravation for many in the community. My father frequently had to "have words with her."

My dad was five and Aunt Agnes eight when Grandad, Floyd Rau, married Mary Melchior. They "took up housekeeping" across the street from the home where Mary grew up, the Melchior home. Both houses were along Route 212, a little over a mile west of Durham.

Dave and Agnes learned immediately upon arrival at their new home with their new step-mother that their first and most vital lesson was how to cross the street safely. Luckily, they had lived in Bethlehem along a much busier street for the first years of their young lives. Crossing the street to Grandma and Grandad Melchior was imperative and much desired because it was a matter of health: physical – getting enough to eat, and emotional – getting some loving. The sweetness, kindness, attention and edibles were to be found on the other side of the street.

Grandma Rau was a woman who attended to business. Additionally, she was eccentric and quite self-contained. It didn't seem to bother her that neither her biological daughter nor her step-daughter liked her. She just went her own way and did her own thing. And the typewriter was an integral part of her efforts.

Grandma was "a stringer" for several local papers, and since she was paid by the word, she became verbose. Because she never learned to drive and rarely went anywhere, she collected her "news" through her numerous phone calls to unsuspecting people who thought they were just having a chat with a neighbor. Imagine their surprise when their words appeared – properly quoted, of course, she did know her business – in the local paper.

One incident I recall clearly was the time Witte's planned a two-week vacation. Grandma Rau wrote this up, quite accurately, and it appeared in the paper like an open invitation to anyone wishing to remove anything or everything from the Witte's home: The Witte's will be gone for two weeks starting on this date and won't be returning until this date. She may as well have said: Their house will be empty and ripe for the picking! (They lived in a secluded spot just across Haupt's Mill Bridge, a rustic old covered bridge, on a hill and out of sight for the most part.)

The Wittes called my father, as everyone seemed to, pleading that he "have words" with Grandma Rau. Off he went. Words were had. She would listen and then slowly slip back into her need to find news. This caused her to lose perspective on what the news might mean to the people involved. Grandma couldn't seem to focus on much of anything except her word count.

She also seemed to lose focus in the kitchen. First of all, let me say that it was the most unusual kitchen I have ever seen. Ever. It was a short person's kitchen, which was suitable since Grandma Rau barely topped 5 feet. Anyone else working in the kitchen would suffer an instantaneous backache from bending over.

I remember one Easter Sunday, stooping over washing dishes after a dozen of us had enjoyed a truly delicious ham. (Ham was a good thing for Grandma to make; it is hard to wreck a big ham.) Grandma Rau was not one of those cooks who cleans up as they go along, and I think I was washing dishes from a week or two before, as well as after, Easter dinner. It was days before I could stand up straight, and I was young and agile then. I know I had to change the water and start over at least three times with a fresh sink full of hot water and suds. Some experiences just stick with a person.

The highlight of Grandma Rau's Easter dinner was always her angel food cake. Mention angel food cake to anyone who was there, and you'll get a snort, a smile, or a shake of the head. This special cake sat on a pedestal cake plate on her desk in the dining room all through dinner. It was a work of art. No exaggeration, that cake was ten inches high and perfectly browned. After the main course, Grandma would bring out the cake plates, which had belonged to her mother, and a knife that looked like it moonlighted as her security system. Brandish that knife at someone, and they'd turn tail. The angel food cake didn't think much of that knife, either.

Maybe she bought the cake; we never knew, but it surely didn't seem representative of her usual attitude toward a culinary task. That cake was exquisite. Magazine covers would have featured it. And then she put that knife to it. It was a travesty. My mother could have cut that cake and it would have hung over the cake plates. Not Grandma Rau. What we were served was no more than a two-inch-high square. Under her carving, the air, which she had carefully baked into the cake, came rushing out. I'm surprised we couldn't hear the "Whoosh." Flat as a pancake. We'd sigh and eat it. It was still delicious, but somehow the whole angel food cake experience was diminished and a little depressing.

The cake was never iced. That would have been another entire debacle!

The entryway to Grandma Rau's home was under a grape arbor. Unusual, for sure, but of course it would be. Grandma grew big, fat, purple grapes which she liked to squeeze into grape juice. I had some once. I had ridden my bicycle to see her one summer day and arrived hot and sweaty. She asked if I'd like a nice cool glass of grape juice. That sounded wonderful.

Fifty years later, I was sitting in dignified silence in a room in Beijing, China being ceremonially served tea. I was on a Medical Mission trip with the Eisenhower Foundation exchanging ideas and treatments for PTSD with Chinese mental health professionals and we were enjoying a break while tea was served. My psychiatrist friend, David Deckert, was beside me and scribbled a quick note to me: "Keep your teeth closed while drinking – tea leaves in bottom of cup."

I took a small sip and almost spit out my tea. Only once before had I ever tried to drink a beverage with all kinds of pieces/parts/pulp mixed in with the liquid: in Grandma Rau's kitchen when I tasted the incredibly delicious but unstrained grape juice.

It is very challenging to quietly and politely drink a beverage containing floating residue. Then, remembering the grape fiasco, I started giggling. I was afraid I'd cause an international incident, but David kicked me under the table, and I straightened up.

Grandma Rau was a complicated character. It was she who always kept a lamp burning in the front window "to cheer the weary traveler." She was fascinating to talk to; she knew a little about a lot. Floyd, her husband, who had worked for the railroad and apparently been a soft-spoken, kind man, died when he was in his fifties during the first year of my life. Grandma lived alone for more than twenty-five years. She never had any money. I took both grandmas, Hindenach and Rau, grocery shopping many times. I remember one Saturday when Grandma Rau spent $4.39 for her weeks' worth of food. (Who could forget?)

Don't you love it: just when you think you have someone figured out, they surprise you. Around the age of seventy-five, Grandma announced she was selling her house and moving to Quakertown to live with Walter Unangst. In typical Grandma Rau fashion, she had spoken to no one about this, well, except, of course Walter Unangst, himself. We assumed she had cleared this with him, although, being Grandma Rau, that could have been a mistaken assumption.

Now, no one knew or was saying what the dimensions of this relationship might be. How long had this been brewing and how hot was the brew? Unknown. Was this a lovely romance come to blossom late in life or a strong friendship that had been building? We only knew Grandma had her own room in Walter's house. Beyond that, everyone seemed to keep his and her noisiness and speculation under wraps.

The unanimous conclusion seemed to be that it was lovely that Grandma Rau, long the loner, would be "keeping company" with Walter, however they chose to keep that company. Now Walter would have a lamp burning in the window to cheer the weary traveler. And, like Grandma and Walter, I keep a lamp burning at night in the window of every home in which I have lived. And I often think of Grandma Rau when I turn on the lamp or bake an angel food cake. Except for communion, I haven't had grape juice since.

Who do you call when there's a house to clean out and sell? Right. Call Dave Rau. In comes my father to sort through years and years of newspapers and STUFF. Grandma Rau wasn't exactly a packrat, but she did hate to throw things away; she had that "you might need it someday" mentality. What fit in Grandma's room at

Walter's was taken to Quakertown, and then my father got down to an all-too-familiar job. He had another house to clean out, clean up, and prepare for sale. No wonder he liked to sit and tell stories after a meal. The poor man never got a break.

UNCLE CHARLIE

So, Grandma Rau's brother, Charles, whom everyone called Charlie, was the topic of many of my father's entertaining after-dinner stories. Uncle Charlie is my friend and cousin Karen's grandfather and her father, Tony's, father. Charlie married Gram's sister, Mary Mae, whom everyone called Mae. (You notice in that family we had sisters named Mary and Martha. Someone read the Bible!)

I know nothing about Mae except what may be surmised from the fact that she married Uncle Charlie. I'm reminded of a therapist friend from graduate school who spent an hour one day complaining to me about how irresponsible her young husband was. "He has used cars parked in our narrow driveway that he's going to fix someday. He owes his parents money, and he always has an excuse for why he's not paying them back. I can't trust him to cover his share of the bills." The litany went on and on. Finally, since she had offered nothing positive about the man, I asked why she had married him. She stopped and smiled. "He's so much fun," she admitted. I think that's what Mae might have said about Charlie. God knows, he has kept everyone laughing for generations.

Charlie and Mae apparently lived with Granddad and Grandma Melchior at some point and for some length of time. One day Charlie was upstairs changing his clothes. He took off all of his old, dirty clothes. This is an undisputed fact; we have witnesses. Simultaneously, Grandma Melchior was holding a meeting of the church ladies in her dining room, directly below the bedroom in which Charlie was changing.

Everything might have gone smoothly and without any disturbance to the ladies gathered around the table drinking tea, except that Charlie forgot one important fact: the floor of his closet was missing. It had been ripped up in preparation for replacement. Charlie, naked, stepped into the closet and dropped immediately and heavily to the dining room floor!

I would love to have heard the various responses when the women were gathered with their families around their supper tables that evening, and someone innocently asked how the ladies' church meeting had gone that afternoon. "Oh, someone dropped in," one of them may have said coyly.

Charlie did whatever farm work was done around the place with his best friend, a mule named, Belle. Like his sister, Grandma Rau, Belle, his mule, was apparently a woman with a mind of her own. She and Charlie had frequent skirmishes. Now, Charlie, the preacher's kid, loved to sing hymns, and he'd entertain himself while plowing with Belle by singing in a loud, strong voice. "Nearer My God to Thee," was apparently one of his favorites. Coincidentally, I'm sure, it was also what the band played while the Titanic sank.

Charlie did not like to exert himself any more than necessary. He was a man with a good appetite and an aversion to exercise, so what Charlie liked to do was get Belle started down a row and then sit and wait for her. She'd come to the end of the furrow and Charlie would call to her to come back. This was accompanied by one hymn or another until Belle lost concentration, or tested Charlie by wandering out of the row they were plowing.

There he'd be, singing "Nearer my God to Thee," and all of a sudden, the same booming voice would echo across the fields: "Goddammit, Belle, get back in the row." My dad acted this out perfectly; he could have won an Oscar for his performance. We'd beg for it time and time again!

The most unfortunate Uncle Charlie story required a tow truck or some such mechanism be brought from Springtown, which was only about a mile away. Of course, someone had to walk that mile, or saddle and ride a horse there to get the towing device. No one called on the cell phone for immediate service in those days, so Uncle Charlie, who had fallen through the floor of the outhouse, was "down there" for a while. Hours. We're talking hours. He was not singing hymns that time. The legend goes that he was fished out by a crane-like attachment, and while he was connected to the towing vehicle, he was hauled right on down to Cook's Creek and dropped in. Apparently, a few hours in the bowels of an outhouse is a pungent experience. Yes, it seems Uncle Charlie had a talent for falling through things!

AUNT KITTY

Katharyn, Dave, and Agnes all loved Grandma and Grandpa Melchior's house. Clearly, the major reason for this was that they loved their grandparents. Katharyn was Aunt Kitty to all of us. Much as she would wash out my mouth with soap for saying so, she possessed a number of Grandma Rau's characteristics. She was independent and self-contained. She was not the type person who talked things over with people and sought consensus. When she had an issue resolved in her mind, that was that.

Like Grandma Rau, she was also a woman way ahead of her time. First, she married a guy who, according to family lore was a real, legitimate bad boy. She had a child with him, and then broke with all the familial and cultural rules and divorced. Divorced. Unheard of. (Thirty years later I was the second family member to do the unthinkable and divorce.)

Katharyn, then, just to keep things interesting, and shocking, married a foreigner! A foreigner from a different country, not only not from eastern Pennsylvania! This man was a former French resistance fighter. Pierre charmed not only Katharyn, he charmed all of us. (Most of us. Walter Unangst was the only fellow to charm Grandma Rau at that stage of the game.) Actually, Pierre was a sweetheart. (Walter Unangst may have been, too. I never met him. But God bless him if he gave Grandma Rau some happy years.)

Then, Aunt Kitty broke additional familial and cultural norms and moved away! What a brave and adventurous woman. Katharyn, Pierre and their four children moved to New Jersey where they purchased and operated a drug store. It was a hard, exhausting life with no chance for time off. Running their drug store lasted about ten or twelve years and necessitated many trips between Bridgeton, New Jersey, the home of a Hunt's ketchup cannery, memorable because the very air smelled like ketchup, and Durham, Pennsylvania, the home of the relatives. I remember one car trip where we were bringing the already cooked turkey and fixings, got a flat tire, and had to unload the entire meal on the side of the road to get to the spare tire.

Two things prompted a change of course for the Bridgeton folks. First of all, Aunt Kitty had been trained as a teacher and wished to return to that occupation, and, secondly, the old Melchior home went up for sale. Aunt Kitty leaped on that, and the family moved back to Durham. She immediately landed a job teaching at Springfield Elementary School while Pierre began working nights collecting tolls at the Quakertown Exit of the Pennsylvania Turnpike. In his view this beat working seven days a week in a drug store.

My family enjoyed a hilarious Grandma Rau/Pierre Hannam Christmas story which begs to be shared. Grandma Rau, poor as a church mouse, did all her Christmas shopping in a thin little catalogue which appeared in the magazine section of the Sunday paper. I don't remember the name of it, but everything the catalogue offered cost 99 cents. It was the original Amazon/Dollar Tree – nothing above One Dollar by mail order.

Grandma's gifts were thoughtfully chosen. The first year I was married, my husband and I received pillow cases with our names stamped on them, lest we mix up our pillows and have a pillow fight, I guess. But this particular year, Grandma bought Pierre a car engine cover. Since it was below freezing at night for much of the winter, and Pierre needed to leave for work between 10 and 10:30 in the evening to get to his 11:00 o'clock shift, this was a very useful gift.

The motor cover, a large, non-descript piece of plastic, apparently had never been seen in France, nor had Pierre ever heard the necessity of covering one's car engine to keep it from freezing on a cold winter night. As an additional complication, our French family member arrived in America as an adult and was never completely fluent in English. All of us, and I mean all of us, tried that Christmas morning to explain to Pierre what he had just unwrapped. It was not happening! I think Aunt Kitty mercifully interrupted the futile attempts to tell us it was time to eat.

Aunt Kitty loved being back among family and settled into the family home. My dad, her older brother, had always been her hero, so she delighted in being around him. She earned a Master's Degree and became renowned for her teaching. She relaxed. She was home.

Siblings: Katharyn, David and Agnes.

DURHAM CIRCA 1956

When we Durham baby boomer kids were ten or eleven years old, it was time to start fifth grade. We would have had Aunt Kitty for a teacher if she had been "BACK" by then, but unfortunately for us, she was not.

Mom had transferred to Durham School from Springfield Elementary, where we would be going this very year, and Aunt Kitty was still in New Jersey, so it was rather scary to climb aboard that big yellow bus for the ride to a new school. None of us could remember for sure who drove that bus, but Charlie Fretz, from the town of Springfield, is our best guess, thanks to the older and more observant Marty Stemler, who remembered him. Marty thought Tony didn't start hauling us around until later. Leaving Durham on a daily basis filled us with apprehension; we were excited, too.

Our fifth-grade teacher was Mrs. Strock. Now, the major problem with Mrs. Strock was that she had given birth to a strange kid, a son named Terry, who happened to be seated, according to her inflexible seating chart, between Suzanne Beshore and me. This interfered mightily with our need to write notes to each other throughout the day. Terry had to cooperate in order for our communication to maintain its necessary level of immediacy.

Terry was never happy about being the intermediary, but he usually went along with us. He had one of us in front of him, Suzanne, and one behind him, me, and he probably didn't want to find out what would happen if he crossed us. If we had been content with just passing tiny little strips of paper, everything might have stayed under the radar.

Neither Suzanne nor I remember which of us initiated the plan, and neither of us is going to incriminate the other, but one day in the middle of math class – which actually sounds more like me than her – we decided we needed to exchange shoes. *Culprits:*

With a girl's shoe in one hand, Terry Strock raised his other hand and sold us out. The snitch of all snitches. The absolute worst part was that the entire class was subjected to a long lecture on the evils of athlete's foot. Really? That was the best Mrs. Strock could do? All she could think of for chastisement was that our feet were going to get red and itchy if we wore someone else's shoes?

Well, Terry hadn't expected the reaction he got: he thought all the boys would side with him. No sir! Nobody likes a snitch. As far as I was concerned, his reputation was ruined.

But then, wouldn't you know it, Mrs. Strock ended up teaching one of our sixth-grade classes, too. Speaking of ruined reputations, I never did get back in her good graces. I have rarely appreciated that saying, "If it wasn't for bad luck, I wouldn't have any," but it certainly applied to me and teachers so far.

One of the awesome things that happened at Springfield Elementary School was that on May 1st we got to dance around a Maypole. We had done this at Durham School, too, but the area there was small and only a few of us got to participate. At Springfield there was a large, open space for dancing! A tall pole was festooned with ribbons of every color and we were assigned dresses that matched our ribbons, so, of course, Gram was recruited to sew up a quick turquoise dress. I remember feeling so elegant and poised as we weaved in and out and intertwined our ribbons.

I laugh now when I think of our rather staid and conservative community participating in an ancient pagan ritual. Obviously, no one knew that May Day was originally a festival held mainly in Great

Britain and Germany to beg the gods for a good harvest. In Great Britain, the May Day dance followed a night of raucous love-making, since it was also a fertility ritual. Apparently, dancers showed up with straw in their hair and quite disheveled clothes. One of the songs they sang while twirling around the Maypole praised a very private part of a woman's anatomy.

Well, the Puritans closed down that whole depraved business for two-hundred years, but, somehow, in the 1950s, a small part of the frivolity was resurrected at Durham and Springfield Elementary Schools. We may have had a music teacher who was a closet Wiccan. Whatever, it was a strange but welcome event.

We had our usual summer fun when school let out. The Riegels, with their never-ending generosity, let us swim in the millrace. We played along the creek, and the baseball games continued in Limantour's field. People didn't seem to "go" on vacation in those days, at least not in our community. Instead, we took day tips to "the seashore" in neighboring New Jersey several times each summer. Those were magical but exhausting car rides. I invariably came home beet red, this being pre-Coppertone times, and had a few miserable days of sunburn afterward, but it was SO worth it to stand in the surf and imagine Spain across the way or walk along the boardwalk chewing on salt water taffy.

When my Durham girlfriends were busy, two of my favorite ways to spend time by myself involved heights and reading. Our attic had a window which opened onto a gently sloping roof that overlooked our back yard. Often, forgetting to thank Mrs. Ross for the gift of reading she had foisted on me, I would sit up on the roof for hours with a book.

We also had a tree in the front yard which possessed an amazingly comfortable, wide, thick branch. When you positioned your butt on the branch with your legs dangling over the sides, you could lean back against the tree truck, comfy and secure. I'd stay in that position until my feet fell asleep.

Most of my friends had chores and parents who were stricter than mine, so I did find myself with time on my hands. The word "chores" was a word I wasn't familiar with. I remember telling you right up front that my mother was "a subtle woman." She would ask for my "help." Who wouldn't be happy to work alongside her mom? I was always willing. Same with my dad. He'd say, "Susan, let's go…" and I'd be putting on my shoes. Who cared where we went? I was going with my dad. Nothing was ever presented as though it was a job or work. These two wise old owls were psychologically astute. Most kids love spending one-on-one time with an individual parent.

Also, the idea of saying "No" to one of my parents, or even "Just a minute," or "Do I have to?" was unheard of. I didn't know anyone who talked back. I was watching The Lone Ranger and Roy Rogers, for heaven's sake, not the Simpsons. I was reading Nancy Drew and Cherry Ames, books where people helped each other and smiled while doing it.

I did hear kids talk about getting spanked or getting "the belt." I just stayed quiet. I had one spanking in my life when I ran across the street when I was two. I was soaking wet and muddy when that poor terrified mother of mine tried to spank me. I think all she accomplished was moving the wet mud from inside my pants on down my legs and up my shirt, no doubt making more work for herself.

Talking back to teachers or any adult was also verboten. That was a sure way to get the family punishment, whatever it was. In my house the family punishment was disapproval, which was all it ever took to keep me on the straight and narrow. We heard stories about belts and beatings on the bus, and they weren't pretty. What would today be called child abuse certainly existed.

One of our girlfriends was literally kicked down a flight of stairs by her father. In our high school yearbook, she wrote this message to me: "Best of luck to a tremendous kid and one of my truest friends. Thanks for the help when I get so low." It was she who told me what her dad had done. I was appalled. My father's hand on my shoulder was always warm and supportive. What must it be like, I wondered, to live in a home where you were scared of your parents instead of protected by them?

I mistakenly believed most of us had decent parents. It wasn't until much later in life that I discovered how rare parents like mine actually were. Despite what some of my Durham friends might have been enduring at home, we kids typically had the run of the village and fairly free access to the activity du jour, especially during the summer. We hated to see the end of those long days, but sixth grade beckoned, so back on the bus we climbed.

The most fun we had all year was Halloween. There was certainly no smashing of pumpkins or throwing of eggs. Those were cash crops. Wasting toilet paper was out of the question. We were the first generation to get beyond the Sears catalogue and the outhouse.

Speaking of plumbing, when I was a little girl, we had no running water upstairs. My brother is still resentful that on bath night once a week Mom would always put me in the big claw-foot tub first. Then she'd get me dried off and shined up and go back downstairs to heat more water, carry the pots and kettles upstairs and let Skip take his bath. How was she not too tired to enjoy a bath of her own?

Back to the Durham version of Halloween: First of all, Halloween wasn't a night; it was a week. Aside from sledding, it was the most continuous exercise we got all year. Every night we'd set off, six or eight of us, at least. We had five or more different routes we could take. I think LouAnn was the brains behind most of our adventures. She'd tell us what time to meet and then announce where we were going. I'm surprised she didn't grow up to be a travel agent.

One year we walked so far to get to one house that, by the time we got there, all we could do was turn around and trudge back to Durham. We certainly surprised the folks in that farmhouse, though. We weren't sure they'd ever had Trick or Treaters before. They heard us coming; we were not stealthy or silent. We were probably making noise to keep the bad "things" away. In fact, if some of the older guys had jumped out and scared us, we probably would have canceled Halloween completely.

But the couple in the farmhouse heard us closing in and by the time we got there, they had a basket full of apples for us. We were not sure the long walk was adequately rewarded by an apple. We all held a strong preference for chocolate, which was not part of the penny selection in Tony's candy case.

We saved "town" for Halloween night; we started early and visited every house. The adults who answered the door actually guessed who each of us was in our homemade costumes. There were two elderly couples who never had their lights on, so we just passed by those two houses, but the other eighteen or twenty homes welcomed our mob of Trick or Treaters. By the time we'd worn our costumes every night for a week, they were pretty ragged, but we didn't care. I think we carried pillow cases for our loot. Somebody always gave us each a quarter, which we thought was wildly generous. LouAnn said recently, "It would be like getting a $5.00 bill today."

PALISADES
HIGH SCHOOL

S kip graduated from high school and started college at West Chester State Teachers' College. Cousin Jackie had gone there, too. Mom had attended Kutztown State Teachers' College, and Gram, and later Molly, graduated from East Stroudsburg State Teachers' College. Pennsylvania was well known for its affordable abundance of Teachers' Colleges, which specialized, of course, in turning out teachers.

Jackie taught special education in California; Skip was a music teacher in New England; Mom taught first and second grade at Springfield Elementary, Durham Elementary and had even taught several years in Saucon Valley, a one-room school near Springfield. Gram taught in two local one-room schools before she married; and Molly taught all kinds of physical education classes before she became a Provost at Springfield College in Massachusetts. I taught high school for two years in South Lyon, Michigan, outside Ann Arbor, and then taught communication classes at The University of Akron for thirty years. I also taught at Kent State, Cuyahoga Community College, and NEOUCOM, the Northeastern Ohio Universities'

College of Medicine. Teachers all, all over the map from our little family!

When Skip left home for college in 1957, I started seventh grade at Palisades High School in Ferndale with a one-hour bus ride each way. To say that it was a consolidated high school doesn't do it justice. We were an odd assortment of kids from little towns, like Ottsville and Kintnersville, and farms, big and small, wealthy and impoverished.

In our graduating class of 91 students, we were divided into college prep, business education, academic, and "general" concentrations. Those were the four choices. Even in seventh and eighth grades, though, we were still taking a lot of the same classes. However, there were three sections of each class and so, for the first time in our educational history, those of us from Durham were split up – our small, tight, familiar circle had to open and make room for a lot of outsiders.

We used the bus rides to hatch plans and commiserate, but our social skills were tested by the new arrangement. The extraverts, of course, did best. Karen could have a stimulating conversation with a fence post or someone who spoke a different language. That's Karen. She was, after all, selected "Most Talkative," she and Stu Johnstone, whose voice I don't remember, shared that honor. He may have been talkative, but he wasn't talking to me. Some of the rest of us didn't fare as well as the more extraverted. I remember seventh and eighth grade as two nightmare years, and, since you know the history of my first six years of school, you know that's really saying something.

At home, though, things stayed pretty much the same: the food was delicious and the people were devoted. My two meals a night, one at a table on each side of the house, continued in full swing with my mother constantly offering to clean up the kitchen if only I'd go and be social. It worked for me. I'd sit with Gram and Aunt Ruth while they ate supper and eat whatever they were having that I liked. I was always willing to try new things, so I found I liked some of the dishes Gram made that my mom didn't make, like tomato aspic and various sauces. My mom never hid her culinary talent under a sauce, but Gram, who was cooking for Aunt Ruth and her fancier preferences, did.

Then we'd watch television together from seven until eight. We watched shows like To Tell the Truth, What's My Line and Walter Cronkite. Aunt Ruth and I often talked during these shows which, I believe, annoyed my grandmother who was very intellectual and liked to try her mind against all comers, especially the hotshots on TV. The last Christmas Gram was alive, a group of about eight of us went to see her on Christmas afternoon at the nursing home and had a rousing game of Trivial Pursuit. We were all beaten and humbled by a 96-year-old.

Back in Durham in 1957, Gram and I had to devise a new schedule. Now I left for the bus at the same time my mother left for her teaching, so Gram and I didn't have our morning games anymore. That was just one of the changes which indicated that seventh and eighth grades were going to be a trial. We Durham friends had been in a sort of incubator. It was just us. We knew what to expect. Now, at Palisades, we were hatched out into what seemed to me to be the real world. Little did I know what the real world really was.

We entered our high school through the back doors where the juniors and seniors stood around to smoke. Yup. High school kids smoking in the back hallway of the school! It was allowed. Walking in through those tough guy smokers on both sides of the doorway, I felt like those big fellows were going to jump out and scare me. This growing up was starting to look like it should come with a user's manual.

Then there was the whole business of changing classes every fifty minutes and finding our way around a school with multiple hallways. And there were ALL those teachers and ALL those unfriendly faces. Who knew the other kids were just as intimidated as I was?

I started learning to navigate my new school with a pattern which I would use in my car-driving for years: I knew one way to get from Point A to Point B and followed it religiously. Any break from the tried and true one path method, and I was a wreck. Mostly, in seventh and eighth grades, I felt like I was in a stupor, wearing a straight-jacket of flawless behavior and trying to blend in with the woodwork.

One of the only times I spoke turned out a lot like my poodle remark in second grade. Mr. Scoboria taught civics, current events or similar classes I couldn't even recognize. I thought what he taught was himself; he seemed so arrogant. Who knows if he truly was or if I was simply unaccustomed to a teacher who self-revealed? Anyhow, he was also the wrestling coach and the track coach. At one point in the year, he broke his arm and came in wearing a cast and a sling.

Somehow, before I could stop the words, I blurted out, "Did you do that patting yourself on the back?" I'm silent for 179 days and ruin my perfect record with one flippant remark. Again. I felt like a stealthy smart alek. I hoped word of that didn't get home to my dad. Impertinence was not appreciated in the Rau household, nor was disrespect.

The classroom beside Mr. Scoboria's, which was the first room on the left after the smoky entrance, was the classroom of the handsome and dashing Mr. Gonzalves. I knew what he taught – English – and I loved English, and I, along with many other girls at Palisades, loved Mr. Gonzalves. Fortunately, he was our seventh and eighth grade English teacher which helped to make life bearable.

Music class was another bright spot: in that class we were allowed to talk and breathe and even laugh. One day someone noticed that Ronnie Keller had come to school wearing one shoe and one slipper. That kept us entertained, everyone except Ronnie Keller. Luckily, he continued talking to those who mocked and scorned him because he would have been the wrong guy to alienate. His family lived along the Delaware River and owned a boat. A few times each summer, we were invited to "go boating," an elegant occasion for us. We were even introduced to water skiing, which was actually possible on the placid Delaware River.

(Twenty years later I was with friends on Lake Erie; water skiing was offered. Thanks to four-foot waves on Lake Erie, I never did get up on the skis. Actually, I was much closer to drowning myself than I was to standing on the water!)

Back to music at Palisades: Mr. Rhea was the vocal music teacher – the first person of color I had ever encountered. We all adored Mr. Rhea. He ran a tight ship and expected some discipline when it came to paying attention to what we were doing, but during the in between times, that man had a smile on his face and could take or make a joke.

Palisades had a wonderful music program. Mr. Homonay, my brother's former music teacher and later friend for life, was the instrumental music guru and Mr. Rhea was the choral instructor. What a team; we had an active musical life for such a small rural school. We entered Bucks County competitions and district competitions, often scoring in the top three. Those two great music teachers put Palisades on the map.

At the end of eighth grade, I "auditioned" for the majorette team. I think there were only about eight of us on the squad, but from ninth to 12th grade, I was a majorette, and we got to do everything and go everywhere the band went. Eventually the very beautiful and svelte Mrs. Gretchen Waterbury became our majorette advisor. Things got a little classier when she was steering the ship. We even had a "golden girl" by that time, someone who marched out in front of us wearing white sneakers, a skimpy little gold outfit, and twirling fire.

Palisades H S Band Marches In Inaugural Parade

(See Page 3)

E. PALISADES HIGH SCHOOL BAND, pictured here during earlier rehearsals, marched in the Inaugural Parade in Harrisburg yesterday as area representatives in the 4-hour long parade. Clear skies and cold weather were the order of the day as units from 36 of the Commonwealth's 67 counties strutted their stuff. (Photo courtesy PSD)

The rest of us followed behind wearing heavy white boots and uniforms that looked imported from some Germanic military festival. We didn't complain. The color guard, which led the band, had uniforms as uninspired and unattractive as ours, *and* they carried either guns or flags. We, at least, had light-weight batons. We marched on the boardwalk in Atlantic City and strutted down the main street of Harrisburg, the state capital. The Governor of Pennsylvania smiled at me. I was certain of it. Exciting, exciting.

We practiced hard before every parade and performance. Somehow Mr. Rhea and Mr. Homonay instilled in us a sense of gratitude and humility. Maybe our behavior had something to do with the times, too. Dr. Spock had not yet guilted parents into easing up on their kids. In the 1950s Father Knew Best and kids were to be seen and not heard. Our community, too, was a hard-working, serious assortment of people. For the most part nobody wanted to stick out, and for the most part, nobody did. Noses were put to the grindstone, and rules were followed. If you were allowed to participate in band or chorus, you were fortunate; you could be spared from working after school. Very few of us could do something as frivolous as join the majorettes.

During indoor band concerts, we majorettes made up a routine or two adapted to where the concert took place. I remember distinctly the routine we made up for a Christmas concert. We tumbled down the concrete auditorium walkways to "Jingle Bell Rock." Not only were we allowed, we were encouraged to be creative and consequently learned self-respect and self-discipline.

We had no football team at Palisades. Our sports were field hockey, soccer, track, cross country, and baseball/softball played outside after school; wrestling and basketball were inside in winter. The cute, energetic cheerleaders had us standing and shouting our support, but, unlike music, sports were not our claim to fame, at least not basketball. In those days, basketball season was a long season.

Mrs. Gackenbach (in case you didn't believe this was a German community) taught the modern foreign language most of us took because we already knew a smattering from home: German. She also taught Latin, which was required for the college prep kids. A dozen years later when my husband and I lived in Rome and went to a concert that the Pope was attending, the program was printed in Latin and Italian. The Pope and I were probably the only two in attendance reading the Latin. As for the three years of German, groan, I can still sing Silent Night in German – the only pleasant assignment

I remember from those five arduous years with Gacky, as she was called behind her back.

Mr. Rohrer taught history--but the reason we all particularly liked him was that he was the Driver Education teacher. That guy was so nice that he took me to Quakertown on my sixteenth birthday in the middle of the school day to attempt my driving test. And I passed! I don't know if his kindness or my passing was the bigger surprise! Probably my passing on the first try.

I would have my only (in the first sixty years of driving) accident the next winter. (I was rear-ended in 2019, but that wasn't MY accident. That one belonged to the girl who was texting while driving!) My accident was a slide into a snow bank that cost $75 in car repairs. I felt like I had bankrupted my father. No one seemed too angry with me, but I was upset enough with myself that they knew I was enduring plenty of self-punishment.

Mr. Hand, the dictator we had for four years of math, was the only human I ever saw stand as straight as my dad. He had been injured, he in World War II, and he walked with a pronounced limp. He called us all Miss or Mister. No first names for him. I remember one day hearing his booming voice when I was searching in my purse for something: "Miss Rau, do you think you could attend to your make-up at a later time?" There was a dose of humiliation not soon forgotten! I probably didn't take my eyes off him for the rest of the time he taught us math. I will have to say, giving credit where it is due, he was a great math teacher. I did not inherit the Hindenach gift for mathematics and/or music, which is apparently the same part of the brain, and yet I can usually hold my own in the basic math world.

Once I put my make-up away, I really concentrated. (I didn't even own any make-up! I have no idea what I was looking for in my purse, or why I even had a purse in school!)

I can't say the same for the world of home economics. Gram and my mother were both too perfectionistic to let me fumble around with sewing or cooking. I'd get a sewing assignment of any kind from Mrs. Maude Kuhnert and tell my grandmother about it, and in a New York minute it would be completed. Perfectly. Surely that teacher knew I hadn't done that flawless work. I still have the apron "someone" made for my Home Economics project. It has perfectly straight ricrac stitched invisibly across the pocket. It's a cute little apron. It just isn't anything I created. My grandmother, a teacher herself, perpetrated this deception! She just couldn't help herself. For one thing, she depended on her sewing machine for some income. She probably wasn't about to take a chance on letting me within five feet of it.

"My" Home Economics apron.

My mother was no more educational in the kitchen. One time, she let me make a cake, and when it called for coffee, I added dry coffee grounds. The entire cake was gritty. We threw it away. From then on, I was assigned to make the salad. In retrospect, it's surprising she let me handle a knife, not known, as I was not, for my coordination or precision. Calamity Jane with a knife! But slice and dice the salad fixings I did. My mother was not risking her reputation so I could learn to cook. The first meal I made for my new husband at the ripe old age of twenty-one was tomato soup and toasted cheese sandwiches. I prepared the soup with water (you're supposed to use milk) and burned the bread. His mother was a terrible cook, so he never even flinched, just sort of sighed that, "Here we go again," sigh.

Come to think of it, it's no wonder I was allowed to stay after school for majorette practice, play practice, glee club and anything else I could find. I'd ride home on Jake Wampfler's "late bus" arriving just around 5:30 when my dad pulled in. Supper would be ready. No need for my help when everything was ready and waiting.

PART TWO

THE WORLD BEYOND DURHAM

After my brother left for college and/or was busy working all summer, my parents and I started traveling. We went to Virginia Beach (and took Carol Chaser along), Washington, D.C., the Blue Ridge Parkway and took various other short trips. It had been years since we traveled. I suppose, truth be told, I was to blame for that. I always thought it was because my brother *then* was not the cheerful traveler he became once HE was driving, but it might have been because of the trip to Canada when I was two, the last major trip my family took. I've mentioned before that the second year of my life was not easy for anybody. If I'd been a pet, they probably would have given me away. Or had me put down.

We had driven to Canada with Gram and Aunt Ruth, and part of the trip was on a ferry across the Saint Lawrence River. Apparently, it was before the "leash days." They took their eyes off me. Even my brother, who would have been nine, was traumatized by my climbing the railing of the ferry. I guess someone turned around and there I was, looking like Bob, sailing, in the movie "What About Bob." Bob, however, was securely strapped in when he shouted, "I'm sailing. I'm sailing;" I was just balanced in all my two-year-old wobbliness on one of the bars of the ferry railing. We didn't travel for a long time after that. For more than ten years we stayed home and away from water.

Most of our traveling, though, whether due to my dad's thriftiness or my mom's love of family, was to visit Uncle Jim and Aunt Marilyn. They were the consummate host and hostess. And they moved every few years. I remember particularly a trip to Detroit in which we went NEAR Niagara Falls. We could see the Falls. I don't remember being allowed out of the car.

Then Uncle Jim and Aunt Marilyn moved to Louisville, Kentucky. That was a long trip and we had to stay overnight. Fortunately, we found a small, clean motel in New Concord, Ohio, and stayed there every trip. After we'd unpacked, we'd find a little restaurant, and then drive around exploring nearby sights. That was how we happened to find Muskingum, a beautiful, small Presbyterian College.

Muskingum was eight hours from Durham. I should have given that more thought, but somehow, I was smitten by the brick buildings and the lake in the middle of the campus, dividing the classrooms from the dormitories. It was and is simply charming. My parents agreed. When it was time to apply for colleges, I applied to Penn State and Muskingum. I was accepted to both with my mediocre grades, amazingly. There's a reason I haven't written much about high school homework: I was too busy watching game shows after enjoying two suppers. That was time consuming and by eight o'clock it was time for a bath and then the hair ritual.

Another aspect of my mother's very charming and attractive perfectionism was that she spent an inordinate amount of time doing her own hair. Had she been able to choose, instead of following in both her parents' footsteps and becoming a teacher, she probably would have chosen to become a hair dresser. Keeping her own hair perfectly coifed was very satisfying to her, but not quite adequate to satisfy her need to fix and fluff. Luckily, she had a daughter.

After washing my hair, I was expected to return to the kitchen and sit on one of the stools at the kitchen counter. I'd lug along the box of rollers and bobby pins. Mom would set my hair, and I was expected to sleep in the contraptions she installed. By morning, I looked like a poodle myself, quite curly and poufy. It was not our most cooperative venture. Typically, my mom and I were on the same page and were thick as thieves. Not when it came to my hair. She persevered. I submitted.

When I went away to Muskingum College, one of the things my mother bought me, with the S&H green stamps she received at the grocery store every week, was a hair dryer. This hair dryer was big and loud. It tucked nicely into its own hat box and had as many tubes as my C-Pap machine. Included with the mechanism was a large plastic cap with elastic to put around your hair. You wore this on your head while you were being blown around by the jet motor of the machine itself. And that damn thing wouldn't break. Years and years later, I finally had to decide to donate it to someone who would appreciate it, because I never had what my mother thought was the proper respect for it.

The only time I ever again wished for my mother to do my hair was during my sophomore year at Muskingum when I had been involved in an automobile accident – not my fault. I have bad luck with drunk drivers, although, doesn't everyone? That time I was riding in the passenger seat and smashed my collar bone on the steering wheel. I can still hear the intake of breath as the doctor read the X-ray. They could have done surgery but the doctor didn't push the idea because apparently that bone was shattered. Oh, well. Life has been fine without an intact left collar bone.

But, for six weeks I had to wear a sling and remain immobilized while the pieces settled into whatever pattern they preferred. Obviously, my modeling career was over, since all those wonderfully slender-verging-on-anorexic girls have sexy, protruding collar bones. That, actually, wasn't my problem.

There had been three of us who roomed together at the beginning of our sophomore year. Cathy and I both had thin, fine, blonde hair. Cathy would have understood my hair. But she, what are the chances, had already been in a really terrible car accident with many broken bones and much trauma and wasn't able to come back to school yet. That left Judithe and me.

Judithe, intelligent, musical, linguistically gifted Judithe, was Lebanese. She had thick, dark, exotic hair which framed a beautiful face which sat on top of a slender, agile body. Judithe was a looker and a beautiful person. But as a beautician for thin, fine hair, she was a disaster. I'll give her this: we laughed our fool heads off at her attempts, and she never stopped trying. I should have worn the hair dryer on my head when I went to class. It would have been more flattering than what she was able to do with my goldilocks.

But I'm getting ahead of my story. I haven't thrown the boys of Palisades High School under the bus, and I'm not leaving this portion of the story until I do that. They deserve it.

Where to start? Charlie, later Chuck. He was the first and most heart-breaking. He actually caused me to cry for three days straight, which is my all-time record, SO FAR. I'm not much of a crier anymore. I think anti-anxiety medicine is really helpful with that. I recommend Buspirone, although it makes your ears ring, but tinnitus is a small price to pay for not getting stuck in the cycle of anxiety.

I met Charlie at church. He was from Durham, two years older than I, and a handsome devil. According to my sister-in-law, who was in his high school class, he's as handsome as ever, even though he's old now. I could have happily lived the rest of my life not knowing that, but he's been a thorn in my side since I was fifteen. Why should it be different now?

Okay, truth be told: he was the reason I applied to Penn State. That's where he went. Thank goodness I chose Muskingum. I would have cried myself through the first two years of college. Let's be clear. He was always polite and kind. He was just never smitten.

Actually, I have never heard anything about that guy which would make me think he wasn't a good choice. It's just that he was one of those beautiful people and I am not. I have lots of good characteristics and much to recommend me as a decent human. Physical beauty is not one of those things. We live and work with what we're given, right?

So, there were a few opportunities where Charlie and I had such a lovely time together that my hopes rose beyond reason. One of those times was a party my brother and I gave in 1961. It was the only party my brother and I ever gave together, so it's easy to remember. Skip had joined the Navy after two years at college. (Apparently neither he nor I took to homework until later in life. We both have master's degrees. It's not that we don't apply ourselves and do the work. We do. When we're ready or see the necessity!)

It was Christmas and Skip was home on leave. For some unknown reason, he and I were actually talking and getting along. Seven years difference in age can be a chasm of uncrossable proportions, but we decided to host a party. Since my brother had lots of friends, we had plenty of guys to invite. But girls? That was rough. Obviously his seven-year older buddies didn't want to hang around with my friends. I was invited because (a) the party was my idea, (b) I was Skip's sister, and (c) I would do all the preparation and clean up.

In a stroke of genius, I said, "Let's invite Molly Thomas." If you've been paying attention, you're recognizing the name MOLLY. That made us think of others in her class at Palisades – like Charlie. If you threatened the life of someone I love, I could not name another person who was at the party other than Skip and Molly – and you know what happened to them – and Charlie and me – and you know what happened to each of us, separately.

It was a great night and anyone who was there, although I can't name them, will tell you that. Skip and Molly retired to the living room after most of the guests left, whoever they were, and Charlie and I retired to the kitchen to clean up the mess. We had, from my perception, a wonderful time doing the dishes and straightening things up so my mother wouldn't go into apoplexy the next morning. She and my dad had come home from a party of their own and had immediately gone upstairs to bed. I remember Charlie and me sitting down at the kitchen counter (which was mercifully free from hair) and having something to drink – non-alcoholic – before he finally went home.

Alas, what had been the beginning of something big for me was simply a moment in time for him. As to Skip and Molly, who knows when things wrapped up for them. I was fast asleep. Actually, as of yesterday, when I last talked to them, things were still moving on for them. Skip and I lovingly call Molly "the little wife." He frequently needs clarification or a fact, and I always suggest, "Ask the little wife." She has a head full of clarifying facts!

But Charlie was just the beginning of the high school heart break. Then came Wally. I'm only using their first names so they can plead innocent and not sue me for whatever it's called when you kiss and tell. Wally was on the basketball team and was a heart throb. When I went away to college, I couldn't wait to get home at Thanksgiving and see him. I drove to Palisades and sought out his sister, Lorraine, who was a friend from the majorette squad and a senior. She and I hugged in the hall between classes, and she quickly told me the news about her brother: he was married. I tried to smile. The bell rang and the halls emptied. I slumped down against the cement wall, alone, stunned. I wasn't heartbroken, just a whole lot wiser than I had been ten minutes before. You know, when you leave somewhere, you expect things to be unchanged when you return.

Oh, but there are so many more. Walter, Joe, Jerry, Lynn's brother (I forget his name), another Charlie, and . . . Larry. Walter drove me home down 212 using his feet instead of his hands on the steering wheel. I never went out with him again.

Joe took me to a fraternity party and introduced me to Scotch and soda. Like driving with one's feet, I was a little too sheltered for such things.

Jerry was a playboy. That didn't work.

Lynn's brother took me bowling and the bowling ball slipped out of my hands and rolled backward, landing on his foot. He never asked me out again.

I have a picture of the other Charlie and me sitting at a swimming party looking pretty cute together. I'm not sure why that didn't go anywhere. He said recently on Facebook that it was his fault. He should have taken me to the covered bridge and kissed me. But, he didn't. (Clue: he thought, and still thinks, he's in charge of what happens in a relationship. Opps! Lucky escape!)

And Larry, who was two years older, went off to Susquehanna University and decided no young high school girl was going to slow him down. He confessed years later that his rule was, "Never date the same girl more than three times." That sort of sums up my high school dating history.

My talent, then and now, seems to be fixing up other people. I have been downright instrumental in a number of long-lasting relationships. None of them included me. My earliest matchmaking was, as you know, with my brother when we had our one and only party and I cleverly suggested he invite Molly Thomas whom he had dated in high school. They're on year fifty-nine of marriage and counting. I guarantee they have not always thanked me, but they've been good sports about it.

Additionally, I have done a lot of "interpreting" male behavior for female friends to help them hang in until their guy got a clue. Luckily, I've had wonderful girlfriends all my life and high school was no exception. Lynn T. came to town and she certainly stretched my perceptions. For one thing, she was a Christian Scientist. This was a religion we had not discussed in Vera Riegel's Sunday School class. (I went to Sunday School with Lynn one time, and when her teacher asked where I lived, I said, "Durham," but he heard "Germ," which to a Christian Scientist was apparently hilariously funny. He never did recover himself.)

Lynn was an athlete, a very accomplished athlete. I was not. I remember the President's Challenge we were assigned in gym class. This was an Eisenhower era attempt to encourage high school kids to move more and develop greater interest in physical prowess. Well, Lynn beat me at every athletic challenge until we competed on ring pull-ups. She did fifty. I was next. I did fifty-one. It about killed me. I didn't know I had that degree of determination in me. Of course, it could have been jealousy or spite, too.

Lynn had a little VW Beetle and we had some adventures in that car. One I will never forget was the night we got a flat tire. She actually knew how to change a tire. She set about the process, but couldn't get the fourth lug nut off. I didn't even know what a lug nut was. I was just standing around communing with the cows who had wandered up to the fence along the road to see what we were doing. We ended up having to walk three miles to her house. Her brother, the one with the bowling ball injury, drove us back to her car, bringing along a tool to loosen the lug nut.

My biggest issue with Lynn, our one serious disagreement, was with Mr. S. He was one of our teachers and she "loved" him. I did not. I didn't trust him. He used to take her ALONE with him into the back alcove of the classroom where he taught, and that made me incredibly nervous. She always swore there were no shenanigans going on, but I couldn't understand, even then, that a male teacher and a female student alone in a back room was a good idea. I never told anyone. I wasn't a therapist, yet, and didn't know about "Duty to Report."

One claim to fame Lynn and I didn't share was acting. I was in the junior and senior plays; however, I never got the parts I wanted. I wanted the romantic lead, of course. But I got, for example, Mrs. Pickles, the annoying busy-body in the senior play. The teacher who did the casting tried to convince me that anyone could be a romantic lead, and only someone with acting skill could pull off the character roles. It sounded like a crock to me but (a) I didn't care, and (b) I was happy to be involved. I was Best Actress in the Superlatives section of the 1963 *Palisadian*, our yearbook, but I think that's only because they couldn't figure out where else to put me.

I may have been voted Best Actress, but my mother, a fine woman and a loving mother, had not done my self-confidence any favors as I was growing up. First of all, there were the silly, fussy hairdos. Then there was her constant refrain of how much I looked like my father. My father was a large man, not heavy or fat, just large. He was 6'2", bald, and wore glasses which rested on a pronounced nose. He had false teeth, which always stayed in his mouth. I forgot to mention when talking about Uncle Charlie that once on a deep-sea fishing trip Uncle Charlie suffered motion sickness, threw up over the side of the boat, and lost his false teeth. My dad was really neurotic thereafter about using plenty of Polydent.

I did not want to look like my dad. I wanted to look like my very pretty, feminine mother. No, she insisted, Skip, my handsome brother, looked like her, and I looked like my dad. Now, as you have surmised, the Hindenach side of the family was known for brains, and the Raus were known for other things. What they were known for depended on who you talked to and who you were talking about. My mom clearly believed my bright and handsome brother a Hindenach and me, such as I was, a Rau.

One of the Hindenach prejudices was the selectivity and specialness of college educations. They pretty much thought a college education separated the haves from the have-nots. This left Aunt Ruth and my father in the dust, with their business school degrees. That strong preference for those with college educations is, undoubtedly, the sole reason I was (without discussion) enrolled in the college prep track at Palisades. It certainly wasn't because anyone thought I was smart enough. In addition to constantly telling me I didn't look like a Hindenach, my mother informed me I didn't have the IQ of a Hindenach, either. Unfortunately, she told me exactly what my IQ was.

Anyone with an IQ of 100 should never be told she has such and is absolutely as average as they come. Especially if she might have been told that her brother had an IQ of 132. Therefore, in our family he was known as the smart one, and he got away with being a moody grump whenever things were not going his way. He was the smart one. All could be forgiven. I became the sweet one. No pressure there. Enter: Little Mary Sunshine.

Years later I realized that one of my three boys was starting to be known as "the responsible one." I put the kibosh on that as fast as I could. Learning from my own rigid label, I wanted to make sure I didn't pass on that negative legacy. I was creative enough to make my own trouble instead of continuing someone else's.

Somehow, I struggled to maintain acceptable grades until I encountered Alice MacDonald. She saw something in me much more encouraging than the number on an IQ test, but that was years in the future.

One of the most enduring gifts my parents gave me was a home full of music. Skip, the musician, played trumpet and loved jazz, so, I, too, listened to Stan Kenton, Maynard Ferguson and so many other artists and bands that he chose and had blasting from the record player. My dad loved Mitch Miller and Lawrence Welk, patriotic music and hymns. My mom loved symphonies and classical music.

Our family went to Skip's band concerts, whether marching band or jazz band. If he was playing in a group, we were all there. And for years my mom drove me the half hour back and forth to Bethlehem and sat in the car an additional half hour so I could take piano lessons. To this day, I thank her and my dad at least once a week when I feel the gratitude of knowing how to play the piano. What joy it has given me over the years.

My dad performed in a few plays and led singing for various church and community events. If the Lion's Club or another organization needed a Master of Ceremonies, Dave Rau was your guy. My mom and Aunt Ruth sang in the Messiah Chorus every year. We would go to Allentown or Quakertown and hear the community bands.

My absolute favorite of all the musical activities, though, was our summer evening drives to Lambertville, New Jersey, to the Lambertville Music Circus, an outdoor tent in the round that offered a different musical performance every week. We saw so many classic musicals – *Oklahoma*, *South Pacific*, *Guys and Dolls*, *Carousel*, *Brigadoon*, *Li'l Abner*, and *Damn Yankees*. If we didn't have the records, we'd buy them after we saw the show. When I was home alone, that was what I listened to – show tunes.

In addition to music, we were a family who loved books. Gram walked down to the traveling library bus, the BookMobile, that parked in front of the millrace for one hour, every other week. My love of reading obviously comes from her. She introduced me to Corrie Ten Boom and we all read James Michener's books as well as historical novels. Books and music. Such gifts for life.

Palisades High School and the last four years of living in Durham were wonderful. My mother loved her average little girl and there were no doubts about my paternity. Growing up in Durham was a great platform from which to jump off into the big, wide world.

A number of us from Durham were leaving town and heading off to college, but the vast majority of kids from Palisades were not. The division, which began when we were split into "tracks" in high school, became more evident as we approached the end of our senior year.

I didn't understand then and don't understand now why "college" is preferred to other ways of learning. I admire and adore people who can do things with their hands. (There's a loaded sentence!) An auto mechanic, a brick layer, a drywall person, a stonemason, an electrician, an appliance repair person, each is brilliant and talented in my book. I wouldn't want to live without them. Then the people who work in nature and grow the plants I put in my garden every year, or those who know how to trim a tree, or those who work with animals, like park rangers, animal shelter angels, or those who own or work in restaurants or movie theatres or trash hauling companies – we'd be up the creek without all of them. What is so special about a college degree? I think it's a classist prejudice.

Things that divide and separate us one from another are really tricky when the divisions are competitive and hierarchical. None of us, absolutely none of us, is better or more vital to life than any other. Each of us in Durham had our part in the community quilt. Tony could butcher a hog and back a bus; Lillian kept the music going; Vera taught a generation or two how to express ideas; Floyd figured out how to create and operate a hardware store/ feed mill/ post office; my dad kept the grass mowed, the snow shoveled, and the township solvent; and, as I said to everyone who came into her room during the last days of her life: Miriam Rau taught more than 600 children how to read. Everyone has his or her place.

I felt, and still feel, guilty that I had an opportunity that many of my childhood friends (and most of the people in the world) simply didn't, and still don't, have. Although I would argue vehemently that the college degree I would receive did not make me special, there is no denying that that degree did open doors and give me advantages that my friends who stayed in Durham never had. Perhaps the price was that I had to leave the secure familiarity of Durham to be able to accept those opportunities. Nothing is free. Nothing.

As things wrapped up at Palisades, we were beyond excited. We went to New York City for an all-day senior class trip and enjoyed graduation parties at church. We talked endlessly about plans; romances seemed to blossom. And then we all came crashing down to earth.

Although we didn't know it, one of our classmates suffered from epilepsy. She was at her home in the bathroom a few days before graduation and had a seizure. Her father heard her and rushed to the bathroom, but she had inadvertently locked the door, and he couldn't get to her in time.

Her close friends as well as those who knew her slightly felt devastated. The death of a young woman on the eve of her high school graduation was, and remains, an unthinkable tragedy. If you ask any of us about our high school graduation, I think the first thing we will tell you is that "Gay" died a few days before we graduated. We had a very somber graduation.

The Class of 1963 dedicated a lectern for the auditorium, "In memory of our beloved Gay Gardner." The Palisadian added a dedication to her as well; she was first and foremost in our heavy hearts as we went through graduation without her.

In the typical ups and downs of life, that summer held a wonderful surprise for me. It was my second summer working as a nurse's aide at Easton Hospital, thank you very much, Aunt Ruth. I might have gotten the job on my own, but we'll never know, because Aunt Ruth moved behind the scenes. Did she move mountains or just whisper the right words, "my niece," in the right ear?

I had liked summer number one, regardless of the steep learning curve. I worked all over the hospital in a different department on a different floor seemingly every day. Those hospital corners Aunt Agnes instilled in us certainly came in handy, as did the Little Mary Sunshine face which greeted some very pitiful patients. I saw people missing parts I didn't know you could live without. Other patients weren't there the following time I returned to that room. It was an eye-opening, gut-wrenching, hands-on education.

I'll never forget the cancer patient who asked for a glass of ginger ale. When I brought it, I had put ice in it. She threw it on the floor. "I don't want ice," she wailed. I brought a glass of ginger ale with no ice and then cleaned up the mess. I learned to ask from then on. Assume nothing. When you have lost control over whether you will live or die, whether your ginger ale has ice in it or not becomes a vitally important matter. As soon as that woman taught me that lesson, it struck me as perfectly reasonable.

Then, in my second summer, I won the nurses' aide lottery: I was assigned to the newborn nursery. I would work there that summer and the next three summers. How I loved those babies. The nurses thought I was a hoot. They knew how to change a diaper without getting peed on. I, of course, did not. It's a skill. They could turn a deaf ear when someone was crying. I, of course, could not. I was constantly picking up the crying baby. The old hands just made fun of me. When I began working in the nursery, we used safety pins and cloth diapers, but, in the few years I was there, transitioned to disposable diapers. We wore hair nets, masks and scrubs while on duty. All was quite sterile.

The newborns stayed in the nursery under the watchful eyes of the nurses. We took them to their moms to be fed and then collected them again, transporting them in sanitized little plastic boxes on wheels. Those babies ate on a schedule, and we kept them in the nursery at night so the moms could sleep. Dads had visiting hours. This was a regimented operation.

I remember the safety pins, particularly. The nurses taught me to keep my hand between the safety pin and the baby at all times. I immediately understood why, as I pierced myself constantly. Between the little boys who loved to squirt me and the safety pins that were constantly pricking me, it was a dangerous but delightful job.

Of course, this being a real job and not an imaginary job, there was also heartbreak and sadness. The most hurtful and harmful thing I ever did in my life, I did that first summer on the obstetrics floor. I walked into the room of a woman who had lost her baby and wheeled in a baby I thought belonged to her. She never had to say a word. Her face said it all. I felt like I had rammed a knife into her heart. Why she was placed on the floor with the newborns to begin with was a mystery – probably just to make it easier for the obstetrician to visit her. Having to listen to the sounds of the infants crying and the noise of the little bassinets rolling down the halls was, alone, cruel punishment. Add to that, some seventeen-year-old who confused Room 359 with Room 358. Agony. Eight years later I would lose a baby myself, and the pain of what I had done to that woman came back to stab me.

Death and sorrow took its toll, but joy and humor helped us along. One of the seasoned nurses found it amusing that I couldn't sit down when I was on the clock. On the rare moments when all the little darlings were sleeping, the nurses would grab a cross-word puzzle or their knitting and enjoy a brief period of leisure. Not me. I'd start cleaning. I'm sure that nursery was cleaner during the summers I was there than any other time of the year. The parental work ethic, which was actually the Protestant work ethic, was loud and clear in my mind. Plus, I didn't know how to knit or do crossword puzzles. I did know how to clean.

Another two lessons in realism I encountered in the newborn nursery were the births of a baby with no, or a very small, underdeveloped brain and a baby born with severe hydrocephalus – fluid in the brain. I was not allowed to touch those babies. The baby with the very small brain caused a lot of discussion among the nurses who all felt strongly that his mother, who showed up every summer to deliver another abnormal and clearly disabled baby, should be "sterilized." This was a great deal of hard-core realism for a new high school graduate. Once again, the ever-present life lesson was that even in the happiest of places, horror and agony loitered in the corners.

Summer passed quickly and I earned as much as possible to help with the unnecessary, luxurious expense of going to a small liberal arts college in Ohio, when I could have gone to one of Pennsylvania's State Teachers' Colleges for less money. I can't say why my choice was allowed; I was never a brat about things and would easily have acquiesced to wherever my parents thought I should go.

Maybe my parents realized I was so attached to them that if I didn't go a considerable distance, I'd be back in two weeks. Clearly, this was a problem other young college students experienced, too. Muskingum had instituted a rule that parents couldn't visit their freshman children for the first six weeks of the school year. Additionally, maybe my parents sensed I was so bonded to Durham, our way of life and sense of community, that all of that had better get shaken up. Maybe they wanted me out of their hair. I suspect I may have been a little clingy.

MUSKINGUM COLLEGE

Thank heaven Uncle Jim and Aunt Marilyn lived in Louisville, Kentucky for a few years, and we passed through New Concord, Ohio on route to visit them. Otherwise, Muskingum College would have remained invisible and unknown to us. This small liberal arts school was almost twice as big as Palisades High School; New Concord, Ohio, was probably twenty times as big as Durham, Pennsylvania. New Concord was and is a small town. Its famous products are Agnes Moorhead, the actress, and John Glenn, the astronaut, and his wife, Annie, who pre-Biden scrutiny was the USA's most famous stutterer.

Also, thank heaven, I had some good roommate karma going on: Cathy Lindsay and I took one look at each other and have been friends ever since. Fifty-nine years and still enjoying each other's emails and pictures. I also have two of Cathy's paintings hanging in my living room. She has become a talented artist, and I am happy to have her paintings of The Bucks County Playhouse and Pears, my mom's favorite fruit, to help me feel close to Cathy all these years later. She is also the artist who painted the beautiful, totally captivating picture on the cover of this book.

Getting accustomed to dorm living was easy. There were so many rules – in by ten every night, lights out by eleven, only skirts and dresses on Sundays, and on and on. It was sort of like entering a convent, just a Presbyterian version. It didn't require thought as much as simple compliance.

Compared to the shock of first grade, it was a walk in the park. And Cathy had the most beautiful collection of sweaters I'd ever seen. She let me wear them whenever I wanted. They came in all colors and had embroidery down the front panels. I can see them now.

I started off as a music education major. When I auditioned for the chorus and the director told me he wasn't admitting me because I sing "flat," I got the first inclination that perhaps music education was not the best choice of major for me. It never kept me out of County or District Chorus in high school, but I figured probably Mr. Pickering had a more discerning ear.

Mrs. Dunning, my voice teacher, didn't bring up this inability of mine, but she was a grieving widow. What I remember from voice lessons is her telling me about her husband's cancer diagnosis and saying that trying to figure out what was wrong was the worst part of his illness. Once they knew what they were fighting, they started the battle. They lost it; but they put up a unified and formidable fight. She was very young and very lovely, and it broke my heart that she had been forced to watch him die. She had to say, "Good-bye."

In the fall of my freshman year, a national tragedy struck. We were standing in the hall outside German class when someone heard on a radio that President Kennedy had been shot. When classes changed and we went in to sit down for class, we begged the professor to allow one of us to listen to the radio and find out what happened. "Verboten!" Absolutely not, he ordered. Somehow, we made it through that long, nail-biting hour. When we left class, we learned that our President had died.

The campus went into silence and tears. It didn't matter whether we had supported Kennedy for president or not. Someone had assassinated the President of the United States of America, and no one felt safe.

The college administration cancelled classes until after Thanksgiving break, and we all scrambled to find a way home. Thirteen hundred grief-stricken, shocked, mourning college students was too much for the college to handle. Send us home; let our families deal with us.

It was a long, sleepless night until we could arrange transportation and leave in the morning. Everyone was red-eyed and head-shaking. How was this possible? How could this happen?

Most of us had come to embrace Camelot and the things JFK stood for. We had an integrated student body. Although there were very few non-white students, those who did manage to find and come to Muskingum were completely accepted. We had an African-American girl from the Bronx on First South, our section of the dorm. She entertained us all with stories of NYC. The only cow she had ever seen was in the Bronx Zoo. She was always making us laugh with her Big Apple tales and her descriptions of how differently she had grown up from most of the rest of us. Her New York stories set her apart more than the color of her skin.

We had been in high school when John Glenn circled the earth, and we agreed with the President that going to the moon was absolutely necessary. We didn't know why or care how. If JFK thought so, we did, too. Then there was that sophisticated French-speaking wife of his and the darling children. It was a family that played sports together and believed in serving their country. We were proud of them and proud to be Americans, then someone killed him and murdered our dreams.

We couldn't see from that vantage point that Lyndon Baines Johnson, sworn in on Air Force One, was actually going to accomplish much of what John Fitzgerald Kennedy had gotten rolling. Bobby was the Attorney General and Ted served in Congress, but the public face of hope had been the eloquently articulate, ever-smiling face of JFK. My master's thesis, ten years later, would be "Kennedy's Use of Myth."

The rest of 1963 was a low energy time until Christmas and the event on December 28th: Skip and Molly's wedding. When I was about ten, I attended Uncle Jim and Aunt Marilyn's wedding, but this was much more exciting: I was going to be IN this wedding! It was a minor role, of course. Good actresses never get the romantic lead. But Gram made a beautiful dress for me to wear. Heart throb, Charlie, was singing at the wedding, and he actually graced me with a dance during the reception. It was fun and uplifting; something positive to end a year which had been so heart-breaking.

It wasn't until late January when we returned to start our second semester that life finally came back to our little college campus. The snows fell, the lake in the middle of campus froze over, and some magic returned to Muskingum. We freshmen had finished one semester, and we weren't sure, but we imagined we could survive a second semester. It would never be as challenging as the one we just completed – nothing in our college career would come close.

During the next three years we changed majors, dumped boyfriends and girlfriends, joined sororities and fraternities, and started to grow up. Started. Drama reigned. The introduction of the draft system in our senior year was a jolt from the blue. Disappointments were endured. And we experienced some amazing and memorable events. For us, life returned, but I'm not sure life ever returned to The United States of America with the vitality it had in the 1950s and 1960s. I believe hope died on November 22, 1963.

During sophomore year we endured a Thanksgiving dinner none of us have ever forgotten. I'm sure some of us have never since eaten turkey, some boycotted stuffing, and some, a large number, probably, became vegetarians. Remember the Thanksgiving before – our freshman year – JFK was assassinated. This year, we were the apparent target.

We had a beautiful Thanksgiving feast the Sunday before we were to leave on Wednesday for Thanksgiving break. Sundays we always had our main meal at lunch time. By about eight or nine o'clock at night there was quite a stir on our dorm floor. Little did we know the commotion was on every floor of each dorm which had partaken in the Thanksgiving extravaganza.

Cathy and I were by this time rooming with Judithe, she of limited beautician talents. Judithe is, and was then, a vegetarian who is gluten intolerant. She may have had the green beans and a salad for dinner. She only came to the dining room to hang out with us. Luckily, then, she stayed healthy while virtually the entire dorm spent Sunday night and all day Monday suffering from food poisoning.

Anyone who wasn't sick would have become sick listening to, watching, and smelling the rest of us in our intestinal agony. Judithe, somehow, managed to take care of a lot of us. She was constantly walking someone back and forth to the bathroom, tucking us back in bed, finding ginger ale and glasses of water. One experience all humans could live their lives without is being part of a mass food poisoning event in a tight, common space like a dormitory. It was unforgettable. Fortunately, no one died, although a few of us wanted to at various moments.

Once again, going home for Thanksgiving was a relief and a blessing. This was my second year as music major. I continued to struggle with music theory, which probably sifts out more wannabe musicians than lack of talent. I ended up getting through that class, though. My next challenge, other than overcoming singing flat, was staying in isolation for hours on end in an assigned practice room playing the piano or singing. I never found myself that fascinating!

Also, as music education majors, we had to learn to play every instrument. I actually flunked the flute final. I was totally and completely unable to ever get so much as a squawk out of a flute. I managed "Mary Had a Little Lamb" on everything else. They let my flute issues slide.

But this first semester of sophomore year I took a required humanities class: Speech. Speech class provided an element previously missing for me: I was good at something – speech. I still labored under the assumption that my IQ was average, and I conscientiously worked down to what was expected of me, but, unexpectedly, I kept getting A after A on my tests and the speeches I wrote. Maybe I was channeling my dad's Sunday school lesson talents. Maybe it was early evidence of what is now called an EQ – emotional (intelligence) quotient.

Whatever it was, I was the star of that dag-blasted speech class, and Miss Moore knew it, and I actually heard some praise and gained confidence. My class even voted me the best speaker, which meant that when we came back from Christmas vacation, I'd be representing us in the speech contest held in the chapel. It was a well-attended event because all the speech teachers required their students to be there. Other than that, the pews would have been empty.

Well, Miss Moore had a teaching assistant she assigned to help me prepare for this auspicious event. Enter the person who shall henceforth be known, spoiler alert, as H#1. The first time I met H#1, I had just come off an all-nighter in a desperate attempt to pass geology class. Rocks and me just didn't resonate with each other. The geology professor was a snore, and I had already learned that I did a lot better in classes with lively teachers who interacted with students. So, there I was, half-asleep, having just done badly on yet another geology test, and wearing – how could I forget – one navy blue knee sock and one black knee sock. I have never done well without sleep.

H#1 took one look at me, set a time to meet the next day, and hurried away. I said to myself, as I say to myself sarcastically to this day when things are underwhelming, like when I drop something or break something or someone gives me the brush-off, "That went well."

We met the next evening to practice my speech in the empty chapel, and when I got through it, H#1 asked, "Do you like basketball? I'm going over to the gym to watch the game." "Sure," I guessed I liked basketball; I faithfully went to every game in high school to cheer for Wally, but I never thought about whether I liked basketball. It was kind of sweaty, actually. However, I like people, and if the people I like are doing something I will probably like the something they are doing. Hunting and criminal activity would be the exceptions, but typically people who hunt don't like me: I'm not the rugged outdoor type. Criminals don't trust me, although I've kept the secret for a couple of pot smokers I've known over the years.

Actually, let me tell you one other thing I really had not liked at all and it entailed spending time with someone I didn't know. Judy Eliasen, she of the prettiest feet in the Durham girls competition, arranged a blind date for me with her boyfriend's friend. The four of us went to a nighttime car race. The drivers just went round and round on this circular course. All the headlights would come at us accompanied by loud roars, zoom by with screeching tires, and then disappear to the back of the circle. This went on interminably. The guy never talked, but he tried to snuggle while watching the race. Added to my discomfort was the fact that he was a smoker and smelled terrible. I suspected I might end the night by throwing up on him, but somehow, I don't remember how, I got home from the longest night of my life and swore off blind dates.

But my new "speech coach" wasn't a smoker and wasn't suggesting drag racing, or whatever that driving around in circles was called, so I guessed it was safe to head off to a basketball game at the gym with someone unknown to me.

Three things followed that basketball game: first, I won the speech contest. No one cared, although I was kind of happy about it. Everyone was relieved that they had fulfilled the requirement to attend, and the chapel cleared out quickly. Second, perhaps because I demonstrated I was capable of choosing matching knee socks, H#1 asked me out on a date; the rest is history. And third, since I said I liked basketball, it was assumed for the next fifteen years that I liked sports.

I don't regret that little misunderstanding. H#1 loves sports and passed that love on to, another spoiler alert, our three sons, which has given them the greatest of pleasure and revealed quite a bit of talent. I've ridden the coattails and watched Gordie Howe play hockey in Detroit, Joe Namath (undoubtedly in his panty hose) play football in Cleveland, and lots of Cleveland Indians play baseball, none of whose names rush to mind at this moment, except the amazing short stop, Omar Vizquel. It was all fun. I love the ambiance of sports in person.

The most astonishing thing happened at a Browns/Jets football game: some guy pinched me on the butt. It made me feel so good, I almost cried. I would have thanked him if I could have picked him out from the crowd. I was eight months pregnant at the time and not feeling very sexy. He probably single-handedly got me through that last awkward month.

Due to my perceived love of sports, H#1 and I spent a lot of time competing in football contests. He'd get the list of games and choose college and professional games for each weekend, and we'd predict who'd win each game. We did this for years. He would study, read about the teams, ponder at length who might win depending on who was playing at home, how strong the rivalry was, which players had gotten hurt and other determining factors. I'd pick the names I liked. Except I always picked Penn State, and we know why. I also always picked Susquehanna University because another old heart throb went there. Other than that, it was all about how the school or team name sounded to me. Gonzaga was always a favorite.

H#1 would become aggravated the few times I won, which I did a couple times a year, but mostly we were both content with his research paying off. We lived in Europe when we started this. There were no computers. He had no choice but to play against me if he wanted to be in a football pool. Now I think he and all three sons compete. They never seem to remember to ask me.

H#1 was himself in a speech contest, this one a national contest, and he won that. Judithe and I were entrusted with the college car and drove to Columbus to the airport to pick up the champion and his speech coach. It was on the way home from that trip, in the college car, that we were hit by the drunk driver and my collar bone was shattered.

My parents were called the next morning. Since my dad was already at Durham School mowing grass, my mom took the call, hung up, rushed to the school, and told my dad. He hurried home, changed his clothes and they jumped in the car and drove eight hours to have a look at me. They apparently realized I was going to survive; they drove eight hours home the next day.

They were needed to sign some papers – no way to fax them – and help make the decision for or against surgery. It was unanimously decided that the pieces of bone would be allowed to settle where and how they might. Any time anyone ever gives me a choice about surgery – or any other type of pain – my consistent reply is, "No thank you." As my dad liked to say, "Let nature take its course." He left me a note on which he wrote, "Fight the good fight." Of course, he'd quote a favorite Sunday School hymn.

That was minor upheaval compared to news of the draft lottery which had most of us on campus in a panic. We were all terrified, as were people across the country, that young men were going to be required to go fight in Vietnam. There was no talk of Canada that I ever heard. If your number came up, you went. The parents and the girl back home and everyone else who knew you supported that decision. This was a small liberal arts school in the Midwest in 1965. I think we were mostly clueless and still very much Eisenhower/Kennedy patriots. (At that time, being a patriot didn't require being strictly for one political party or another. A reason why they are called "the good old days!")

H#1 graduated – first in his class. We're not going to even discuss his IQ. He went on to The University of Michigan Law School, and I finished my last two years at Muskingum. After the accident, I was unable to sing or play the piano for the rest of the semester; that was enough to catapult me to finally change majors. I became a speech major, and the last two years at college were immensely more pleasant than the first two. My grades and GPA skyrocketed. I had totally missed the clue: if you are getting low grades, you may be studying the wrong things. Find your strength – it's what comes naturally.

One aspect of the joy of those last two years was that Judithe and I, who had been singing together in our dorm room the past two years, started singing in public. Judithe has a beautiful voice; she never sings flat. Additionally, she plays the guitar with finesse and gusto. We sang for Homecoming and other, smaller venues and events. We were hired to sing at a bar in nearby Cambridge, Ohio. That was really exciting. We made arrangements to borrow a car to get there.

We practiced and practiced. If I sang flat, Judithe didn't care, she just played the guitar more loudly. She needed me because I had the chutzpah to stand in front of people, and she had the talent to perform. Later in her life, she and her husband recorded a great deal of professional music, including a fabulous CD on Ohio History which should be used in every Ohio History class. It makes the events which formed Ohio fascinating and easy to remember. *Ohio Echoes: Chuck and Judithe Craig.* (Sweetsong Productions, 193 Meadville Road, Parkersburg, West Virginia 26104)

So, the big night comes when we're finally going to be professionals – that is, we're going to be paid. Judithe and I get to the bar. There are about eight people hanging around--not the crowd we were hoping for. It gets worse. We walk in, and the bartender says to us, "Didn't anyone call you?" We shake our heads. He points to the wall. There is a very large television set tuned in to wrestling. "We decided to get a television set instead of having you perform." Our first professional gig, and we're replaced by a television set.

We had a few other mishaps in our singing history, too. Our roughest concert was for the Shriners. We planned carefully. We had one bawdy song which ended in the punchline, "Your papa ain't your papa but your papa don't know." That was going to be our finale; we'd "leave them laughing." The Shriners didn't even clap. We had no idea if they didn't get it, or if they were just so uptight and stiff, they couldn't laugh. As I type this, another possibility occurs to me: maybe it hit home and they were all thinking it over. Anyhow, to say we were a flop would be putting it nicely.

Twenty-five years after college one of our college friends invited us to sing for the reception after her son's wedding. Judithe and I made arrangements to get together and practice; then we drove the eight hours across the state of Pennsylvania for this grand event. Upon arrival, we were informed that the bride had changed her mind: she no longer wanted us to sing. Our dear friend was mortified. Judithe and I did the one thing we have always done even better than sing: we laughed.

We laughed and cried as we graduated from Muskingum, too. My dad had made it very clear to my brother and me that we were going to have college degrees. We both do, and then willingly we both earned master's degrees, as well. And that Hindenach prejudice for brains certainly influenced our choices of mate: we both married really smart people. My dad further decreed that once I had my college degree, I was free to marry, but not a day before. I graduated on June 13, 1967, and H#1 and I were married on June 24, 1967.

MICHIGAN, WASHINGTON, DC, BELGIUM AND ITALY

T hen off we went to South Lyon, Michigan, where we lived in a brand-new apartment building built like a motel. The six units were strung out in a straight line. It was an interesting first summer. Number one, I had to find a job.

In the process of job hunting, I was searching the South Lyon newspaper and there, staring back at me from the page, was a picture of me in third grade. The thin blonde hair, the glasses, the shy smile – she couldn't have looked more like me. Her picture was featured in the paper because she was available for adoption.

I was loaded for bear when my husband of a few weeks came home that evening. Within an hour, we had figured out how we could manage this. He took no convincing at all. He was all onboard. The next morning, I was on the phone to the Children's Services people and the lady on the phone was as excited as I was. We spent about a half hour going through all kinds of background information and then she said, "We're almost done. Just a few more questions."

She asked how long we'd been married. "Since June 24th, but we've known each other almost three years." She was furious. I had wasted her time. "We would never consider newlyweds!" she snorted. Sigh. The seed had been planted, though, and it would come to fruition, but the little girl who looked like she was my daughter was not to be our girl. I only hope she quickly became someone's beloved child.

My first teaching interview was at Ypsilanti High School, the town which was home to Eastern Michigan University where H#1 taught while going to law school. The interview went well enough that the principal decided to show me around the school. It was during this impromptu tour that he opened the door to a classroom and dislodged a cup full of milkshake which had been placed as a booby trap to spill on the next person who opened that door. The principal had politely stepped back so I could enter the room first. That was a surprise: totally drenched with milkshake. Chocolate.

Luckily, I had a second interview scheduled, which turned out to be non-eventful. This one was at South Lyon High School, three minutes from our apartment. I was a speech and communication major, but South Lyon only had one speech class. It was already July and they were desperate. I was hired. $4,900/year to teach the only speech class, two sections of college prep sophomore English, and one two-period class of ninth grade "special education," which consisted of a period of history followed by a period of English.

A first-year teacher with four different subject preparations every day! Thankfully, I had no idea how daunting that would be. Just an innocent sheep walking cluelessly into the slaughter house. The last history class I had was Art History, which wasn't going to be too helpful, but thank the Good Lord I had had some really superb English teachers in high school, like Mr. Gonzalves, Mr. Miller, and Mr. Magrogan, and that helped me sail through the English classes.

Our contract allowed for one sick day per month. Fortunately, I had gotten my illnesses out of the way early and was now incredibly healthy. But once a month I called in sick and spent the day trying to prepare history classes for the following month. I loved those kids and am so glad they are now called "Exceptional Children." I had sixteen students in both of the two years I taught that class. They taught me so much. I just recently came across a note from one of the girls telling me what a good teacher I was. Probably the main thing I taught them was that they were loveable and valuable.

I remember talking with them once and suggesting they ask their parents about something that night at supper. All I got was blank looks. It took me a minute. They patiently waited. "Do you eat supper with your parents?" Fifteen of the sixteen didn't have family meals. That's a statistic I've never forgotten. I've always remembered the correlation between academic success and family meals, which seemed so basic and ordinary to me. "You're not in Kansas anymore, Dorothy," I reminded myself. Not everyone had my family-oriented childhood. But for that family of mine, I might have been in special education classes instead of teaching them.

The sophomores in the college prep track also surprised me. I'd think of the hardest and most creative assignments I could for them, and they always outdid themselves. I asked them to re-write Romeo and Juliet and the re-writes – except for the eloquent language – put

Shakespeare to shame. He won the flowing, flowery prose, but they demonstrated the ability to maintain the plot while moving the setting and characters to another century and culture.

After law school graduation, H#1 joined the United States Information Service, also known as the Foreign Service. He traveled to Washington for extensive interviews, while they sent someone to Michigan to interview me. The day and hour the interviewer arrived, I happened to be cleaning the oven. I guess they like to surprise you so they can see you as you really are. I invited the interviewer to sit at the kitchen table. He declined anything to drink. I admit the house smelled awful; I've already complained about the scent of Easy Off. I apologized, but he made a hasty exit. The United States Information Service probably changed their policy and started calling in advance.

The women and men in the Foreign Service are sent to embassies all over the world. They promote understanding and appreciation of United States policies with newspaper reporters, television stations, diplomats in the home country, universities, and libraries. Any cultural or informational programs or events which might increase cooperation and conciliatory relationships are devised and delivered—classes, concerts and cultural exchanges build tolerance and humanize us for each other.

Our first stop on this journey was Washington, D.C. We found a small apartment in Landover, Maryland. The most notable thing that happened there was that the neighbors had a dog they were abusing. That poor thing was tied on the porch all the time. One day after the neighbor couple left for work, I took that dog on a long walk to a very nice neighborhood. When he sat down, I turned around and walked back. He didn't follow me. I always chose to believe that the family he picked out that morning turned out to love him very much. I gave him a chance, I felt. Hopefully, he chose wisely. Dogs are very smart and intuitive.

About ten years later, when we were back in Ohio and I was teaching speech at The University of Akron, one of my students gave a speech on "how cruel it was to drop off animals." I thought I was going to pass out. Somehow, I listened to what a horrible thing I had done in Landover, Maryland. Trying to spin my karma around a little bit and earn myself some grace, I gave that student a really good grade.

The other memorable event from that period of time was the weeks I substitute taught in Washington, D.C. public schools. One of the things I learned there was that I was not suited to fifth grade. After one day teaching fifth grade, I told them I would teach younger kids or older kids, but no middle school, fifth through eighth, for me. In my opinion, anyone who can teach those grades, like my brother did for years, goes automatically to heaven, regardless of having taken an animal for a walk, or lusting, as Jimmy Carter confessed, or whatever else you may have done. Total absolution if you can teach fifth through eighth grades.

The next incident happened in a high school class, where I, at least, had a fighting chance. One of the lessons I learned at South Lyon High School was don't try to call roll by pronouncing students' names. I had a student whose last name was Paddleford. That class never let her or me forget the way I murdered her name. Phonics is not foolproof with names.

So, in this particular high school class, when I asked their names, I was getting some amazing names from some of the guys who were clearly on the football team. Finally, one of them gave me a football name I recognized from pro ball, thank you very much H#1 for all the sports trivia. I looked at that student with a knowing smile. "And I'm Rosie Greer," I said. It was a moment in the sun for me. "She got you," his buddies guffawed and hooted! I had earned enough points that they cooperated the rest of the period, and word spread, apparently, that I was okay and deserving of respect. Every time one of them saw me in the hall they laughed and called me, "Teach."

Then the classes for Foreign Service wives started. First, I had to take French class. I had the coolest teacher from somewhere in the Caribbean. He was a beautiful man with a beautiful accent, and he was a hoot. He always wore a plain black tie. We teased him about it until finally he showed us his ties. On the underside of each was a swimsuit model from Playboy or Sports Illustrated. Risqué. Suggestive.

In order to get into those language classes, you had to pass an entrance exam designed to uncover whether you were capable of learning a foreign language. This required a score between 140 and 180. I got 145; H#1 got 179. Show off!

The same part of our brains which lets us hear nuance in music is necessary for foreign languages, as well. Judithe, roommate extraordinaire, was a foreign language major as well as a talented musician. I do better in English and speaking rather than singing. Good to know. But, muddle through French, I did. When H#1 and I went to Paris, he asked me not to talk. They'll peg us for Americans if you try to speak French, he reasoned. I couldn't be offended. It was true. I was dutifully silent in Paris. And, maybe a little offended, anyhow.

The fun part of training, though, was "wifely duties." We were expected to be able and willing to entertain and to be discreetly proper whenever we left home. We did a crash course in cultural differences around the world, how to set a table, manners, what clothes were appropriate for which occasions and other diplomatic necessities.

We were told sternly that before we did anything, even opened a bottle of wine, we were to check, check, check. Each embassy had experts who specialized in the cultural nuances of the host country. They knew whether lamb was considered a delicacy or forbidden. And they knew everything else we might need to know to prevent an international incident or even a small insult. (I would go on to teach many Intercultural Communication classes at The University of Akron. It was a very helpful, practical prelude.)

What they couldn't have predicted was allergies. I took an opening rosebud in a glass vase to the first diplomat's wife on whom I called. She immediately started sneezing.

The longest night (for me) of our diplomatic stint was an Italian dinner party of twelve with one English speaker in the group who did not know much more than a few food names in Italian. The dinner was delicious, but I did have a hard time staying awake.

Before we left Landover, we were delighted to learn I was pregnant, so we set off for our first posting in Brussels, Belgium, feeling like we had won the lottery. We were assigned to Europe which never happens to young diplomats. Europe is the reward for years in Africa or Asia. But here we went with what we thought was the greatest excitement, yet, growing inside me.

We were in Brussels about six weeks and I was fourteen weeks pregnant when our hopes for a baby were dashed. A trip to the small embassy physician's office in Brussels confirmed our worst fears, and that night we were transported by ambulance to the SHAPE (Supreme Headquarters Allied Powers Europe) hospital an hour from Brussels. We traveled quickly through the dark night, mostly on rural two-lane roads, H#1 and I both crying, the ambulance siren sounding just like the movie ambulances of WW II, wailing that minor chord, the sorrowful two-note repetition warning of disaster.

That was April 14, 1970. It's a day I hold in my heart every year – fifty-two years now. She, I know in my heart our baby was a little girl, was not to come then and was not to be our little girl. That doesn't stop the loving of her or the acknowledgement of her time with us, as brief and unseen as it was. It was deeply felt and she was a precious treasure. The smell of bacon made her sick. That was how she first announced her presence.

The obstetrician was wonderful and very wise. "This is the way nature handles things which aren't forming correctly and wouldn't have a chance in the world," he explained. "One in every ten pregnancies ends in a miscarriage," he continued, "especially the first pregnancies of those who had been on birth control." That was what he said, and then he added: "Wait three months and then try again. You'll be back here next year having a healthy baby."

Andrew David was born a year and eleven days later at the same SHAPE hospital. (This hospital and health care complex has been run by the U.S. Army but staffed predominantly by locals since 1955. They provide care for Americans stationed overseas as well as NATO personnel from Belgium, Luxembourg and the Netherlands. When I was there delivering Andy, the only English-speaker was the doctor, who, as obstetricians like to do, slid in at the last moment. Husbands were not allowed in the delivery room. Those poor nurses probably thought I was really non-compliant because I didn't understand a word they said.)

Before that joyous arrival, though, we grieved. Helpfully, the embassy grieved with us. It was a small group of mature, seasoned diplomats; they had been excited about the prospect of a baby. Former President Eisenhower's son, John, was the ambassador at that time. His wife, Barbara, came to see me as did most of the other wives. They brought flowers and food and small treasures, but mostly they brought encouragement and hope.

Then the embassy arranged for us to travel to Berlin, Germany for a week -- just the change of scene the doctor ordered. When we returned to Brussels, I started a job with the Fulbright Foundation, which sees international education as a powerful force for peace. In our office of four women, we were two English speakers and two French speakers. I learned smiles need no translation, and we found sturdy common ground as we worked together to bring Americans to Belgium for study and cultural exchange as well as send Belgian students to the U.S.

J. William Fulbright, Senator from Arkansas, is the longest standing chairman of the Senate Foreign Relations Committee. The Fulbright Scholars Act of 1946 started what has become today's Fulbright Foundation which gives 800 awards annually to place students, teachers, artists, engineers and others in 135 different countries. Senator Fulbright believed: "It is the task of education, more than any other instrument in foreign policy, to help close the dangerous gap between the economic and technological interdependence of the people of the world and their psychological, political and spiritual isolation." (fulbright@fulbright.no) Unbelievable what one man's foresight has brought to fruition for the last seventy-six years.

The most well-known wife of a diplomat in the Foreign Service was Julia Child, who became a world-famous chef. We heard stories about her all the time. Apparently, she was always entertaining whomever was available because she constantly had new recipes to perfect. Everyone wished for a posting wherever she and her husband, Paul, landed. Word on the street was that when she was working on a recipe, she served it every night until she felt it was the best it could be. No one seemed to feel sorry for her husband or the embassy folks who were invited as guinea pigs, even if he or they did eat the same thing for days at a time.

On weekends, H#1 and I traveled as much as we could possibly afford. We had a sixth sense that this time in Belgium was limited, and we needed and wanted to make the most of it. Europe is so small, our travels were like going from Pennsylvania to New Jersey one weekend, to New York another weekend, to Ohio or Delaware or Connecticut the following weekend, and so we did.

I feel in love with Paris, although it was a smelly city in those days, and, of course, I wasn't supposed to talk. Still, it was Paris. Judithe and I had a song about the Seine, and here I was walking beside that famed river. I'd studied the Notre Dame Cahedral in Art History. The Louvre. Mona Lisa. To my astonishment the bathrooms in Parisienne restaurants consisted of a wooden booth with a step up and two footprints on either side of an opening in the floor. A stand-up outhouse! It was probably wise I was silenced – what might I have blurted out?

And in the countryside, we'd be driving along and randomly, on the side of the road, would sit a deserted tank from World War I or World War II. We might happen upon a huge cemetery with acres of white crosses in perfect lines. Out of nowhere, we'd come across a little shed which sold not ice cream, as we might find in the United States, but pomme de terre frites –French fries. They were served in a piece of paper shaped into a cone, salt and malt vinegar the only condiments. Yes, they were better than the freshest ones from McDonald's—thick and fresh and wickedly crisp.

My parents came to visit and we had a wonderful time touring. The only low note was a near death experience on a train track. The train tracks in Europe at that time did not have warning lights or crossing gates – at least not the one we were crossing -- and a train came barreling at us out of the blue. H#1 floored our little green Maverick and the wind from the passing train shook the car as it brushed by us, missing us by divine mercy. Well, my mother and I, in the back seat, having had a clear vision of what might have been, got to nervously giggling. We simply couldn't stop. The two men in the front seat were very annoyed with us. Years later, my mom and I would giggle about it again. Why imminent death struck us so funny is anyone's guess.

Traveling in Europe is so different from traveling in Indiana or Idaho. At least every hour, wherever we were going, we'd happen upon something we'd read about, studied, seen in a National Geographic or remembered from a movie. The cathedrals were awe-inspiring. We'd drive through a small town, somewhere, anywhere, a town we'd never heard of, and there was yet another magnificent church. Cobblestone streets were bumpy but charming. Window boxes seemed to be everywhere, overflowing with a Crayola profusion of vibrant flowers.

One of the most delightful experiences we had was the day we set out to find Chartres Cathedral. It was hilly, I remember, and finally, off in the distance, we spotted a spire. But as we drove down into the valley the spire disappeared. Back up the hill, and we'd see more of what we imagined to be the church. Finally, we crested a hill and there was Chartres. I believe, except for a newborn baby, it was the most breath-taking thing I've ever seen.

Moments in time, a few in an entire life, touch our souls and reassure us that we are part of the entire fabric of life's quilt. Chartres is a long way from Durham, Pennsylvania, and yet the little church on the top of the hill in eastern Pennsylvania and the towering cathedral out in the middle of the countryside of France seemed the same to me. Everything felt connected.

H#1 and I went back to Durham that June with two-month-old Andy in tow. He was the best traveler ever. On the trans-Atlantic flight, they had a little hammock for him in the front of the plane.

He slept like an angel, awoke, had a bottle, got changed, and the minute he was back in his hammock, with the soft noise and the movement of the plane, he was asleep again. I think the stewardesses were a little disappointed not to be able to walk him around the plane. My brother came to JFK Airport in NYC to pick us up, and I remember he was a wreck transporting the first grandchild.

John Kennedy described himself as "just the man who accompanied Jackie Kennedy to Paris." We were just the parents who accompanied the hit of the party back to Durham. Gram was thrilled with her great-grandchild. Andy was baptized at First Presbyterian Church in Bethlehem where H#1 and I had been married four years before and, although in a different building, the same church where his grandfather had been baptized fifty-nine years earlier. It was gut-wrenching to leave Durham to return to Brussels, harder than the first time, but we had a new adventure coming up.

We received our second assignment which was even more exciting than our first: Rome. H#1 had been studying Italian for the last year and he would be helping Italian newspapers interpret (positively) US news, politics, and public affairs. It was the time of Angela Davis, Simon and Garfunkel, Richard Nixon, and the arrests of 12, 000 militants in Washington, D.C. He had a lot to interpret.

The embassy found a fabulous apartment for us three blocks off Via Veneto. The living room was furnished with matching red silk couches, and it had a maid's room. We didn't have a maid, but it was a kick to have a room for one. The kitchen was remarkable, too. Grandma Rau would have loved it. Everything was low. There were no upper cabinets, only lower cabinets.

One of Andy's favorite games was emptying the cabinets. He'd crawl around the kitchen, open a cabinet, and take every glass and plate, or pot and pan, out of it. He'd place them one at a time on the floor, and then put them back. He never broke a single thing. It was a fascinating game he made up for himself. He had some little contraption with wheels that he could ride and he rode that, fast, up and down the hallway. He'd crash into the front door and then twist himself around and start back down the hall. This was all before he could walk. I wondered if there was a leash or harness in his future.

Italian women walked their babies in the park, so I did, too. ("When in Rome, do as the Romans.") We had a baby carriage that a group of women friends in Belgium had bought for us. Off Andy and I would go to one of the many parks. The difference was that the Italian babies were all dolled up and looked like little princes. The mothers must have drugged them because none of them ever moved. Andy's clothes came from the Sears catalogue and his permissive mother would buy him ice cream cones, so he always looked like he'd been sleeping and eating in his clothes for weeks. He was happy, though!

Again, we traveled as much as possible, this time with baby in tow. We drove around Italy and once flew to Sicily. The airport in Sicily butted up against a mountain, and it looked for all the world like we were going to crash into the rocky slopes upon landing. After that heart-stopper, we had to board a bus, for the bumpiest ride imaginable, to get to the other side of the mountain and our hotel room in Palermo. The adventures were endlessly different, but all entertaining and educational.

I took classes at a University of Maryland branch campus in Rome. H#1 saw Venice by himself on an embassy trip, but we made it to picturesque Florence and saw more art that we recognized, thanks to Louis Palmer's art history class. We also went to Pisa to see the Leaning Tower which does, indeed, lean, right there in the middle of town. It is fairly small. I don't think it would do too much damage if it did finally topple.

The closest commissary was an hour from Rome, so we made that trip monthly. The commissary had disposable diapers and other necessities we were familiar with like toothpaste, aspirin, razors and tampons. Everything in Rome was frightfully expensive. We bought no clothes despite the fabulous quality and style. We may have been diplomats, but we were at the bottom of the pay scale. Of course, actually, we should have been paying the Embassy for the experience and the privilege. What a life-changing opportunity we were given.

I drove once in Rome, right after we got there. In the days before car seats, I put Andy in his little plastic baby carrier on the floor in front of the passenger seat. I forget where we were headed because we never got there. We happened into a traffic circle. This particular traffic circle in the middle of Rome, had about five lanes of traffic circling it. I think there were six options for getting off the circle, should a driver be able to get into the outer lane to be in position to exit.

It was summer, August, when I ventured into this matrix with a four-month-old baby. The signs were in Italian, of course; no such thing as a GPS existed. The map on the passenger seat was useless because was no way was I taking my eyes off the road.

In Italy no one uses turn signals. They blow their horns for all driving communication. I started off taking it on the chin and thinking of Charlie on the MTA. "And did he ever return, no he never returned, and his fate is still unlearned," I sang to Andy. That got us around the circle a number of times. And then I felt a premonition.

I'm not sure which of us started crying first. It was as hot as Hades is reputed to be. Andy, best baby in the universe, had had enough of the little oven in which I'd placed him, and I'd had about enough of being honked at. I'm not even mentioning the gesturing that was going on. Italian men, in a fit of pique, can actually stretch most of their upper bodies out of a car to reprimand a foreigner whom they believe to be a driving menace. I truly thought Andy and I were going to be circling until some merciful police officer came and stopped traffic so we could exit. (I knew the German word for exit: AUSFAHRT, AUSFAHRT, AUSFAHRT!!!!!!)

I would love to be able to explain how we got out of there. I believe it might have been as miraculous as the parting of the Red Sea. Somehow, there was a path and I took whatever road it was, and, again, somehow, I found my way back to the apartment and rehydrated Andy and me and cooled off. There was no air conditioning, but we did have cold water, some of which I sat Andy in until he cooled down; and then, when he was exhausted and asleep, I eased into a tub of cold water myself.

That was almost the only driving disaster – there was one other and then there was the walking incident. The other driving event happened almost a year later when I finally had the courage to drive again and was pulling out into traffic. Now, as anyone who has ever ridden with me will testify, I am the most cautious puller-outer ever. My mother used to say, "Susan, I would have gone three times already." This particular time when I pulled out, I had plenty of room. The fool coming toward me sped up and brushed my rear bumper. I imagine from how loudly his voice boomed he was saying it was my fault for pulling out in front of him. Luckily, not understanding Italian was actually helpful because he just gave up and drove off. It really does take two people to fight.

The pedestrian incident was a little more dramatic due to the Good Samaritan. I was walking across a street in Rome and a car actually hit me hard enough to catapult me up onto the sidewalk and knock me off my feet. The driver didn't stop. A fellow pedestrian hurried over and practically held me down as I was trying to sit up. "Say you're pregnant," he told me in English with a lovely Italian accent. "I'm not," I whispered. This had to have been the strangest conversation of my life. "Yes," he said, understanding, "but they'll never know, and you can get a lot of money if you say you are." Then, he saw a police officer walking toward me as I lay on the sidewalk where I had been deposited by the car. The very opportunistic Good Samaritan vanished, and the police officer helped me stand up and steady myself. I went home and took Motrin for a number of days.

The only other commotion I caused was at the greengrocer's one of the first times I ventured into that little shop. In Italy it took a long time to gather groceries because each store had only certain items. There were no super markets. You went to the place that sold chickens if you wanted chicken, and believe me, it didn't come in pieces. If you wanted chicken, you got a whole chicken with everything that chicken ever possessed (except its feathers and head) tucked back inside it. That was interesting. My mother had spared me so many of life's messy details.

The greengrocer was located across the street from our apartment and due to my love of vegetables and his proximity, he and I soon became acquainted. On this early visit, I wanted an eggplant. I had previously seen eggplant in his store, but this day I saw none, so I asked for one. The grocer didn't know the English word, "eggplant" and for the life of me, I couldn't remember the Italian word. I estimated the size and shape of it with my hands. Then he started throwing out some color words – enough color words that I knew he was asking me what color it was. I didn't know the word for "purple." He didn't know what purple was. He asked me if I spoke anything other than English. I actually understood the question; we were getting somewhere. I said, "German." He went out on the street and found a man who spoke German. (I couldn't make this up.)

The German man and I greeted each other in German and he asked me what I was trying to buy. I didn't know the German word for eggplant or purple, either. The German speaker and I muddled around a little in my rusty German. Then, in a moment of either desperation or insight, the greengrocer went into the back room of the store and re-appeared with an eggplant. You would have thought one of us had just donated a kidney to the other. The three of us did the happy dance. The grocer charged me an arm and a leg for that little eggplant, but I think he added in something to compensate for all the time he had spent on me.

Two other remarkable things about the greengrocer were the celery and the price of wine. The celery was wilted and limp instead of stiff and crunchy like our celery. The first time the grocer gave me a stalk, I thought he was giving me an old, second-rate stalk of celery that no self-respecting Italian shopper would have accepted. But, time after time, if you got celery, it was floppy. They must have grown it differently. It tasted like celery. Oh, and delightfully, if you bought a tomato, you were given a small bit of basil with your purchase.

Then, in a break from having only vegetables and fruit, this enterprising green grocer introduced wine. One kind of wine: Chianti, with a lovely woven basket surrounding the bottle. I wasn't a wine drinker in those days, so Chianti was as good to me as anything else. "When in Rome…" And the clincher of the deal was that one of his lovely bottles of wine cost 600 lire. At that time, that equaled $1.00. The greengrocer's Chianti and taxi rides were the only two bargains I discovered in the Eternal City in 1972.

Once again, as in Brussels, all the sights were enthralling. Things we had studied or only seen in pictures were right around the next corner. The Spanish Steps were the home of the flower market and the beauty was unparalleled. Everywhere, window boxes burst with color and texture. Churches and cathedrals were tucked into every nook and cranny. Some sprawled for city blocks. The Coliseum was exactly as it appeared in pictures but much larger. Trevi Fountain was much smaller than we thought it would be and tucked into a small plaza. We almost missed it.

One of the most breath-taking things we saw was the catacombs under the City of Rome. Christians had hidden in these tunnels.

They had slept on the three-tiered stone pallets which were narrow and crowded together. They had eaten and rested and worshipped despite the Coliseum, the hungry lions, the hatred and the danger. We saw drawings of the symbol of the fish, exactly as one sees them today on the bumpers of cars. This symbol was etched into stone two thousand years ago by desperate people trying to practice their faith and stay alive.

How discouraging to realize that centuries later, we have not become any more tolerant or loving. How awesome to have witnessed the early endeavors to stand up for freedom of religion, to have traced our fingers into those painfully drawn fish – our heritage, our hope. For me, the catacombs were another of those moments in life when all the dots connected and everything belonged. I felt peace and serenity, the sense of continuity which had graced my early life and kept me "moored to the millrace" even in ancient Rome.

Again, we took every single-day car trip we could take with a child under the age of one. Each trip was a breeze compared to our entrance into Italy in August of 1971. We had managed, through sheer ignorance, to time our trip so that we entered Italy on the very weekend most of the country was on the road. For two weeks in August, almost everything in Italy shuts down for the country-wide vacation time. We new kids coming to town had no idea. The multiple lanes on the main north/south road in Italy would only kindly have been called an "expressway." In most of Italy, we found, there was little that was express. Everything seemed to have its own incredibly slow pace.

So, unbeknownst to us, as we passed through beautiful, green, lush, cool Switzerland, was what awaited us when we entered Italy -- it was like landing in a big, brown sauna. All of a sudden nothing looked very inviting, the sun was beating everything into lethargy, and we had hours to go before we'd be in Rome. We also had a hot, thirsty baby with hot, thirsty parents trying to soothe him. Plus, we found ourselves in the middle of a slow-moving parking lot. Cars were crawling at about Andy's speed of crawl as everyone jockeyed to get to where they were going for the two weeks of vacation. It was a nightmare.

Ice, we found out that day, was unavailable in Italy. We finally had to buy Andy a sweet, orange soda because there was nothing cold available and certainly no way to make any of the formula we brought. No bottles of water in those days. He liked his orange soda; it was the first sweet drink he'd ever had. Thank God it didn't make him sick.

We arrived in "Roma" late that night and located the "pensione" where we were staying until our apartment was available. The lovely woman who ran the place had a basket of fruit and crackers, a bottle of wine, and a carafe of water, room temperature water, waiting for us. She asked if we wanted anything else. "Ice," I requested desperately. She looked aghast. "You have two," she conceded and went to get them. She returned, with two very small ice cubes in a teacup, and said with authority, "Ice not good for you."

To this day, except for my piano, the ice machine in the refrigerator is my favorite item in any house. I always keep plastic ice cube trays on hand so I never need fear an ice-maker malfunction.

The year in Rome was a year of delight as we watched Andy grow from a four-month-old, who showed us he could roll-over by rolling off a bed, to a sixteen-month-old who was active, adventurous, happy, and who could make a game out of anything and amuse himself for hours. We befriended two college girls who were studying in Rome for a year, and they watched Andy for us so we could get to the commissary or go to social functions at the embassy.

The most tragic thing that happened while we were in Rome was a phone call from my dad telling us that Aunt Kitty had been in a terrible accident and was not expected to live. I remember sliding down the wall beside the phone and sitting on the floor. My legs wouldn't hold me up. No, he said, I was not to think about trying to come home. He would keep us informed as things progressed. Life felt very fragile, and I was bereft to be away from my family. Aunt Kitty lived and regained her intellectual and emotional resiliency even as she was trapped in a body which had betrayed her. This is the first half of the double tragedy I'll talk about next.

By winter that year news came that our next assignment would be to Africa, since H#1 spoke fluent French and Italian. We had met diplomats who had been assigned all over the world. They unanimously told us that a posting in Africa had a big advantage: you were going to save your entire salary. There was nothing to spend money on, and most of the embassies were considered hardship posts, so housing was provided as well as many other perks. The big disadvantage was that 99% of diplomats who were posted in Africa came home with a life-long intestinal parasite. If it had just been us, two adults, we probably would have gone. No way were we taking a chance like that with our precious son.

H#1 called a friend from college who was teaching at The University of Akron. It happened that the friend was leading a group of students to London the following week, so H#1 flew to London and was interviewed on a park bench for a teaching position at the University. He was hired on the spot. We made reservations on Flight 111 which left Rome August 11th. I don't remember the airline, but once the decision was made, we couldn't get back on American soil fast enough. It had been a life-changing, perception-altering, exhilarating, fast-track-to-maturity adventure. We'd only been gone three years, but we'd had ten years of experiences.

I got in trouble with a security officer at the airport before we got out of the country. He stood sternly in front of me and asked me what the bulge was in the pocket of my dress. I guess he suspected I had a gun. I slowly pulled out Andy's collection of pacifiers. He didn't even crack a smile. The plane ride was much longer with an active sixteen-month-old. Bless her heart, the older woman in the seat behind us had a coin purse with a variety of coins in it, and she must have played with that child for three hours. They did serve ice on the plane.

THE SECOND
DOUBLE TRAGEDY

By Memorial Day weekend of 1972, we had a year-old baby and fewer than three months left in Rome. Back in Durham, it was cousin Rebecca's sixteenth birthday. A picnic was planned at Aunt Kitty's to celebrate. First, though, there was a parade to attend, because Rebecca marched with the color guard who led the Palisades High School Band. She was following in Molly's footsteps.

Aunt Kitty stood along the side of the road cheering as the band passed by. Then she hurried up the hill to her car to drive home and prepare the family birthday picnic. An elderly woman was driving down the hill Aunt Kitty was climbing; the elderly woman lost control of her car. She hit Aunt Kitty, dragging her a long way. When the ambulance arrived, Aunt Kitty was barely clinging to life. She died three times on the way to the hospital. Those angelic volunteer paramedics revived her each time.

Aunt Kitty, our vibrant, outspoken, slender warrior who was a gardener, an active church member, a fighter for the underdog, and a crusader for justice, would be a quadriplegic for the rest of her life.

Months of rehabilitation resulted in no return of mobility. From her neck up she was in one piece, her voice and her brain as indomitable as ever. This is not a victim story; she'd quickly correct us if we erroneously thought it might be.

After months of rehabilitation, Aunt Kitty came home to the house and family she loved. The room which had been the scene of Uncle Charlie's fall from grace, the former dining room, became a hospital room. The old back porch was converted into a handicap accessible bathroom with lots of windows added. Aunt Kitty dearly loved looking over those Pennsylvania hills.

Christiane and Rebecca, her two daughters, the nursing student and the high school junior, learned how to care for her. Aunt Kitty accepted her daughters' care only temporarily. She would not have her children's lives altered or their futures diminished by being responsible for their mother. She had some money; she would spend it getting the care she needed. Additionally, she belonged to an active, loving, service-oriented church in Springtown. The people from the church, as well as those with whom she taught, the neighbors in the community, and various family members, stepped up and made it possible for Katharyn to live at home.

Every day, someone brought a meal or someone showed up to cook a meal. Once, when I was visiting, the woman who was going to be cooking supper came to ask Aunt Kitty what she'd like her to make. The answer was "a pork roast." Then Aunt Kitty proceeded to tell the woman where the roast was in the freezer. It was under the wire basket on the left. There were two roasts there. Aunt Kitty wanted her to use the smaller of the two. Now, this freezer was in the basement and Aunt Kitty hadn't been in the basement for about four years. It took me a while to figure out that Aunt Kitty knew where every single item was in her home.

As impressed as I was with her knowledge of the whereabouts of everything, from the meat in the freezer to the cleaning supplies under the sink, I realized that someone (or multiple someones) had been patient enough to go over with Katharyn what she had and where it was. Then Aunt Kitty, with her amazing mind, had retained this information, adding and subtracting everything either emptied during the day or purchased and brought into the house. To say that Aunt Kitty was controlling was an understatement. To say that it helped save her sanity and her dignity, probably wasn't.

She had been the first person I knew who refused to buy things unless the items were made in the USA, whether a car or a paper plate. She was a conservationist, a recycler, and a proponent of cloth napkins and "real" table cloths. She hated waste and despised laziness. She had no lukewarm opinions.

When my husband, the one with his name on the pillowcase, ran for state representative in Ohio – we had obviously moved back from Italy –Aunt Kitty was the only person in the family to give him a donation for his campaign. She wrote a typical Aunt Kitty note along with the donation. "I don't like Democrats," one of which he was, "and I don't trust men with beards," one of which he had, "but I believe you to be of good moral character, and that is more essential than anything else." She sent him $50.

She also wrote to me during my first year of teaching. I had laryngitis, and she told me it was a good thing I couldn't talk.

"Teachers talk too much. Use this as a lesson. See how much more you can accomplish with less talk." She was right. All those repetitive commands and bossy directions? Not needed.

For the first two years after her accident, she prayed non-stop for the use of her hands. She bargained with God and asked all of us who knew and loved her to bargain on her behalf. If she could simply use her hands, she'd accept being in a wheelchair for the rest of her life.

Nothing changed.

Finally, she told me, she decided God had listened but God had a different plan.

She requested her typewriter and slowly, laboriously, taught herself to type using a stick she attached to a finger. From then on, I received short, typed notes from her. She even wrote for local newspapers. (Another similarity to Grandma Rau, of course.) She was creative and unstoppable.

Here is one of her letters, typed so carefully to me soon after I was divorced:

Dear Susan, I've just lost two books to the floor. The crows and blue jays are calling me to come out. Pierre and the dogs are napping. Christy just left. And I have the first head cold in years. There's no use in gretsing because no one will listen, ergo, we get out pretty paper and think about other things. The clean surgery of divorce is over and recuperation takes place. Last night I listened to Children of Divorce and I listened through the minds of your boys. The children themselves brought out that single parent is a euphemism; they have two parents, no matter what happens to the marriage. Your lovely and loving mother has such serenity and is sure "in the long run" your separation is for the best. I just keep quiet, because, thankfully, she never had a lonely night or a lost love. My husband was rotten, too, but forty years later, I still mourn the death of my marriage. Well, we survive. Affectionately, Aunt Kitty

A fascinating thing started happening as Aunt Kitty accepted "what is" and focused on survival: People began to realize Katharyn was always home. They started stopping by, "just to talk to Katharyn and see how she is." That became the opposite of the reality. They started stopping by because she would listen to how they were. She was crafty and cunning in the advice she'd give. She became, for the next eight years, the village psychiatrist.

Just as I only saw my mom cry once, my mom only saw Katharyn cry once. It was ten o'clock at night, and since Pierre was on his way to work, Katharyn was home alone. A blizzard was raging outside. My dad and his cohorts were at a meeting and not paying attention to the weather, so he wasn't home. My mom was in bed when the phone rang. She immediately worried for her husband who wasn't back yet, but it was Katharyn.

"The door blew open," she said. "Get Dave to come latch it."

My mom said, "Okay," and they hung up. Mom dressed and set off in the snowstorm with the winds blowing a whiteout across the road. She got to Aunt Kitty's, and whether it was because it was my mom and not my dad, or because there was snow on the bed, or both – Aunt Kitty burst into tears. A one and only crying jag.

Fortunately for Aunt Kitty's modesty it was my mother who showed up. She dried Katharyn, put a warm nightie on her, then changed the bed and cranked up the heat to get the chill out of the room. When she finished, she turned around and headed back to Durham with the outside door of Aunt Kitty's room firmly latched.

I visited Aunt Kitty whenever I was home. During one of those visits, when we were deep in discussion, she dated an event by saying, "It was right around the time when your grandfather committed suicide."

And there it was. The secret that had been kept, at least from me, for twenty-six years.

"Who?" I asked, not immediately understanding.

"Grandad Hindenach. I think you were about ten."

I was nine. Close enough.

And then she proceeded to tell me how he had killed himself.

Aunt Kitty was the consummate realist. Information hidden from children or anyone else was anathema to her.

While she returned to the conversation we had been having, I watched the pieces fall into place: my mother wailing, Gram and Aunt Ruth having to hurriedly get away from where it had happened, everything moving with such urgency in Durham, the changes in the tone when I walked in on a conversation, Gram's stoicism, Aunt Ruth's depression . . . click, click, click went the pieces of the puzzle.

I made up my mind then and there that I was not going to throw Aunt Kitty under the bus or ruin two and a half decades of secret-keeping. I knew now, and now it was my secret to hold. All those devoted to keeping the secret from a little girl are gone. Depression is better understood. I trust we have come far enough that no one reading this feels anything except compassion for Grandad.

Aunt Kitty lived ten amazingly productive years after her accident. She saw those years as pure gift, including playing with her oldest son's boys, and holding Sarah, her older daughter's first child. A few months before she died, I happened to send her flowers. She typed a thank you note that said, "Don't put flowers on my grave, give them to me when I'm living." So exactly an Aunt Kitty message. I didn't realize it would be the last time I'd have a chance to send or give her flowers. We never realize when the last chance is that we'll have for anything, do we?

When I think of her, which I do often, I see her sitting in her wheelchair outside her beloved home, her sister, Agnes, sitting beside her. I'm there, and my three boys are running around. They start playing in the dog house on the porch. Aunt Agnes, the nurse and health expert, says, "Boys, get out of there. That's dirty and full of germs." I say nothing. The boys are preparing to listen to the stern voice of reason.. Aunt Kitty pipes up: "Oh, Aggie, leave them alone. They're kids. Play wherever you like," she smiles at them.

PART TWO OF THE SECOND DOUBLE TRAGEDY

Aunt Kitty's accident was the trauma on the Rau side of the family, and Aunt Cicely's surgery to remove a benign lump on her neck was the trauma on the Hindenach side of the family.

Now "the boys," as Gram always called them, the two sons who followed the two daughters, won the jackpot when they chose their wives.

Uncle Lee, child #3, met Aunt Cicely in church, the same way both his and her parents met, and the same way my dad met my mom, and all in the same church. She came from the big, happy DeSilver family that lived about two miles from Durham. Cicely's earliest claim to fame was that she was a twin. There was no evil twin in this pair. I think her sister's name was Peg and Aunt Cicely was usually "Sis" or "Cissy." Finding two sweeter, kinder girls, both smart and creative, would have been impossible.

Aunt Cicely's much-admired talent, other than her legendary patience, was her artistic talent. She painted realistic scenes from her childhood, and, then, later, from everywhere she traveled, which was all over the United States and Europe. She captured the feel of what she saw because she felt deeply and saw the world with kind, accepting eyes.

Whereas my mom adored Uncle Hollis, my dad adored Aunt Cicely. She was a great deal like my mom in temperament, and the two couples got along well – until my parents went to California to visit Uncle Lee and Aunt Cicely. Typically, in Pennsylvania, shared meals had been served at the DeSilver home, where a big picnic accommodated the crowd, or at the Rau home, my mom cooking any time Uncle Lee and family came to visit.

When my parents stayed with Uncle Lee and Aunt Cicely in California, one noticeable difference between my mom and Aunt Cicely emerged. My mom was a planner; by 8 a.m. the supper menu was air tight. Meals, chez Miriam, were served at specific, scheduled times. She might have been off by two minutes on a rough day, but that's about all the leeway she needed. Her kitchen ran like the Swiss railway system.

The first night Aunt Cicely cooked for my parents and her family, she reportedly sat down with the adults to enjoy a cocktail and conversation. Around six o'clock she said she thought she'd drive over to the grocery and see what looked good for dinner. My dad was totally unprepared for her to fall so drastically from the high pedestal on which he'd placed her. According to his stomach, her departure for the store coincided with the time the meal should have been on the table, give or take two minutes. Aunt Cicely shopped unhurriedly. She came home and made a delicious dinner – which was ready around 9:30!

Years later, Uncle Lee and family moved back to the east coast and settled in Connecticut, near brother Jim and wife Marilyn. Aunt Marilyn was another sweetheart. My dad, in fact, was overheard on separate occasions telling each sister-in-law that SHE was his favorite. Much visiting was done among the siblings, with Gram and Aunt Ruth in tow, most of it after the kid generation had left home and the adults had time to wander about the eastern seaboard.

Uncle Lee and Aunt Cicely considered building a home in a lovely development about a mile from Durham. A huge, hilly and fertile field across the street from the Nicholas' home was to become Durham Farm. My dad, township supervisor extraordinaire, was a strict and adamant proponent of zoning. Durham Farm had hilly, spacious, five acre lots which appealed to Lee and Cicely. Everyone involved, especially Aunt Ruth, who would have loved to have had them near-by, was ecstatic about the plan.

It never happened, though. Aunt Cicely went into the hospital for a minor surgery on a benign lump on her neck, and something went catastrophically wrong. She spent the next four years in a coma. Uncle Lee had recently retired and they had foreseen a lovely new chapter in their lives where they could finally concentrate on each other.

When they married, Uncle Lee immediately went into the service. It was World War II and he had enlisted in the Army; Uncle Jim enlisted in the Navy. Gram considered it one of the greatest blessings of her life that both of them returned home after the war "without a scratch," as she liked to say. When Uncle Lee came home from the war, he was a father, and then three more children followed.

Now, devastated, he either went to see Aunt Cicely every day or made sure someone else was going to be there. He studied and read everything he could to try to create a miracle, but, except for a brief period when she seemed to rally a little, it was a dismal and unproductive four years in terms of any quality of life for our wonderful Cicely.

I suppose everyone is missed when he or she dies, but some people are such bright, steady lights in the world, quietly helping and supporting, adding warmth, that when they leave the land of the living, the empty space that belonged to them seems never again to be filled. Such was the case with Cicely DeSilver Hindenach. And surely no one missed her more than her twin, the only person who had never drawn a breath but that Cissy drew one, too.

Aunt Cicely drew or painted the family Christmas cards every year. Coventry Cathedral, old and new, was the 1986 card.

PART THREE

BACK TO THE U.S.A.

So, our little family of three headed for Durham on August 11, 1972. Andy and I would hang out with my folks while H#1 found us a place to live in or around Akron, Ohio. He quickly found a house to rent on a farm outside Wadsworth, Ohio, a near-by town, and we stayed there four eventful years.

Meantime, in Durham, Andy was having trouble breathing. Aunt Ruth got him right in to a pediatrist who immediately transferred him to an oxygen tent at Easton Hospital. His daddy made a flying trip back east because his son's condition sounded so serious. But by the time H#1 arrived, that resilient little Andy had absorbed the steroids they injected straight into his chest, gotten some antibiotics circulating, and was thoroughly enjoying the oxygen tent.

In 1972, for a sixteen-month-old, the oxygen unit went entirely around the bed. It was taller than he was, of see-through plastic, and Andy could breathe so well he invented another game for himself. He started at one end of the bed and ran to the other, bouncing off the plastic, knocking himself silly with laughter. By the time his daddy had rushed to the emergency, the hospital was ready to send us home. Andy would fight with croup for a few years and allergies the rest of his life, but that wouldn't stop him from becoming quite an athlete, even running marathons. As my mom was always quick to point out, "It didn't hurt his golf game any, either."

The farmhouse in Wadsworth was perfect for us. We immediately joined the Methodist Church and met lifelong friends, some of whom we had known at Muskingum. H#1 got set up with a great teaching assignment and came home the day before classes were to start to ask if I wanted to get a master's degree. A teaching assistantship no one had claimed could be mine if I would teach two sections per semester of the basic speech class. They'd pay me to go to school? No brainer. I never expected I would be teaching there for thirty years.

As a newcomer, I attended one Welcome Wagon meeting in Wadsworth and so did Judy Moffitt, whom I happened to sit beside on the sofa at that meeting. She and I have been dear and trusted friends since – fifty plus years and counting. Our husbands played baseball and tennis together and served on this and that board at the church. Judy and I religiously went to years of Bible Study at a conservative church in town, which made for a great, substantive theological background for us. She would go on to earn her master's in theology.

Our most important and cherished activity, though, was that we raised our children together and shared countless suppers at both homes, all because we were lucky enough to each choose the sofa at a meeting which was completely out of character for either of us to attend. (Neither of us ever went to another Welcome Wagon event!) What are the chances? God is in the details, I like to say. Actually, I've taken to more accurately saying: God IS the details.

One story about that Welcome Wagon meeting always makes Judy and me smile. We were told to take turns saying where we had lived previously. I said, "Rome." One woman asked, "Rome, New York?" I shook my head and was trying to open my mouth when another woman said, "Rome, Georgia?" I again shook my head. It was Judy Moffitt who grinned at me and said, "Rome, Italy." We knew then that we'd be friends.

H#1 ran for the Ohio House of Representatives in what was obviously a doomed but dues-paying venture. Running against him was the Republican Representative who practically "owned" the Ohio House and had already served numerous terms. But politics is like acting. You have to be willing to play the small unsuccessful, unnoticeable parts if you ever want to be in line for a starring role. "Take one for the team." He did. It was another amazing learning experience. And, of course, it gave Aunt Kitty a chance to send him that $50 check, even though she didn't trust Democrats or men with beards.

Far and away, though, the best and most important decision for us, while on the farm in Wadsworth, was that we took the opportunity to expand our family. Andy had always been around adults, and we figured he could use an older sibling to show him the ropes of being a kid. (We were looking for another nine-year-old little girl like the one we had seen in the South Lyon, Michigan newspaper.)

We went to adoption seminars and found an adoption organization which seemed to be willing to trust us with a child. They came to check out our house and left after about ten minutes. That Pennsylvania Dutch cleanliness of mine paid off. Also, the fact that we each taught college was the deal-maker.

We had asked for a little girl between the ages of four and eight. They offered us a four-month-old biracial baby boy with minor foot problems. "Close enough," we said, and went to another city in Ohio to meet this little guy.

The sixteen-year-old biological mom had asked only that he grow up in a home where he would have the opportunity to go to college. The powers that be figured the home of two college teachers was about as good a bet as any. The foster mother, who had totally resolved his foot problems by doing the suggested exercises, misunderstood and thought we were taking him home. So, we did. He came to us, July 22, 1974 in a tan onesie with a train on the front, clutching a tan and brown bottle. Foster mom sent one extra diaper and a jar of green beans.

The case worker walked in the door of the room where H#1, Andy and I waited carrying a broadly smiling, adorable, curly-headed boy who was hilarious from the word go. He had a belly laugh, and anything and everything Andy said to him, he thought was funny. They developed their own secret language and would have long, boisterous conversations no one but the two new brothers could understand.

When the social worker appeared, I, helpfully, froze. I couldn't move. H#1 rose to the occasion and went to take the baby who happily reached for the stranger who would be his new daddy. The three of us talked and laughed and tickled and oohed and aahed. When the social worker returned to say the foster mom had mistakenly gone home, we said, "No problem." Obviously, this guy was a keeper.

We might have stayed in Wadsworth in the rented farmhouse. Eddie, Andy's new brother, loved all the room and the two of them ran their little hearts out. Eddie adored the horses that came to the fence beside the house. He gave me a couple heart failures by crawling under the fence to get closer to the huge animals. He was not the least bit intimidated by their size. The horses, wisely, always backed away from him. He was probably more of a wild card than they were, but I didn't know that.

Eddie also "cut his eye teeth" by climbing on the roof of our car – I don't know how – and jumping from the roof onto the only cement on the entire thirty-eight-acre farm, the sidewalk in front of the house. He knocked his teeth up into his head but, like the dentist assured us, they came back down. My blood pressure never has.

Eddie was the messiest and most daring child I ever saw. He pulled a glass pitcher of iced tea down on himself while H#1 and our friends, Jim and Judy, were at a church meeting and I was watching the four children. Miraculously most of the glass shards scattered landing on the table and the carpet instead of becoming embedded in his skin. Did I mention that he's also fast and lucky? I wasn't so lucky the first time I gave him some rice. If there was an award for mess-making, Eddie would have won it. Knowing him now, you'd never guess what he was once capable of; he presently travels with a hand-held steamer to remove the wrinkles from his clothes. Astonishing transformation!

Eddie settled into our home with only one other little problem, which he still has today: he doesn't sleep. For the first nine months we had him, he awoke six or eight times every night. He'd fuss, not really cry, just sort of make enough noise to wake me; I'd go pat him on the back and talk to him for a minute. He'd fall back to sleep, and then, in less than an hour, we'd do it again. Finally, I took him to the pediatrician and begged Dr. Nafziger to drug one of us. I was hinting broadly that I thought it should be me. He said to give Eddie some cough medicine with codeine for a few nights. It only took two nights and we were both, mercifully, exhaustedly, sleeping through the night.

The bicentennial summer of 1976 brought an accomplishment: my master's in rhetoric and communication. More exciting by far, it brought a new beginning: October of that year son number three joined his two big brothers. While I headed to the hospital for that event, my parents came to babysit. After about a day my dad headed back to the quiet of Durham, assuring my mom he'd come for her when she was ready to go home. My mom saw Andy on and off the school bus for kindergarten and was entertained by little Mr. Fearless.

Luckily, she was there to help me make sense of just what happened when we brought the baby home. This beautiful, perfect, eight-pound, seven-ounce baby named Nicholas screamed, and I mean screamed, every time I put him down on his back to get changed. My mom and I examined his back in great detail. When he snuggled up against a shoulder, he was fine. We could feel nothing out of place. Still, when we put him on his back, he'd wail. I was practically inconsolable. I thought we had to get him to the doctor.

"Susan," my wise mother said, finally. She sighed. "I'm afraid," she hardly knew how to state her hypothesis, "I'm afraid," she looked kind of sorrowfully at me, "that what we're seeing is . . .stubbornness. I think he just doesn't like being on his back."

I had never heard of a three-day-old being stubborn. My mother, however, had hit the nail on the head. One day about four years later when my parents were visiting and I had just dressed the boys for church, Nick came down the stairs wearing something quite different than what I had just put on him. My mother looked questioningly at me, asking wordlessly if I had dressed him in that mishmash. "Obviously not," I shook my head no. She nodded at me and smiled and called to him to go back upstairs with her. In a few minutes she came downstairs looking a little smug. She had him in matching clothes. A few minutes later, Nick came downstairs dressed in the mismatched things he was determined to wear.

"Off we go," I said. In my very permissive world view, there are few things in life worth fighting about. My always meticulously dressed and coiffed mother did not agree, but she had tried her best to reason with a headstrong four-year-old and it hadn't worked. Her words when he was three days old resonated soundlessly between us. She had nailed it! Stubborn, headstrong, obstinate, willful . . . my vocabulary grew to accommodate his personality traits.

Despite our happiness in Wadsworth, the local paper came out in the winter of 1977 to announce that the good people of that small Ohio town had counted and reported that a total of 79 people in town were not white. When H#1 came home from work that night, I announced that we were out of there. He had no objections. Probably not a good idea to raise our biracial son in a town where they were counting.

Unbelievably, the next day H#1 talked to a music professor who was moving to California and was about to list his home in West Akron. I went to see the house that same night after teaching. Actually, I crawled there in the car and later crawled back to Wadsworth because we happened to be in the midst of a blizzard. I would have walked. That house was not going on the market the next morning until I checked it out.

It was a beautiful colonial in a firmly integrated neighborhood. (We didn't realize how firmly, but it didn't matter to us, and I think it proved to be an amazing advantage to all three boys.) My dad quickly loaned us the down-payment complete with 5% interest – he was an accountant and this was a business deal – and suddenly we couldn't wait to stop renting and have a home of our own.

Another amazing stroke of luck or blessing was that there was in this music teacher's living room something after which I had always lusted: a baby grand piano. (Gram had given me a charm of a baby grand when I was about thirteen.) Not being feasible to move a baby grand piano from Ohio to California, they'd sell it to us for $1,000. I owned a life insurance policy my parents had purchased for me when I was a baby. Cash-in value? One thousand dollars. Should I have an early demise, my ashes would have to be placed in the piano.

When Andy started first grade that next year, there was one other white kid in his class. It turns out many of our neighbors lived in that neighborhood because it contained a very popular and well-respected Catholic School. As a child from a long-line of teachers and the daughter of a thirty-year tenured school board member, I was a strong advocate for public schools. The boys, none of them, ever complained about attending public schools.

One night when Andy was in college and driving around with a few of his fraternity brothers, who happened to be white, a car full of black guys pulled up beside them. The two groups were starting to talk trash to each other when Andy recognized a guy he'd gone through school with, and the almost-rumble became a little reunion. That is just one of the reasons I'm a believer in integrated public-school education. You have to know people different from you to realize how similar they are.

We had wonderful neighbors in Akron. Odd, but wonderful. A Catholic family with five mostly grown kids lived on one side of us and conveniently provided two babysitters; a family from Germany lived next to them and provided a good friend for me; and a family with three grown sons lived on our other side. That family happened to have a swimming pool which they shared, but the odd part about that family was their choice of pets: a dog and a monkey.

Two quick notes about Marga, my friend from Germany, before we get to the monkey. Number 1: We spoke English together. Number 2: Marga was the niece of the Von Trapp family, the family who famously sang to escape from the Nazi's. It was their story which became *The Sound of Music*. Marga was polished and cosmopolitan, unlike the monkey nearby.

Butch, the monkey, wore diapers. Lucky, their dog, did not, but he liked to wander. The boys became experts at calling Lucky back home, although it was an expensive venture because Lucky only 'came' for a piece of lunch meat.

Butch was mostly house-bound and on a leash when outside. Supposedly. Unless he escaped, which he was slick at doing, when someone opened their door. A three-foot-high cement wall divided our properties, and Butch had no trouble sprinting over the wall to terrorize the boys.

I'll never forget the time Eddie came rushing in. He was always the first to bring news: "Butch just stole Nick's bottle." Sure enough. There sat Butch drinking from Nick's bottle. I have to admit, that bottle went in the trash. (You'll understand why a not-yet-two-year-old was toddling around the backyard with a bottle when you remember my mother's pronouncement and my overly permissive nature. I'm sure the statute of limitations has expired, but I do want to add, in my defense, I was in the kitchen and none of the boys could leave the back yard without my seeing them. Not to mention the fact that getting any nourishment in Nick was an achievement. He went eighteen months on white milk and chocolate doughnuts. (He got over that just before my own mother had me arrested. I just felt the need to explain!)

Once, I was unfortunate enough to walk into the neighbor's house and surprise Butch. I had been invited in, but it had apparently not been cleared with Butch. So, more accurately, it was he who surprised me. Mary Kay, Butch's mom, was telling me something and stopped when tears started running down my cheeks. She looked down to see Butch holding my leg in his toothless but very strong jaws. I was so shocked; I couldn't even talk. Just like any mom, she called his name in a certain tone, and he dislodged me.

Butch's parents, Mary Kay and Paul, had a game they liked to play when they went out for a drive in their huge bright turquoise Chrysler New Yorker. (We called it The Land Yacht!) They would install a baby carrier on the large front bench seat. Then they would dress Butch in a frilly bonnet, place him in the baby seat between them, and ride around with him to see people's reactions when they caught a glimpse of the baby's face.

None of us ever really warmed up to Butch, who lived for thirteen years, but we were all pretty found of Lucky-the-dog, who didn't bite or steal and taught us to keep a good supply of lunch meat on hand. Mary Kay would just step out of the house and start calling, "Lucky," and the boys would run to the refrigerator, procure a slice of lunchmeat, wave at her, and trick the dog into coming home. It was a small price to pay for the luxury of being allowed to swim in their pool on a hot afternoon.

The only stipulation for being permitted in the deep end of our neighbor's pool was that you had to be able to swim the length of the pool with an adult beside you before you were deemed ready. Eddie was sure he was ready. Remember, this is the daring one. He talked me into swimming beside him. We were almost there when he had misgivings and threw his arms around my neck. I was not a strong enough swimmer to keep us both afloat, but I did manage, from underwater, where he'd pulled me, to push him toward the side. Other than that, we had no disasters in the pool.

We had a disaster brewing at home, however. It was a quiet, civilized disaster, which was probably part of the reason it was a disaster.

Before the disaster unraveled, though, we had a major triumph. H#1 had never taken the bar exam because after law school we were immediately off to join the United States Information Service. When we resettled in the U.S., H#1 started studying, with the help of the tireless question-asker who had stepped up during the last two years of law school and who was re-invited, during this study period, to ask every question imaginable from the content before me. I thoroughly enjoyed it. It was learning with absolutely no pressure for me.

H#1 passed the bar on his first try. The day the letter arrived announcing the news, I threw together a party for that evening which was great fun and a well-deserved celebration.

Despite such joint efforts and shared devotion to our three sons, the writing was on the wall that this marriage would not be sustainable. We went out to dinner one evening, and by the time dinner was over, we had decided to divorce. There was little animosity in the decision. We were both sorry.

I stayed as busy as possible while things changed dramatically, and we sought a new, separate normal. One of the things I did was to start taking English classes. I had really enjoyed teaching high school English at South Lyon, so I thought I'd prepare to teach high school again. I loved the classes. My teachers were all particularly kind to me, an older student and a faculty member. But one of my teachers changed my life with a single statement.

Alice MacDonald was as classy and intelligent a woman as I have ever met. She was dignified, articulate, well-informed in so many different areas – a Renaissance woman. While returning one of the first papers I handed in, she stood in front of me. I can see her now in her dress and heels, standing in a model's pose. Quietly, she said: "You are really smart." I remember clearly that I turned around in my seat to see to whom she was speaking. She looked at me and smiled. "I'm talking to you." She led me, alternately pushing and pulling, goading and encouraging, to reassess my abilities. She and I became friends when that class was over and throughout the years we held on to, supported, and bolstered each other.

The second life-transforming event, in addition to Alice, was that I took an evening class, for no credit, "Writing for Fun and Profit." I had just completed a creative writing class, and my fellow students had enthused over what I did with an assignment. We were to take an existing story line – as I had asked the sophomores at South Lyon High School to do – and rewrite it set in a different time and place.

I chose the Biblical story of Ruth and her mother-in-law Naomi. At my wedding to H#1, I had recited the pledge, "Wither thou goest, I go," and I was bereft not to have been able to keep that pledge. I needed to re-write that pledge in a story that was going to be true to that intention. I needed, literally, to re-write history. That short story for a creative writing class would become Chapter Six of a novel I would go on to write.

The woman who taught the non-credit "Writing for Fun and Profit" called herself a literary agent, although she had never sold a book. She read my short story and handed it back with these words: "There's no money in short stories. Turn it into a novel." Since I was about to become the single provider in a household with three children aged nine to four, I was going to need more money than I earned in my part-time teaching gigs, although I had managed to triple how many of those I had.

While my marriage was disintegrating, I wrote a romance novel. If I couldn't live it, I'd create it in my imagination and bring it to life on a page. I sat at the kitchen table, in front of the yellow and white checked wall paper, and typed and typed and typed. Finally, I reconnected with the woman who had taught the class – the "agent." She read it and threw it back to me. "There are no tags in this," she huffed. I didn't even know what a "tag" was. A tag is what comes before, after, and around the spoken word, like "he said," or "she moaned," or something which establishes who is talking and how they're talking.

I went back and added tags.

Didn't she just take it to New York City and offer it to four different publishing houses! Two publishers got into a bidding war for it. Bantam Books won. They offered $10,000 for *Heart* in a three-book deal. The title came from an old song I often sang to cheer myself up and give myself courage: "You've gotta have heart. All you really need is heart." I was hoping my heart would get me through these uncharted waters. I had never imagined I would be divorced. Oh, Aunt Kitty, how you must have felt all those years before.

No one, of course, could believe it, least of all me. I was making chicken soup from the backs and necks of chickens when the agent called with the news. My first congratulatory note came from Alice. I received $3,334. upon signing the contract. Fifteen percent went to the now official agent. I bought the kids new mattresses and had the roof repaired. And I kept teaching at The University of Akron, Kent State, Cuyahoga Community College and NEOUCOM, the North Eastern Ohio Universities College of Medicine. Some mornings I'd be so tired I'd start driving to the wrong job.

H#1 and I had agreed that I would stay in the house and he would take the car. The child support payment of $450, which he never missed, paid the mortgage, which was $425. I bought an old car (for $400.) boasting two bumper stickers: one for square dancing, the other for the NRA. Clearly, this was not a car which showcased my interests. The boys begged me not to pick them up at school, and they went to a school where lots of dilapidated and last-legs cars arrived every afternoon, but this one was truly a disaster. I didn't blame my sons. I abided by their request.

Bantam flew me to New York and paid for lodging so the editor and I could put the final touches on the book. I had never been away from the boys and spent an inordinate amount of time creating and wrapping a present for each of them for every day I'd be gone.

The "final touches" on the book turned out to be a slew of corrections. The editor said of my writing, "This is so provincial." She also told me the story of what she had done the day before she walked back to her NYC apartment with my book in a shopping bag. The previous day she had been worn out and disgusted, carrying that former day's manuscripts home to read, and so, on her way home, she threw the whole bag of them in a dumpster. The next day, she walked home and started reading *Heart*. As always, God is in the details.

The editor's name was Cathy Camhy, and her job, as she saw it, was to keep me humble. I explained to her that I was a communications teacher, comfortable speaking in front of audiences. If she needed me to go on the television shows and promote the book, I could do that. (I don't think I exactly said that, but I hinted.) She said: "When you've turned out about nine of these, we'll get you on the circuit." Yes, ma'am. I understand. Back to the typewriter.

Who knows where Cathy and I might have gone together, but she got canned. Bantam hired a new editor in chief who was all glam and glitter. Cathy happened to be an amazing editor, but she dressed in polyester suits and librarians' shoes. She was brilliant but did not fit the new image Bantam was about to launch. Her replacement, to whom I was shuffled, apparently passed a dumpster on the way home one day, and I was history. I took refuge in the knowledge that the woman who wrote *Gone with the Wind* only had one best seller, too. Actually, to be less flippant and more forthright, I was amazingly and humbly grateful for even the one professionally published book which sold more than 200,000 copies. How awesome is that for the average girl from Durham, Pennsylvania? Totally.

Things settled down. The royalty check from Bantam allowed me to buy a new car, for $8,200. Channeling Aunt Kitty, who would only buy American and always had Nash Ramblers, and working toward world peace, one small step at a time, I bought an Alliance, which was jointly made by AMC and the French firm, Renault. It was a great little car with only one flaw. It had no pick up. It was impossible to enter a freeway at any rate of speed, and it was a stick shift. I have always loved driving stick shift, ever since my brother let me drive his VW beetle –once – until I mistakenly shifted from third back down to second while descending the hill in Durham, causing both of us to hit our heads on the windshield. (I have never since driven while he was in the car.)

More people honked at me in that pretty little dark green Alliance than at any other time, except the traffic circle in Rome, and it was because they were so relieved not to have rear-ended me on the entrance ramp. They thought it was my driving. Nope. It was that cute, slow-to-accelerate, car.

So, for more than four years, the boys and I returned to near poverty level, but they will tell you, we had a good time. Our house was the neighborhood hang-out. We seemed to have kids of every size and color, usually at least seven or eight, and I don't remember any fights or disasters except, of course, the broken windows. Some of their games, thanks to recreation director Andy, were inside. Oh, well, there was the time Keith Swisher peed in the non-working toilet in the attic. Mostly, it was just baseball games with occasional broken windows in the family room.

I think the favorite game of this gang of young fellows was Hide the Flag. This required my entire supply of washcloths, many of which were never recovered. They'd divide into teams and have to find the "flag" the other team had hidden. They also played soccer and basketball; miraculously no one ever required a trip to the emergency room. The back yard wasn't big, but they used every inch and refreshed themselves with Kool-Aid and whatever snacks, pretzels or licorice, might be around.

Every vacation was spent in Durham, which was not only free but beyond awesome for me and for them. On the way, we'd sing all of Billy Joel's latest hits. Eddie threw me under the bus once. I was a little worried about having inherited my father's ability to fall asleep at the drop of a hat, and so, when I was driving the boys to Durham, I would buy a pack of cigarettes and when I felt sleepy, I'd light up. (I think cigarettes were about $3.50 a pack in those days.) I didn't like smoking; I never even learned how to inhale, but keeping my hands busy with a cigarette acted as an insurance policy. We got to Durham the first time I did this, and we were not even in the house when Eddie announced, "Mom smoked on the way here."

Back in Akron, one of the things we all enjoyed, the boys and me, was our trips to the nearby Pizza Hut. At that time, Pizza Hut had a $5.00 Special: a cheese pizza and a pitcher of Coke for $5.00. We were all over that. It was the only time the boys and I went "out" to eat. (I mention prices I remember because they are so different from prices we are paying today!)

Two gifts came to me in that way that life has of balancing the difficult and the delightful. One was delivered by Mary Kay, Butch's mother, and the other by a man named Phil Hockwalt.

The first Friday after H#1 moved out, he came to pick up the boys for the weekend. I was bereft and had just gone back into the house to sit down at the kitchen table and have a serious cry when Mary Kay called from her driveway, "Come over and have a drink with us." That seemed more appealing than a solitary melt-down.

But Mary Kay had an ulterior motive: as the person in charge of recruiting volunteers for the emergency room at the hospital, she was recruiting me. She handed me a smock and said, "Be at the ER tomorrow around 3:30. They're expecting you. You are not staying home and wallowing." I did as I was told. And, then, I did it every Saturday night for the next four years. Turns out, I loved volunteering in the emergency room.

That first evening, I was there all of three minutes when a nurse came up to me and said, "Go sit with the white-haired lady in the waiting room. Her husband fell off the roof and he's in X-ray and she's a wreck." That was my training. Nothing but one order after another.

"Take Room Four to X-ray." Never mind that I didn't know where X-ray was. Signs were posted all over the hospital. "He can go in a wheelchair, but get a blanket for him. I think we took off his pants." Never mind that I didn't know where the blankets were. How many closed doors could possibly conceal a linen closet?

Everyone was glad for another pair of hands, another pair of feet, and someone else who could move between the "department" and the waiting room with messages. Every once in a while, they had time to teach me something, but most of the time it was a war zone. Anything and everything came through those doors from elegant wedding parties who had encountered some disaster on the dance floor or in the buffet line to shell-shocked families who had been called because someone they loved was brought in unconscious from a car accident.

I was immediately introduced to emergency room humor and the staff delighted in telling me stories of their wackiest experiences, like the man who impaled a delicate part of his anatomy inside a vacuum cleaner hose and couldn't get himself released. One woman got a peanut stuck up her nose. And the accidents caused by stupidity or negligence were frequent and unimaginable. Every Saturday night was a new adventure.

I became friends with one of the nurses and one of the doctors. Jan, the nurse, introduced me to The Course in Miracles which was the first spiritual work I had been involved in since Judy Moffitt and I did that Wadsworth Bible Study. It taught me again, as the theological bent of the Bible Study had, that you don't have to agree with everything to learn from it. Just keep an open mind, and you'll learn to see from multiple perspectives.

The doc, Jack Bradford, and I taught a humanities course together at NEOUCOM, the local medical school, and he hired Eddie to mow his grass. He was a D.O. and I loved watching him work. He would always get people out of bed and moving because he could diagnose so much more accurately when he saw how their bodies were functioning. Fascinating.

One day he came to find me and said, "I need you to hold something." He wanted me to hold these steel hooks to keep a man's forehead open and exposed so he could suture an underlayer of stitches. I made the mistake of looking at that exposed skin, bone and tissue and turned green, or perhaps white. He said, "Look at a spot on the wall and don't move." Somehow, we made it through that, and the guy was stitched up, but my stomach didn't like it at all.

My lack of training made life really miserable for one young fellow who came into the emergency room. A frazzled nurse brought me a cart holding a gallon jug of water, a glass and a bucket. "Guy in room seven took a lot of pills to try to kill himself. If we can't get him to throw up, we'll have to pump his stomach. Get him to drink this water." She walked away and turned back. "All of it."

I smelled him before I entered the room. He was the worst smelling human I had ever encountered but under the scruff and the dirt, he was a nice-looking young man. He was not happy to see me, and I was not all that pleased myself. I put on my mother voice. "We're going to be drinking this water so you don't have to get your stomach pumped, which is excruciatingly painful." I had no idea if it was painful or not, but it sounded awful. If you want someone to cooperate, you have to make the alternative sound worse, right?

Immediately, both from compassion and curiosity, I wondered what had brought him to this moment in time. I needn't have worried about prying the story out of him. I was about to hear it all.

I think it took us about an hour and a half to get a gallon of water down his throat. Neither of us enjoyed the process. However, between sips, he started talking and before long I was listening to his pain: discharged from the Army only to find no work, no place to live, no way to adjust to civilian life, jilted by the girlfriend who had moved on, etc., etc.

Finally, he threw up. New horrendous smells. I rushed to empty the bucket, brought him a cold washcloth for his forehead, helped him lie down and went to find the nurse to tell her we had triumphed.

"I'll be right in to examine the contents of his stomach."

She read my face.

"You didn't?" she asked, appalled.

"I did," I replied, ashamed and equally appalled. Who knew someone had to check the "contents?" Some things are so inherently disgusting it's no wonder no one talks about them. "How was your day at work?" asks her husband as they sit down for dinner. "Great. I got to check the regurgitated contents of someone's stomach. How does a day get finer than that?"

"It shouldn't take as much water to get him started again," she reassured me. All I told the victim of my ineptitude was: "It wasn't enough." It did give him time to tell me more of his story, a story of PTSD before I knew how many faces there are to PTSD. That young man's story inspired my writing of *The Many Faces of PTSD* twenty-five years later.

I also wrote "A Night in the Emergency Room," a short story about volunteering in the emergency room which was published by the Akron Beacon Journal. The Akron Beacon Journal Sunday magazine editor then assigned me two other pieces to write, and that was my very short but highly enjoyable foray into professional journalism.

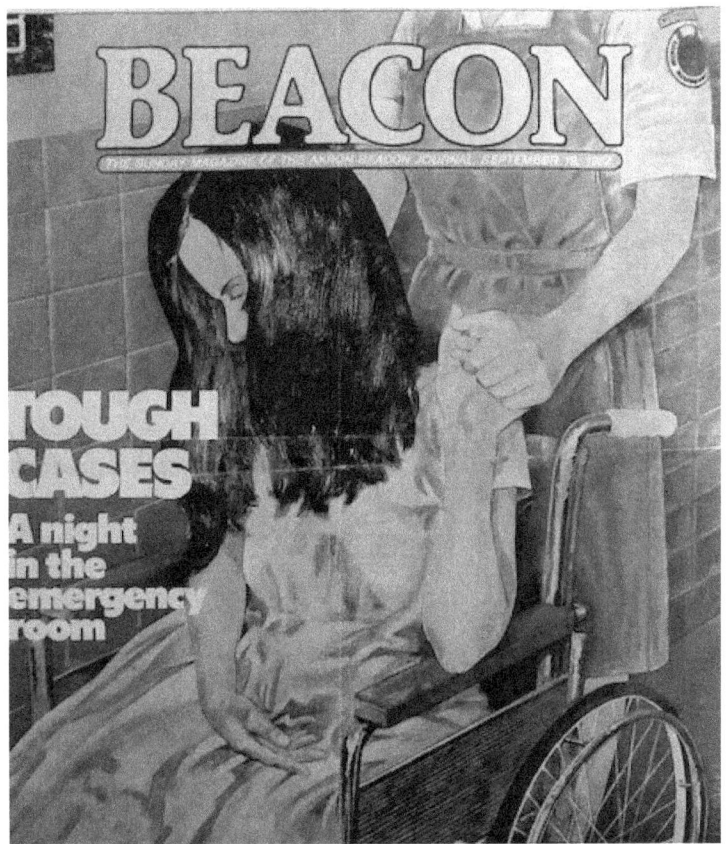

Akron Beacon Journal cover illustration for my article.

Teaching at the med school with Jack Bradford worked into a part-time job there, doing some writing and event planning for the humanities department. I shared an office with David, an impoverished young medical student. One day he was telling me how hungry he was for a real food, not fast food, like maybe a whole roasted chicken. When I finished work that day, I left him a note and five dollars and told him to stop and get a chicken on his way home. That simple gesture was the beginning of a strong, mutually supportive friendship which lasted many years. We worked together, I babysat his three girls, who taught me all kinds of new, imaginative games like Restaurant – they named their "game" restaurant The Golden Goose. (My boys did not play restaurant!) David and I co-hosted music parties at his lovely home, and it was he who heard about the trip to China which was a life-changer for me in positive and negative ways, as most things in life tend to be.

Three of us from that humanities program did some traveling together, and I went on exciting trips to conferences with incredibly wise and articulate speakers, especially doctors who had started writing about their work either in prose, like Oliver Sacks, or in poetry, like John Stone. The three of us also published a book about our work which I helped write. The world just kept getting bigger and more enriching.

My boss there, who shall remain nameless, asked me to edit his doctoral thesis. I think he paid me $75. for about $750. worth of work. I had to basically translate his casual, mistake-laden writing into "thesis writing" which is very different from chit-chat or a breezy little article. Luckily, I had written my master's thesis under the direction of Dr. John Bee, who was a stickler for propriety, form, and content and those high standards became my own. (Anecdotally, I still use his wife, Lee's, Italian vinaigrette recipe. Life is such a winding road.) So, I re-wrote nameless man's thesis, it passed muster, he was awarded his PhD, and then he fired me. My friend Alice always said, "No good deed goes unpunished!" I got a lot more than he took from the whole experience.

In addition to Mary Kay and all the gifts she handed me when she gave me that volunteer smock, Phil Hockwalt was the other big gift which appeared immediately after my divorce. How I met Phil is another of those "God is in the details" stories because it combined the strangest person and the most unusual process which introduced him to me.

I was waiting in line for a Diet Coke in the Student Center at The University of Akron where I had an hour to sit down and grade papers. I had learned that the more noise there was around me the better I could concentrate, so I decided to sit in the downstairs student section instead of upstairs in the quiet faculty dining room. A woman I had never seen rushed up to me, grabbed my arm, and said, "I saw you at church. I need a friend. Will you be my friend?"

Helpless to refuse such an honest but bizarre request, we sat together for that precious hour of mine and she poured out her story. (One of the early clues that therapy might be a good choice of career for me. People love to tell me their stories.)

As I stood to leave to go teach, she asked about me. I said, "Recently divorced and struggling." She advised me to see her neighbor who was "a marvelous therapist" and gave me his name: Phil Hochwalt. It had not occurred to me that I might be in need of therapy. I went home after school, looked up his number, and made an appointment.

The first three therapy sessions were a trial for Phil. All I did was cry. Seriously. For an hour at a time, three times, 180 minutes of him having to listen to tears. He earned his money. He was a great therapist, a fabulous mentor, and a truly good man. He said two things in particular, one of which helped immediately and the second which altered the course of my life.

I had been having nightmares every night the boys weren't in the house. If they were there, no nightmare. If they were with their dad, nightmare. It was always the same: I dreamed that I heard footsteps coming up the stairs. Some unknown someone was coming to get me. I was terrified. I didn't know how to protect myself. The "someone" was smart enough not to come if the boys were home.

Phil said, "I don't think you're afraid someone will come, I think you're afraid no one will ever come again." The proof is in the pudding, and once I had sobbed over the truth in that, I never had another nightmare.

The next session he said, "Look. You're on the wrong side of the desk here. Go back to school, get a counseling degree, and the minute you graduate, I'll hire you to work with me." Now, I already had my three remaining part time jobs, from which I had not been fired, and my three children, why not go back to school?

I couldn't get in. I had no background in psychology. The dean said, "I'll let you take twelve hours without being accepted into the program. If your grades are good enough, we'll admit you."

So, who should I get for the first teacher of the first course: Steve Perkins. It's hard to talk about Steve Perkins without making him sound larger than life, because he really, truly, was larger than life. He should have been at Harvard Business School teaching people how to be leaders. He was extraordinary.

Once he established a therapy practice, Akron Family Institute, he began bringing in people to work with him. From the beginning, he made no decisions by himself. He was one of a five-person management team. He had two people interview everyone who wanted to work there, and many people did. He was the epitome of integrity.

Steve Perkins was also the best possible place a beginner could begin if she wanted to learn "systems theory," which is the basis of Marriage and Family Therapy. A family is a system. A business is a system. There are things that make systems work well and things that tear systems apart.

Steve was not a particularly good teacher. He was constantly disorganized and flying by the seat of his pants. But, boy, could that guy improvise. He'd find a video on his way to class and play it, although he'd never seen it before, perhaps a video of a therapist interviewing a husband and wife. We'd watch it. He'd ask us what we saw.

Then he'd start kindly and gently telling us what we might have seen if we were looking through the eyes of systems theory. You just wanted to be in the same room with him and hear him think. He was so masterfully intuitive. He stretched everyone with whom he came in contact. I attended one Marriage and Family Therapy (MFT) class that Steve taught, and I knew I had found my calling and my niche. I had come home.

I had such an interesting talk with Paula Britton, the PhD student tasked with helping three of us learn the MFT world. She was already a practicing therapist but was new to teaching at the

University. I was a seasoned university teacher new to therapy. We realized, when we became friends and started trading secrets, that she would sweat when she was working with a client but not when she was teaching. I would sweat in front of a class but not when talking with a client. That told us a lot about where we each belonged.

That five-year period of being a single mom, a part-time teacher in Cleveland, Kent, and Akron, and a part-time graduate student was full of ups and downs, but the constant good cheer and fun was that which the boys and I invented. Nothing was more of a joy than our trips to Grandma's and Grandad's. My boys were ages nine, seven, and four when we started our peregrinations; fourteen, twelve, and nine when we concluded our four-person travels.

Every Christmas but one and every summer in August we would head east for at least a week, longer if my teaching schedule and their school schedules permitted. Skip and Molly were there every Christmas, and if they couldn't come to Durham when we did in August, we'd often split our trip and drive to New England to see them.

The little green Alliance made the trips handily, give or take a slow freeway entrance here and there. The boys and I would sing our hearts out – Billy Joel remained our favorite. We'd stop whenever we liked for fast food and drinks. In summer we'd travel east on Route 80 because there was no toll; in winter we'd cross Pennsylvania on the turnpike, paying a toll of $13.65, because the toll road was generally kept plowed and snow free.

Christmas was a child's dream vacation. Grandma and Grandad were available constantly for games, cards and book reading. Skip and

Molly had two girls, Kirsten, a year younger than Andy, and Gretchen, a year younger than Nick. With five adults and five kids, nobody ever got the short shrift and temper tantrums were unheard of because we were all too happy.

In the corner of the living room stood the Christmas tree, small and simple but beautifully trimmed with bright colored lights, and beneath it, the largest most exciting and enticing number of packages imaginable. Grandma must have started preparing the minute we left in August -- there was no other way she could have shopped for presents and wrapped them in time every year. I think our parents were amazingly grateful to have two grown children, Skip and me, who wanted to come "home" for Christmas. It was always a delightful time.

Molly's mother and her family lived in nearby Bethlehem, so it was a double win for Molly and Skip and their girls to come to eastern Pennsylvania. Since Molly's family attended a gigantic Christmas Eve extravaganza, we always had Skip and his family all of Christmas Day. Gram and Aunt Ruth joined us and someone, often Skip, went to pick up Grandma Rau and Aunt Agnes. It was a family celebration of great joy.

One Christmas when Eddie was little, maybe three, he came to wake me in the middle of the night because he heard Santa's sleigh bells on the roof. I settled him back in bed with the reminder that we didn't want Santa to see us or we'd spoil the surprises he left for us for Christmas morning.

Actually, Eddie always heard things the rest of us didn't. He heard a buzzing sound in an Akron department store he found difficult to tolerate. Years later someone told me that buzzing was part of their security system. With that piece of information, I came to believe Eddie really had heard Santa's sleigh bells.

During another Christmas visit, when Andy was three or four and Kirsten two or three, the two of them were playing on the steps to the second floor. Andy stood at the bottom of the stairs while Kirsten waited about four steps up. We adults were all in the living room when we heard the sweet invitation Andy issued: "Jump. I'll catch you!" Kristen jumped before any of us could react and both kids crashed against the wall, narrowly missing the big plate glass window at the bottom of the steps.

Another near disaster involved only the three boys who had headed out along Cook's Creek one winter day, bundled to the hilt and ready for adventure. A while later, after exploring, they returned along the millrace and one of them wondered whether the ice on the race was frozen solid. Being smart boys, they sent the youngest and lightest, Nick, out on the ice to test it. Oops. It wasn't frozen solid, and in he went. They fished him out and then Eddie, either remembering something about falling into ice water being bad, or from fear of what was going to happen to them because they sent their little brother to test the ice, started chasing Nick home, screaming like a banshee. Grandma and I hustled Nick into the tub and he was no worse for wear, but none of the three of them has ever taken to any sports on the ice. Maybe just a coincidence.

I'm sure no Christmas any of us has had since rivaled one of those Durham Christmases. The five grandchildren were small; Grandma and Grandad were vigorous, welcoming and openly loving.

Each of us was accepted exactly as we were at every moment in time. We actually did live Norman Rockwell's drawings. It wasn't that anything was extraordinary. It was that everything was so incredibly ordinary, calm, safe, predictable and loving.

My parents were so affirming that I can actually remember the two times my father expressed displeasure with me. The first time, when I was about ten and being confirmed in church, I happened to look out at the congregation and smile at someone. That was considered "inappropriate." And, the second time, at a restaurant I stirred sugar into my iced tea with too much vigor and made too loud a noise. Calling attention to oneself was not acceptable. I'm not sure if the moral of the story is that my dad was too easily pleased with me, or that I was amazingly quick to pick up on what was required and obey the rules. Who knows?

(Interestingly, I recently read that "good" children – often little girls – who intuited what their parents needed and wanted from them frequently became anxious adults. I am a case in point. Add to that my need to keep Aunt Ruth and Gram happy. Being too eager to please certainly didn't help my marriages any, either. Once again, the yin and yang – every lightness containing darkness, as well.)

My dad and I had created a mutual admiration society, but so did my mom and I. Skip and I agree, we won the parent lottery – the grand prize. I have a little framed verse in my bedroom that says: "Of all the gifts life has to offer, loving parents is the greatest of them all." I had given it to the loving parents I was given. When we cleaned out our parent's apartment at Westminster Village, I tucked it in with the things I was keeping. It sits beside Aunt Agnes' teddy bear.

Our parents were far from perfect. They could have listed their own faults and shortcomings as well as each other's. They could have listed my brother's and mine. Perfection was not required for love in our home or family. All of us were quirky and odd in this way or that. My dad's comment usually was, "Oh, that's just Aunt Agnes," or whomever we were talking about. You still loved them, helped them, supported them, checked on them, and gave thanks for whatever they added to the family stew.

H#2

In early 1985, I received a nasty letter from the IRS (Do they send any other kind?) In a moment of pride, I had listed myself on a tax return as an author. DON'T DO THAT. The IRS thinks that is your main source of income and they start snooping and assuming and taxing you differently. My dear Alice happened to edit the writing of a lawyer who produced a weekly column for the Akron Beacon Journal. "Never fear," she said, "my lawyer will help you."

With the IRS on my heels, demanding that I had underpaid my taxes after receiving revenue for *Heart*, Alice introduced me to the lawyer for whom she worked. Merlin, the lawyer, turned out not to be a magician. After shaking my hand, he called for his law clerk to come take care of whatever I needed. Out comes this barefoot kid, at least a decade younger than I was. We sat and figured out what had gone amiss. He'd write a letter. It would be looked into. Anything else? Nope.

Imagine my surprise when, a day or two later, he called and asked me if I'd like to go to Cleveland that weekend to hear the Cleveland Orchestra. Yes. I would like to do that.

But why was he asking me? He was not quite thirty, and I was forty with three children. I decided he just couldn't find anyone else who liked symphonic music. Actually, after my music theory classes, I didn't much like classical music either. But a trip to Cleveland to hear this renowned orchestra sounded quite lovely.

He brought me a yellow tulip at the end of a long winter. On the way to Cleveland that first evening, I mentioned something about our age difference. He pulled over to the side of the expressway. "Does it bother you? Because it doesn't bother me. I can take you back home."

We went on to supper. Our feet were intertwined while we ate.

At the concert the heating pipes in the concert hall made loud noises throughout the performance. He simply held onto me, his hand holding my legs against his.

We talked easily and laughed like long-time pals.

He took me home and gave me a sweet kiss on the lips.

I slept with a light, happy heart for the first time in years. I had no idea I'd just met H#2, but it was all so easy. Everything. There was no hesitation. We joined forces. He bought me a new dress to wear to his law school graduation. I invited his whole very large family to my house for a graduation party. Falling in love was like rolling off a log. He was an old younger man, and I was a young older woman. We met in the middle.

He was authoritative and had his ways. They were predominantly good ways which felt familiar. His background was as Germanic as mine, so hard work, cleanliness, frugality, and the earth were important to both of us. The differences were less noticeable in the beginning when we were both deliriously happy with the similarities and the chemistry.

I was flexible and more than willing to get back into the "passenger's seat." I had been in the "driver's seat" for five years. I wasn't a feminist or a fighter; I was a partner and a woman easy with conciliatory compromise and concessions. What I mostly wanted was a man of kindness and integrity with whom to share the journey. Where we went or how we got there was of little importance to me. We were crazy about each other and good friends. It would be fifteen years before he said or did anything I had to stand up to.

We were both in Akron from February, when we met, until August when he headed for Dayton, four hours away, and his first job as an attorney. We weathered a year of long distance.

The boys and I were in Dayton visiting him for the weekend when my dear Gram died. I remember calling the florist to order flowers. I was crying so hard, I couldn't talk. Aunt Cicely, shortly before her own disastrous surgery, put a rose in Gram's casket for each of the eight grandchildren. Gram was ninety-six and, in Aunt Ruth's words, "Life had become tedious." She was simply tired of working so hard to stay alive. She died quietly and peacefully, all alone, on January 31, 1986. They say more people die in January than any other month.

While H#2 and I managed a year of long-distance romance and love, neither of us liked it. H#2 found a job in Akron, and we married in August of the same year, 1986. As always in life, things are not all good or all bad. I lost Gram and gained a partner.

We settled in, and in our home I was able to return to the comfortable job of wife and mother. I had not liked being both mother and father. Like my mother before me, I was not a disciplinarian or a woman who could hold the line. In fact, I became increasingly lax with each child. Of course, Andy, the oldest, was incredibly easy to discipline. He was a child who colored inside the lines, unlike Eddie, the middle child, who pretended he didn't see any lines, and Nick, the third child, who saw the lines but didn't give a flying fig if he colored at all.

The one place they listened was in church. Everyone thought it was so cute that I sat in church with my arms around them. I wasn't hugging them; I was restraining them!

We all laugh about my episode with two-year-old Nick around the dining room table. He had done something outrageous, and I went to grab him to tell him, "No," and he turned and ran the other way. That little imp got halfway around the table and turned to look at me. When I started in one direction, he ran the other. We did this a few times, Andy and Eddie staring with their mouths open, thinking Nick was really going to get it, and finally I simply sat down and started laughing. So, when he was two, I lost control of Nick. That never changed.

H#2, oldest brother in a family of six, who had been tasked with a lot of parenting and sibling maintenance, had absolutely no problem with boundaries and inflexible expectations. He had my complete support, with great relief. He and Nick actually, amazingly, became good friends and undertook some massive projects together, like building a garage out back. Nick, being the youngest, spent far and away the most time with us.

H#2 also, being a male, was able to explain some of the mysterious male teenage behavior. "Why is he taking all these baths?" I remember asking of one of the boys. H#2 asked if I would leave the kid alone if he explained what he was doing in the bathroom. Just from the look on his face, I had a glimmer of understanding, and I conceded I'd leave him alone. I didn't want any explanation.

Another time one of the boys, who did not yet have a driver's license, decided to take one of our cars out for a spin. H#2 knew exactly how many miles were on each car. The underage driver was busted. It wasn't pretty, but could have been downright ugly if not nipped in the bud.

The boys weren't always happy that things had tightened up for them, but, as Eddie said to his grandmother, "It's nice to see Mom happy." Their dad, H#1, had been remarried for about four years, and I don't know whether that gave them hope or not, helped or hindered.

In those first years, three memories stand out. First, there was the day I got a flat tire and called H#2. He left work, arrived in his suit and tie, changed the tire, and sent me on my way. He was astonishingly capable. Here I go with the double entendre again, but he was very good with his hands.

The second memory is of the morning I arrived at my office to discover my goldfish had died. I called H#2 in a tizzy. I thought it was a very bad indicator for a therapist to have a floating gold fish in her office. Again, he immediately went to the pet store, bought two goldfish, and came and made the switch so that things were once again going swimmingly by the time clients arrived.

And the third outstanding memory is of the time he left a beautiful red rose and a love note on the car windshield.

H#2 enjoyed traveling, and we went to the beach for a week every year with the boys. Nick was remembering recently that right after Christmas, the pamphlets would arrive with pictures and descriptions of houses to rent. We would all pour over those pamphlets choosing just the right spot for our week at the Outer Banks.

One year all three boys were busy with sports or jobs and H#2 and I went, just the two of us, to the beach. We had a magical experience that year. One rainy morning we went out for breakfast and did a little shopping before going back to our rented condo.

By afternoon, although it was still raining and the beach was empty, H#2 said, "Let's put our suits on and go swimming." It was amazing. We felt like we were one with the ocean. The rain was cool, the water was warm; the rain was smooth and soft, the water salty and gritty. It was a wild array of textures and smells and sensations, and we were the only ones enjoying it. Just as we girls in Durham had "owned" the millrace, H#2 and I "owned" the big, wide, deep ocean and the gifts of that glorious rainy day.

Back home, H#2 and I were busy taking tests. I had to take my counselor licensure exam in Columbus, and he had to sit for the bar exam, also in Columbus. Nick went to Columbus with us for my exam, and we celebrated that evening in a repurposed fire station which had become a restaurant. The waiters slid down the fire pole with our meals and drinks.

We passed those exams, and H#2 immediately started studying for the C.P.A. He also studied and took the test for an electrician's license. He wanted to rewire our house, and it couldn't be insured unless a certified electrician did the work. H#2 was driven with ambition.

Two years after we were married, in 1988, my parents celebrated their fiftieth wedding anniversary. They invited family and friends to Cascade Lodge in Durham Township, just off 611 in Upper Bucks County. My dad was well acquainted with the Knuth's who owned the Lodge: Paula, widow of Captain Ernest Knuth, and her son, Howard. The Knuth's bought the property in 1939, a year after Miriam and Dave were married. Cascade Lodge had developed a great reputation for food and hospitality.

Having looked up the Inn, thirty-two years later, I see it has been renamed Durham Springs and the restaurant is called The Cascade. It was beautiful in 1988 when the anniversary party was held, and again, in 1998, when a few of us returned to celebrate the sixtieth anniversary. Today, under management by a team of restauranteurs from New York City, it is positively elegant and ethereal.

The countryside surrounding the Inn is lush and lovely. The original 1730's colonial style has been recreated. The springs for which the Inn is named have been developed into ponds, and every imaginable modern convenience and posh accoutrement is in evidence. I think the Knuth's and my dad would be delighted. It is a sight to behold. And I noticed that they buy some of the fresh produce for their restaurant from Trauger's Farm Market, the scene of the 1955 flood disaster, which is apparently still in the family and flourishing. More good news for my dad. That would make him so happy.

Miriam and Dave Rau.

Fifty years later, they still have their heads together like newlyweds!

Fascinatingly, although Gram (in 1986) and Aunt Kitty (in 1982) had died before 1988, every member of the bridal party was alive and well enough to attend the anniversary shindig. My parents insisted on no gifts, but we did manage to get the guest list and write to everyone to ask if they would send a memory or a message, so we had a lovely big album of sweet and funny stories, loving thoughts, and best wishes for them to read and re-read. Jackie, coming from

California, had come the farthest, but others came from New England, upstate New York, and, of course, Ohio.

The morning after the celebration, Skip and Molly and their two girls, Mom and Dad, and H#2 and I and the three boys set out in a caravan for the Outer Banks of North Carolina. Except for an accident the first evening when some grease from a frying pan splashed onto Skip's foot, we had a charmed and delightful week. Pinochle was played A LOT and some little group or other was always over on the beach. I remember mom and me peeling shrimp until we thought we'd be doing it in our sleep.

The whole anniversary celebration was such a poignant reminder of what Dave and Miriam Rau valued. No one was left out. No "things" like presents or flowers or gift bags were wanted. They invited the **people** with whom they had spent those fifty years and showed their children and grandchildren, who would carry on, what family and friendship looked like. Then they took their few most valued people, their offspring, to the best place in the world, the ocean, for an extended celebration.

We parted knowing Grandma and Grandad would be coming to Ohio for Thanksgiving. That was the year they were a little late. A deer ran out in the road when they were no more than a half hour from home and somehow, on a holiday, my dad got the poor dented deer attended to – he was devastated that a deer had chosen his automobile – he loved deer and would not have hurt one for anything. Then, somehow, they decided to keep moving, since the car was drivable, although badly dented. He wasn't worried about the car, only the deer.

One month later we packed up and drove to Durham for Christmas. Skip and Molly and the girls were there, of course. I'm not sure we ever missed a year. Who would? It wasn't the plethora of presents. Truly, none of us would have lamented having no presents, despite how much fun it was to sit for hours and open presents and ooh and aah about each thing, from a can of black olives to a new shirt or pajamas.

I remember the year Skip and Molly and H#2 and I gave Grandma and Grandad something technological – a CD player. Mom was so excited. She read that manual from start to finish and had the whole thing up and running the next day. If it had been up to our father, it would never have been unpacked from the box.

Did I mention the worst fight I ever knew my parents to have? They had purchased a television stand for the small television in the dining room. The stand came in a box, assembly required. My mother gave my father the box; he took all the pieces out and laid them on the dining room table. Then he commenced to putting the thing together. A while later my mother walked back through the room and saw my father was having issues with the construction of the TV stand. She picked up the instruction manual and started telling him what he had done incorrectly.

Who would have imagined that in more than fifty years of marriage it would be a TV stand that would cause the most animosity? Not me. But that was the case. I believe, although I'm not sure, because no one hung around to see, that my dad stomped out of the room and my mother, reading the instructions, put the frigging thing together. It was never a topic of conversation and, as far as I know, not mentioned again. Sometimes, it really pays to sweep things under the rug and move on.

Back in Ohio, H#2 decided on two projects simultaneously: build an addition on the house in Akron and search southern Ohio for a piece of land. Thank goodness for the land-searching project; it gave us a chance to sit. Meanwhile, H#2 got right to knocking out walls and designing a huge addition which was going to be magnificent and completely modernize our old colonial. As usual, I was excited and on board. I found him very creative and enjoyed his vision.

I had been totally contented with the house as it was, but a whole house vacuum system, a new master suite upstairs with a fabulous big bathroom with fancy tub, and a full bath downstairs next to the lovely new recreation room all sounded like dreams I hadn't even had the imagination to dream. We were clearly going to be the entertainers in the family, much to my delight, and I loved the idea of a home enlarged for family gatherings.

We found a construction company to perform the structural changes and a drywall man. H#2 had his limits, and drywall was one of them. We did everything else. This was a project that was going to take years, but H#2 wanted to do all the work he was capable of doing. I thought it was like a wolf peeing in the corners of his area of the wilderness – marking his territory. I admired his ambition. I didn't mind living ten years with no drywall or finished walls, just boards and studs, in the living room and dining room. It was dark, but there was so much other lightness in my life, that unfinished walls seemed a small price to pay.

When Aunt Ruth died, Andy and I made that trip together to Durham. She had fought a battle against uterine cancer, a battle not easily won, and she didn't win. Andy had time to go with me before starting back to college in the fall. Again, the bitter with the sweet.

Once both Gram and Aunt Ruth were gone, Mom and Daddy started planning their move to a life care center. I could not believe they were going to leave Durham, but my mother was adamant. I worried it might kill my father. Luckily, we all had a little time to get used to the idea, since there was much to be done before the move.

They had one more house to clean out – a home they had lived in since 1939. My dad had about ten jobs to clear off his plate, some tenures to complete, some resignations to submit, and Mom had a knee replacement to endure. Being their careful, planful selves, they talked to lots of people about the homes they were considering, went to eat meals at each, made various scheduled and unscheduled visits, and settled on Westminster Village, a life care center supported in part by the Presbyterian Church. Eddie graduated from high school the same year they moved in to their fifth-floor, two bedroom/two bath, full kitchen, lovely balcony apartment.

I was bereft, but silent. My anchor, Durham, was gone. For forty-six years my mooring had been at the millrace. My girlhood bedroom looked straight down on that small body of water, the mill to the right, Tony's store to the left. I had the catbird view of Durham, and I had well and truly drunk the Kool-Aid. The sense of community, the values of the towns' people, the stability of such deep roots were all part of my blood and bone.

THE FARM

The thing that saved me and made the permanent move from Durham bearable was my belief that H#2 and I were about to start growing new roots. They would be nourished by the same Protestant work ethic, the same love of the land, the same sense of small, stable community, with the additional benefits of an actual farm: land, animals, barns, creeks and a pond, room for family gatherings, and only one street light which was attached to the house and turned on from our kitchen.

While H#2 and I were working on the house in Akron, we were hunting for a piece of property in southern Ohio. We had so much fun setting off on a Sunday morning, stopping for breakfast, and then following one dirt road after another to investigate land for sale. We found a couple of wonderful farms, but each of them had some missing element. To say that H#2 was fussy would understate things. He couldn't completely articulate what it was he wanted, but he knew he would know it when he saw it.

Actually, we both knew it when we saw it. We had found "The Farm." It was down a dirt road, had no nearby neighbors, was lush and green, and the house had been completely and sweetly remodeled.

It contained the loveliest kitchen I ever had. A new version of an old-fashioned black cast iron cook stove was the first thing you noticed. The oven was small – a turkey was a tight fit – but it produced the best cookies I ever baked. A huge work island occupied the center of the kitchen. Opposite the kitchen door was a wall of windows looking out over the rolling hills of southern Ohio. We had a big family-sized table in front of the windows.

You entered the house from a small porch on which we hung a porch swing. At night, H#2 and I would sit on that porch and drink in the sight of the starry sky and the smell of fresh, country air. Here, again, was a dream I had never had the imagination to dream, and I was living it.

We both wanted gardens. H#2 rototilled, and I planted and weeded and harvested. We'd stay up until 2:00 in the morning the weekend the corn was ready. Together we cooked it, sliced it off the cob, and prepared it for the freezer. I bought a canner and canned vegetables. We devoured the delicious salsa from a recipe on the last page of the Ball Canning Book.

Every Sunday night when we headed back to Akron to our day jobs, we'd pack buckets of flowers and bushels of whatever vegetables we had harvested and share our bounty with neighbors, friends, and work colleagues. We had a pumpkin patch and actually sold our pumpkins to a natural food store. (I think the truck load of pumpkins netted us $111.00.)

Every spring we took a week off and spent that time planting pine trees, believing that we'd have a Christmas tree operation in the future. We had a system, just the two of us, but in the early days, before starting college in 1994, Nick would help. It was back-breaking, blister-making work, but so satisfying. We planted over 8,000 Christmas trees. They say every tree you plant provides oxygen for 3,000 people.

Walking down row upon row of pine trees of all different sizes was mesmerizing. The rows would go on and on, fifty trees per row. We could tell the age of the trees by comparing their sizes. Everyone who came to visit seemed to love to "mow" the trees, no one more than my dad, of course. He may not have been able to walk without a cane, but he could operate that riding mower! He enjoyed the wild flowers that grew around the trees and the butterflies and dragonflies that feasted on the wild flowers – it was a nature panorama. Every year H#2 would shape the future Christmas trees by hand with a long, sharp knife. At the end of the day his arm would be trembling and throbbing. My part of the process was arm and back rubs. Long arm and back rubs.

Our future Christmas tree farm.

We became friends with a salt-of-the-earth couple, Kenny and Lena. The four of us would go out to eat on a Saturday night. We'd get them talking and save ourselves from so many mistakes because H#2 was delighting them with his questions, and they were intriguing us with their answers. Kenny professed love for my cookies but I thought most of it was his ability to charm. Lena was a former professional cook.

We learned about deer whistles for the front of our car so deer would not run out as we rounded those curvy roads in the country; giving shots to livestock and the delicate process of emasculating cattle; which equipment was necessary and which was luxury; which fields to mow for hay; who would bale your hay (Kenny's son); and the how's and why's of southern Ohio farming. Kenny and Lena were the living, breathing Google of the day; they seemed to know all the answers.

H#2 decided we'd go into the cattle business. Later on, he thought, we'd switch to buffalo, but we'd start with cattle. We went halves with Kenny and bought a bull. My father cautioned us that we better own "the important half." Soon, on the field across the dirt road from our house, we had not only cows traipsing back and forth on the cow path but also calves. They really are delightfully cute.

We had more to learn. Always, more to learn. First of all, cows, surprisingly, although they are not small, can get through seemingly invisible holes in fences. We'd arrive at the farm to find the front yard spattered with cow pies, and Kenny would stop by to tell us, "The cows were out." Yup. We noticed. We spent hours fixing fences. One Sunday night, working by the light of the truck headlights, we mended fences until after midnight. Then, after repairing every hole we could find, we still had a two-hour drive back to Akron. On arrival in Akron, we'd grab a few hours of sleep and get up for work early the next morning.

On a special Saturday at our farm, we became the proud parents of twins. We were really excited, but by Sunday, mama was crossing the hillside with just one baby. We wondered if the other baby was sick or deformed. We hopped on the ATV, an all-terrain vehicle being a necessity on a 158-acre farm, fearful we'd discover a dead calf. Nope. We searched for a while, and finally, there in the bushes, alive and well, was that little face staring out at us.

I drove the ATV, H#2 held the calf, and we took the second baby to its mom. We were appalled she couldn't keep track of two offspring and worried she was a negligent mother. She headed off with both calves following behind but not an hour later, she was down to only one baby again.

Thankfully, Kenny and Lena happened by, or the mother may have had to run away from home. Kenny didn't so much as crack a smile, but Lena couldn't help herself; she doubled over laughing. Seems when cows have twins, they exercise the new babies one at a time, and hide the other in the bushes, then go back and trade off. Hm. City-slickers!

Kenny has written a number of books about farm life and family life in rural southern Ohio. They are wonderful stories of the values, foibles, idiosyncrasies, goodness, charm, characters, and community in which he and Lena have spent their entire eighty years. The stories make me laugh and cry. He is a poet, raconteur and dear friend.

When a man known to Kenny and Lena divorced his wife, Kenny was introduced to "the new woman" for whom the man had left his family. Later, when Kenny had a chance to talk to the abandoned former wife, Kenny said, very seriously: "If she, meaning the new woman, was the only woman in the world and I was the only man, it would be the end of civilization." I'm sure it was balm to the betrayed woman's feelings. (She may or may not be telling this story.) That's just how loyal and kind Kenny and Lena are. They had welcomed and treated both of us with such warmth.

A mile from our farm was Seneca Lake, thirty-nine miles in circumference and set in an undeveloped and serene area. H#2 decided we needed a boat, so we'd do something relaxing instead of simply working every minute we were at the farm. Sounded great to me. Researcher that he was, H#2 found a perfect boat for us, and all of the family enjoyed time out on the lake.

However, not all the time at Seneca Lake was relaxing: we managed a near death experience with Jen, Nick's girlfriend, and for the past twenty-three years, his wife. For fun we would drag tubes after the boat and take turns going "tubing." When it was my turn, whoever powered the boat just slowly pulled me around. Almost everyone got a gentle, nonetheless exhilarating, ride. Even in the calmest of "dragging," you really had to hold on to keep from being engulfed by water and pulled under.

Jen was an athlete. H#2 decided to give her a ride. He'd pull her across the wake of the boat, and the more he challenged her, the more she sent him a "thumbs up!" Finally, he pulled her at great speed across the wake and then back across in the other direction. Forced to let go of the inner tube on which she had been sitting, she flew into the air. Truly, she went at least twenty feet up.

Nick laughed.

I gasped.

Jen landed with force on her head and neck. I seriously feared we had killed her. She climbed back in the boat, dizzy and disoriented and suffered from headaches for days. I have always considered it a gift from God that Jen lived through that ride.

We only had one other fearful experience which was exacerbated by my mother and me setting each other off, as we had in our giggling fit on the train tracks in Europe. This time, on a rainy Sunday morning, we sent Nick, a new driver, in the car with Andy, his older brother, to the store for a Sunday paper so Grandma and Grandad could work on the crossword puzzle. The store was only about eight minutes away but after thirty minutes the brothers still weren't back.

The Raus at the farm. (photo: Judy Moffitt)

The road around the lake was curvy and, mom and I fearfully told ourselves and each other, perhaps the route was too treacherous to have sent them on this mission. Forty-five minutes later, we imagined them in the lake and by the time they reappeared, over an hour later, we were almost inconsolable. Turns out they had had to drive to a nearby town, twenty-five minutes away, to find the paper we had requested. They were fine and happy. We were exhausted from our imaginary terror. My mother and I shared that capability. No one benefitted from leaving us alone together when there was any possibility of someone being hurt. They say the more you love something, the more you fear losing it. Cell phones, of course, would have prevented the whole debacle.

Of the many people who visited the farm, H#2's father and step mother were probably the most unexpected. When H#2 and I met, he had been estranged from his dad for years. They were totally out of contact once H#2's parents divorced.

We had been married a few years when we went on vacation to Florida. I didn't realize we were going to be staying near where his dad lived. When we got there, H#2 wondered if he should contact his dad and invite him to meet us for a drink. "Absolutely," said I, a woman who could not imagine being out of touch with her dad. H#2 offered. His dad accepted. We met and that was the beginning of the reconnection and some attempts at resuming a relationship.

H#2's dad and his wife came to the farm a number of times. Their visits were challenging: they had different ways of speaking, different ways of thinking, different experiences. They were much less gifted than their son and I in education, opportunities, and life's possibilities.

Who were we not to welcome them and embrace them into what they had purposefully or inadvertently passed on to those of us in the next generation? They spent a number of weeks with us. Like my dad, H#2's dad loved driving the tractor and mowing the trees. Having grown up on a small farm about an hour north, he appreciated everything about this farm. We welcomed him and his wife. I had been taught at the millrace that everyone was welcome, everyone had value, and everyone belonged.

The Sunday School lesson was ever present: JUDGE NOT. Thank you, God, for Durham, Pennsylvania, the Lutherans and the Reformed, Vera Riegel, John and Mildred Frankenfield, Gertie Koch and her Christmas Eve extravaganzas, Lillian Melchior and her music, and my family. What happens to children who do not grow up in sheltering arms? I'm reminded of the African proverb: If a child is not embraced by his village, he will burn it down to feel its warmth.

H#2 and I had many beautiful experiences at our farm, but clear and away the most amazing happened one night when H#2 awoke me and put his fingers over my lips. He moved his head slowly to indicate I should turn and look out the window. There, not twenty feet from our bedroom, stood three deer, up on their hind legs, eating apples from the prized tree in our front yard. (My mom and I made gallons of award-winning applesauce from those apples! Well, we never won any "awards" but it was unanimously the best applesauce anyone ever tasted.)

Now we watched silently the grace with which the deer feasted on those apples, and our ringside view felt like an "other-worldly" gift.

The deer lowered themselves to chew, then rose again to circle the tree for the next ripe piece of fruit. It appeared to be a well-choreographed ballet. Finally, they all landed on their feet and by some secret signal slowly melted into the dark night. H#2 and I looked at each other in awe, shaking our heads in wonder. Wordlessly, we snuggled down together to go back to sleep.

We had serene times, just the two of us, out on the lake in our little blue boat. We would float around for an hour at the end of a day of hard work. Watching the sun set on the water was a spiritual experience. Watching the stars from the porch on a warm night was another soulful time.

Once we bought our farm, my involvement with the church in Akron came to a halt. The boys had been raised there, had enjoyed

Sunday School, suffered through church with me sitting with my arms constraining them, and delighted in Joe Woods' Youth Group. They'd gone on mission trips and made good friends. Now it was time for them to make choices of their own in terms of involvement with organized religion.

For me, I felt I had transitioned to The Church in the Garden. Since the earth is God's, planting pine trees, tending cows, growing vegetables and flowers are all sacred tasks. I was so grateful to H#2 that he loved the earth as much as I did. Sharing the farm with family and friends brought us both deep pleasures. We had the crazy dog-eat-dog business world during the week, and then on the weekend, we had manual labor, sweat, things which were growing, like the cows, because we cared for them, and things that we grew, like the corn and potatoes, because we cared about the simplicity of self-sufficiency.

I wrote in a journal: "So much to be grateful for. This is truly the best time of my life – my parents are safe and sound, my boys are grown and responsible adults, and my husband and I are buddies and pals and blessed with love." That's what I believed.

WESTMINSTER VILLAGE

In 1992 Eddie graduated from high school after a stellar athletic career, and my parents moved into Westminster Village, a Life Care Center located in Allentown, Pennsylvania. Barely across the city line from Bethlehem, Allentown was made famous by Billy Joel's song.

A life care center has three levels of care: totally independent, the level my parents moved into; medication management, which both my dad and then mom advanced to; and nursing home care, which both my dad and mom transferred to after hospital stays before returning to their apartment. They each died in the nursing home section of Westminster Village.

Since Gram and Aunt Ruth were gone, my parents were free to sell the house in Durham. Aunt Agnes had moved to Bethlehem and died a few years later, so they were no longer needed to care for her. Grandma Rau had died a few years after moving in with Walter Unangst, and so my dad was no longer called to bail her out of trouble.

A few years after Aunt Kitty's death, Pierre moved back to France. He and his new wife, Denise, invited my parents to visit them, and they had a marvelous trip to the French countryside and saw not the tourist sites they had seen when visiting H#1 and me when we were in Europe, but the way actual French folks lived. They were charmed by Pierre and Denise and felt warmly welcomed. But, Pierre, too, was gone now. The former Melchior home once again belonged to people outside the family. So, obligations to care for others in the family were fulfilled, and Miriam and Dave were free to concentrate on each other.

My brother and his daughter, Gretchen, (Molly was traveling for her Provost position at Springfield College and Kirsten was away at college,) moved Mom and Daddy into their apartment, hung shelves, unpacked boxes, and placed furniture exactly where mom had measured it would fit. Planner extraordinaire, Miriam had each item organized and looking beautiful. Despite my prodding, in the fifteen years she lived there, every single piece of furniture remained where she first placed it. She even determined that one of Gram's needlepoint creations would cover the unsightly fuse box hanging in the living room!

They kept a few antiques: a rocking chair from Grandma Rau's house; a desk from Durham; and some bookshelves and curios. Everything else was purchased to fit into the new, smaller space. The apartment sized furniture was more than paid for because all the furniture from the house in Durham was sold. The man my dad had hired to help with the many other houses my dad had emptied took everything, and then presented a check for the worth. Since all that they owned was in perfect condition, the check greatly exceeded what they had expected, and Mom had a nice bankroll for her new purchases.

They had, for the first time in their lives, twin beds, only because they fit better in the new bedroom. The den had a sleeper sofa so Skip and Molly or H#2 and I could come and stay with them. The apartment consisted of a bedroom, a den, a living room with dining area, a kitchen, two bathrooms, one with stacked laundry, and a delightful, small balcony. It was perfect for them. My dad would be there seven years; my mom would live there fifteen years.

Outside their apartment door they placed a Captain's chair which Captain Adam Rau had used on his ship in the 1700's. Beside that was an antique plant stand on which mom kept a lovely, old pitcher (which is presently on the island in my kitchen) filled with vine, pine branches, or flowers, depending on the season.

Across the doorway from the Captain's chair, they set up a card table with jigsaw pieces laid out on it and four chairs. Mom designed a little sign that invited people to sit and fit pieces into the puzzle any time they wished. Most of the residents of the fifth floor, which was their floor, came now and again to work on the puzzle.

I grossly underestimated my father's resiliency. (I apologize, Daddy!) I was certain he would be bereft without being needed to manage the Village of Durham. Nope. He simply shifted his management skills to Westminster Village. In two years, he was the president of the Resident's Association, which magically, under his clever and watchful eye, went from financial red to black, despite adding birdfeeders and gardens to the grounds.

Dave Rau became the "fixer" for all things amiss in his new village, and people came to him with their complaints as the neighbors had come all those years ago when Grandma Rau needed some reining in, or something didn't look quite right on the roads of Durham Township.

He and mom went to church on the Westminster bus. They signed up for every outing offered from day trips to concerts and the theatre. They played pinochle or bridge with various couples a few times a week and delighted in welcoming new folks to Westminster and reacquainting with old friends. A cousin on the Meffan side of the family and a few people known to my dad from Bethlehem Steel already lived there.

For the first time in their lives, they went to the grocery store together. Mom said she could barely rip him out of the produce department. My mom was an incredibly savvy shopper; she knew whether she needed three or four peaches for the week. She hated waste, was a wizard at cooking so there'd be no leftovers, and at shopping so there'd be no spoilage. My dad, having newly encountered the vastness and delight of an entire department of produce – probably reminiscent of his days going to the Farmer's Market with Uncle Hollis – wanted to take home some of everything. My mom adored that her husband was shopping with her, so I'm sure his enthusiasm won out over her thrift most of the time.

A lovely nurse, Paulette, was in charge of the independent living section of Westminster Village. She took a particular interest in Dave and Miriam. They were a happy, healthy, intelligent and vigorous couple. They didn't whine and complain. Paulette expedited whatever they needed medically, from prescription drugs to blood tests to comfort items, like the massage cushion she found for mom's back. Paulette Goddard was a Godsend!

My parents also really liked that they could just lock their door and take off for Skip's house or my house. They were still making those trips. The first six years they lived at Westminster Village, my mom told me, were "the happiest years of our marriage." Finally, for the first time, they spent quality time alone together.

GROWING THE FARM

Because of the farm, H#2 and I were focused on the seasons. We continued with our day jobs which financed our weekend passion as well as our usual vacation location: the farm.

We attended livestock auctions and farm auctions, looking for good stock and the hundreds of necessary pieces of farm equipment needed for planting, growing, mowing, harvesting, tilling, baling and moving those huge, heavy bales of hay. We bought a big, round, red metal container to keep the hay off the ground so it wouldn't rot before the cows could munch it down. We needed a thousand-pound cement drinking trough for thirsty cows; we needed medical supplies. We built, by hand, H#2 and I, a large wooden pen with a chute for separating and immobilizing the cows for the various procedures. Then there was the dag-blasted fence to mend. Constantly.

Oddly, H#2 and I loved it all. We dug ditches for pipes and raked weeds from the pond. For this H#2 used a pitchfork, I transferred the piles of stinky, smelly wet gunk to a cart behind the ATV, and then we dumped the contents of the cart into the woods. Neither of us will ever forget the pitchforkful he hoisted over his shoulder with about a ten- or twelve-foot snake impaled on the tines of the fork. (And it was another black snake, just like the one that terrorized Karen and me in the millrace forty-some years before!) This was not work for the squeamish. We both got tetanus shots. We got dirty, bruised and cut in more ways than I knew there were.

We planned the future any time we weren't working. Buffalo, we agreed. Well, he planned and I acquiesced; I already had everything I wanted and needed. We had plenty of room and went to visit the few buffalo farms we could find in the state. We envisioned knocking out windows in the kitchen and putting in sliding doors which would lead to a sturdy deck. We figured out a way to fit a garage under the house. We needed room for a big freezer or two; extra storage space in the house would be helpful.

H#2 also had a German shepherd puppy on his wish list, so Madi the beautiful, sweet dog joined the family. H#2 got up with her every night for six months and trained her strictly. She was his dog unless we were driving back and forth to the farm. Then, she insisted on being my lap dog. This became increasingly challenging as she grew. She had a fondness for McDonald's hamburgers, which she ate like a lady, gently taking only the bite offered and then waiting until fed a bite more. We'd arrive at the farm and in no more than five minutes Madi'd be in the pond soaking wet. And smelly. She always had a bath before we headed back to Akron.

Recently, re-reading some old journals, I found this entry:

I told H#2 that I wanted a little girl, and after seven years, he gave me Madi. Three years later, ten heifers. Am I not being clear? And dare I ask again? One dog and ten cows later, I'm not sure I should chance it.

He'd probably get me an emu or some sheep or something. Maybe I'll just tend my garden and count my blessings.

That was where my head and heart were.

MEANWHILE
BACK IN AKRON

In 1997/1998 I reconnected with the young man named David with whom I had shared an office when I worked at NEOUCOM, the local medical school. I had a client who saw him as her psychiatrist, so we consulted for her care. We met for lunch several times, and H#2 and I had a few evening meals with him.

He was going to China on a Medical Mission trip, exchanging information for Post-Traumatic Stress treatments, which had become my specialty. He invited me to go along. It was right down my alley, and I was truly excited about the opportunity. Therapists didn't get invited on trips like this. (In fact, there was only one other therapist and sixteen doctors in our group.) My psychiatrist friend David promised H#2 he'd make sure I returned home safely.

It was a once-in-a-lifetime experience and despite what it ended up costing, and I don't mean financially, I'm glad I went. H#2 did not want me to go because it was too expensive. I wouldn't work for eighteen days, which meant no income. For the first time in fifteen years, I didn't capitulate to his wishes. He called a number of times while I was in China and seemed fine when I got home. I had learned a lot and felt like a professional in my field after that time spent with psychiatrists and psychologists. The young psychiatrist then asked me to join his practice, and I did that a few months later.

I had worked for Phil Hockwalt for ten years. He had been the first therapist I had ever met or known and was a brilliant mentor, but we were not on equal footing. He would always be the teacher, and I, the student. I pointed out to Phil the way our clients always referred to us, giving Phil credit for anything they liked that either of us contributed. It had been a ten-year advanced study program doing co-therapy with him. He would pick up on my intuitive statements and quantify them with the name of a book, often including the page number, where what I said could be found. He was all head; I was all intuitive heart. Together, we had the language needed to talk to everyone.

I used to imagine that our co-therapy was like this: I jumped into the pool and swam around with our clients, and he sat in the lifeguard chair and whistled for us to come out when the hour was up. Among so many other things, Phil taught me to react less and pause more. He role-modeled listening patiently and letting clients figure out what they were doing not by naming it but by asking pertinent questions. Any conclusions people arrive at themselves are always more valuable than any which others suggest.

In typical Phil fashion, he told me he thought it was a good idea for me to leave the nest. He also told me I was always welcome back. We stayed in touch until he died, too early and too tragically, from

Alzheimer's. He was such a teacher and I was much more self-contained after ten years working with Phil and Doug Cole, his partner. Doug specialized in ADHD. He worked with kids, but he taught me a great deal about working with their parents. Thirty years later, I still work with one client whose son saw Doug; Doug recommended me for her care.

The next four years of my professional life were spent in an office with a psychiatrist which was again an amazing learning opportunity. He would talk to me about our shared clients. His different vantage point taught me to look more broadly at the clients who came to see me. I started going beyond therapy issues and counseling concepts to medical, neurological and psychiatric contributing factors. Excluding medical problems first became a new, valuable standard for me.

One of the things I learned in China was that the Chinese treatment for PTSD included sending the patient back to his or her family. Surrounded by love and stability, Chinese psychiatrists believed, a patient would recover much more quickly. I think the basic premise was brilliant except where the family had been a major cause of the trauma, as with childhood abuse in the home. The Chinese treatment reminded me of the wisdom of the Native American treatment, where a trauma survivor was enveloped in the warmth and protection of his tribe and given time and space to recover.

Other Chinese ideas just caused us to watch and listen without comment. Chinese hospitals used calligraphy, cards – as in playing card games –and they had a "drinking room." The "drinking room" was empty except for a large tin bucket of water with a ladle. One could go in there and have a drink of water whenever one wished. The strangest treatments, in my mind, were both a total blood transfusion and/or a total oxygen transfusion. Most of what the Chinese offered PTSD patients was more humane than the "shock treatments" we Americans were offering. I don't know what might have been more effective.

Once H#2 got a job as a tax attorney, he quickly moved to an office with a window, on his way to a corner office. He did not enjoy his work like I enjoyed mine. His was a job; mine was a calling. He was diligent and devoted, but the only time he was happy was when we were working on the house or at the farm. I would feel his mood lighten as we headed south and feel the tension return when we headed back north. I remember watching him walk toward the house in the evening and his face would be a mask, as though he had to keep his true self hidden away all day. The farm was years from being self-sustaining, and it was his salary which supported his passion. I explored jobs near the farm and felt I could work in southern Ohio. But the option to work in southern Ohio would be practically impossible for him and certainly not at his current salary. I thought we were temporarily stuck; he apparently had started feeling something much more dire.

MORE GAIN, MORE LOSS

December 1, 1998 my father experienced a very serious health crisis. Here's what I wrote about it at the time:

"When your father is dying, your sanity lies in the details. Numbers you never knew about, natural functions you take for granted, all of these become reasons to celebrate or panic.

His diastolic blood pressure needs to hit 60. You learn to watch the monitor. (It's at 44.)

Never have you stared so hard at his face, watched his chest rise and fall. At one point your brother and sons stand around his bed discussing the color of his urine.

He's always hated hoopla. 'Now, don't fuss,' he said more times than anyone could count.

You remember everyone's name. Colleen, who is there two of the darkest nights, is a red-head. This he would like. She has a dog named Wilma who just had a hysterectomy. You inquire on the second night how Wilma is doing.

He never sees Colleen, or Marion, or Pat – he is lying flat in bed with a ventilator in his mouth, wires in his chest, and fourteen lines of tubing.

What could possibly prepare you for such a sight? You can easily picture him standing at the dining room window in Durham at any time of the day or night you might have been expected. He would be waiting and watching, and the lights would go on. He's too Scotch to turn on the light before you get there.

Now, you rub his head, bald and rough with scar tissue from the many small skin cancers, dry from the days in bed, bumpy from the thousands of bopping's life has given him. You rub his head and tell him things he knows very well: you're there, Mom's there, you're holding on to him, he's not alone, you love him, and you tell him that you know he loves you, because it would be essential to him that you know that.

He has been in the hospital eleven days. He's 87 years old. He and Mom have been married 60 years. He's had nine units of blood. He's been on the 6th, 5th, 2nd, and 4th floors."

Your mother takes two Xanax before bed and still she can't sleep. Your brother has turned on the air conditioner in the den and she knows it's making a troubling noise – something inside ices up and then leaks into the apartment below and people who allow their air conditioners to do this get hollered at. My brother reassures her that NO ONE will holler at her this week.

It was eleven o'clock at night when you first made it to the hospital. You were at work and felt some urgency to call and check on him. Your mother says they're moving him to cardiac intensive care. You know you must go immediately.

Your husband finds a plane. You tell your boss, the larger-than-life Steve Perkins, who is also a soul mate, that your dad's blood pressure is 77/44. He looks into your eyes and says, simply, "Go." You hand him your appointment book and head home.

You take your two good dark dresses, one has some pink stripes, but it's all you have, so it will have to do. You take your blue jeans, a sweater, a jumper, a turtleneck and all your clean underwear. In all the millions of articles and books you've read, you've never read how to pack for this.

You call your boys on the way home and scare them half to death, because at the sound of each of their voices you begin sobbing uncontrollably. They can barely understand you. Andy begs you to pull over and you pull to the side of the road.

Your husband comes and quietly takes you to the airport. "You'll need money. How much do you want?" he asks. He would, you imagine, give a million dollars not to be sending you on this trip. "Sixty," you tell him. He gets you $200.

You talk to no one on the planes. You sit and cry. In the Pittsburg airport, you stare at a poster advertising Paris and you thank God that you father, with your mother by his side, got to Paris.

You feel, actually, more appreciative than anything else. This father of yours has been such an extraordinary man living such an ordinary life. He worked for the same company for 41 years. Always drove a Chevy. Never missed church. Helped found a Lion's Club. Helped save a town. Paid his bills when they came. Made friends everywhere he went.

On June 2, 1999 I write:

It's been six months and one day since he stopped breathing. Since then, it's been a nightmare rollercoaster ride – apartment, hospital, nursing home, apartment, hospital, nursing home. Congestive heart failure on top of prostate cancer. Nephrostomy tube. Catheter. Infections. Tears.

Now it's June and my mom reports he's been crying and asking why God doesn't take him. We spend the night at my mom's apartment and Wednesday morning we head off to the hospital, H#2 and I, leaving mom to take her time getting ready. She warns us he's not very communicative and is very depressed – we should be prepared.

We find the room and he is staring into the hall. His face lights up in immeasurable joy as he sees us. "My Susan," he says. "Thank you, God, for allowing me to see her." He is thrilled to see his favorite son-in-law, and says so, repeatedly.

He is animated, lively. From his bed in his blue pajama top his blue eyes sparkle with joy and peace. He talks about heaven. He is looking forward to seeing his life-long friend, Russell Hess, and his beloved Grandpa Melchior. I tell him John Murphy will be there, too, and they'll be surprised, Catholics such as him, to find themselves with us – or to find us with them.

He kisses me repeatedly and tells me he loves me. He tells us how blessed he has been all his life. Strange coming from a man who lost his mother when he was two and broke his back when he was eighteen, spending six months strapped to a board in a hospital. He had worked incredibly hard and planned incredibly well so that he and mom could pay $90,000. to spend their last years in the security and safety of Westminster Village.

Mom arrives and he tells her he loves her. She says, "I love you, too."
He questions her: "A lot?" She laughs as she has laughed for the last sixty-
one years. That man could always make her laugh. "Yes," she grabs his
hand. "A lot."

H#2 and I are heading to Massachusetts for Skip's retirement party. We will be back on Saturday to see Daddy again and Skip will be coming also. This news makes him very happy. He instructs us to tell Skip he loves him. And Molly.

We tell him again that we'll be back Saturday. I lean in to kiss him and he tells me I have pretty eyes. Now, I laugh. "Daddy, they're your eyes." He smiles. That man could always make me laugh, too.

We try to change gears as we head to Massachusetts and a very happy occasion. Skip is celebrated, and we enjoy hearing all the praise and the stories. He has taught everything from elementary beginning students to seniors in high school who would go on to be professional musicians. He was a highly respected and well-loved teacher.

We feel the urgency, and drive back to Bethlehem the next morning, Skip following in his car.

Daddy has been moved back to the nursing home. One of the maintenance men thoughtfully removed the second bed from the room so we have the room to ourselves. A nurse explains gently that he is not expected to live through the night. H#2 heads off on the eight-hour trip to the farm. "I'll come back and get you," he starts. He doesn't need to say the rest.

Daddy is sitting up, propped against the bed. My mom and Skip and I spend the afternoon with him. A minister none of us have ever met stops to say a prayer with our dad. Daddy says to him, "Where are your people from?" It is the most perfect Dave Rau question imaginable. Everything for our dad was about connections – who belonged to who – where were you from – who were your cousins and ancestors. Who are your people, and where are they from? He was always pulling people together, finding common ground.

His favorite nurse comes to see him. She leans over to give him a kiss, saying she'll be back later. He pats her on the fanny which is apparently some old joke between them. Both of them and my mom laugh. We never did find out what the story was behind the pat, but our father was prim and proper almost to a fault, so it was nothing sleazy or inappropriate. It was sweet to see him laugh and here he was, making another person laugh as he lay on his death bed.

They bring us supper in the room and we pick at a little food. Daddy has fallen asleep. Mom mentions her back is hurting and Skip talks her into returning to the apartment for a little while to lie down and stretch out.

I move in close to my beloved father and start softly singing all the hymns I can remember from his leading of the singing at Durham Church. Those Sunday School hymns are imprinted in my heart forever. I sing to him, as quietly as possible, for almost an hour. The sun is setting; it's twilight.

My mom and Skip come back and Mom touches Daddy's face. He slowly opens his eyes. He groans, and a tear runs down his cheek. Mom tells him it's okay; she knows he has to go. We all say, "I love you." I have one hand on his forehead and the other on his chest. I feel the most amazing thing. His heart doesn't stop. It explodes. I feel it clearly. My minister friend, Lynn, said, when I told her later: "Of course. His heart exploded with joy at his first sight of heaven."

Mom leans over to kiss him and rub his dear cheek. Skip leans over to hold Mom. I am on the opposite side of his bed, and I start walking around to them.

At the bottom of the bed, I stop for a moment and look at Daddy. A small, almost invisible puff of white substance – a cotton puff, a feather -- rises from his chest and floats out the window. I never knew you could actually see a soul, but I know with total certainty that the dear man lying on that bed, the rock who had steadied me and taught me how to live, had also just shown me how to die.

The next afternoon I was alone in Mom's car at a stoplight in Bethlehem. Suddenly the windshield was covered in white butterflies. Luckily, there was nothing behind me, because I couldn't see when the light changed or see to drive. The butterflies flew away as suddenly as they had materialized. It must have been an arduous trip, but they followed me a few weeks later to the farm and spent the summer hanging out in the garden.

I can't explain any of what happened around my dad's death. I just know what I know. That is what happened, and that is exactly how it happened. Those are the gifts I received from either my earthly father or my heavenly Father. Or both -- in cahoots!

H#2 and I had a beautiful summer at the farm. We worked hard. Family, friends, kids, and grandkids came and went. Kenny and Lena continued as our best resource and dear friends. Things flourished and grew. Life was good. Daddy was no longer on earth but never gone, either. We kept in close touch with Mom.

She had been in misery with her back from the day Daddy died. After the funeral Skip and Molly took her to Massachusetts with them but she didn't stay long; she was in too much pain. Skip brought her back to Westminster Village so she could see the doctor. Mom had sciatica and needed surgery. Skip, newly retired, would stay with her.

The surgery was fairly easy and miraculously successful. The surgeon confided to her that he loved doing that particular surgery because once the nerves were freed, the pain was gone. His patients thought he was a genius.

H#2 had a teaching gig in Florida in October, and we planned for me to fly down to meet him afterwards and we'd vacation for a few days at Disney World. It was slow season at the farm, and we'd had an exhausting summer so a few days relaxing sounded great. That was over Halloween.

For Thanksgiving we hosted a big celebration with H#2's family and the boys. We set up a long table in the partially finished new family room. H#2 was cranky and withdrawn – not an unusual mood for him if his family or a lot of children were around. The rest of us had a good time, and when he and I drove to the farm the next day he seemed to cheer up. We brought back a carefully chosen Christmas tree from our plethora of planted trees. It was the first we would enjoy. I had no idea it would be the last, as well.

Nick and Jen were getting married December 4th and Skip and Gretchen were coming and bringing Grandma, too. (Molly was once again out of the country on a business trip.) It was impossible not to like Jen and her darling four-year-old daughter, Briana. We were all excited and delighted.

The morning of the wedding H#2 went to get a haircut and then came back and walked Skip all around the Akron house telling him in detail the remodeling plans.

The wedding was beautiful. While the ceremony was underway, someone broke into the bride's room and stole $600.00 from Jen's purse, their honeymoon cash. We took up a collection and replaced the money. Anytime the problem is money, you don't really have a problem: you find another job and make more money, aka Dave Rau.

That evening everyone was going out to continue the celebration, but H#2 refused to go. At the wedding he had hugged Nick and called him, "Son," telling him how proud he was of him. Now he wouldn't go have a drink to celebrate. Mom and Skip and I stayed home, then, also, and Gretchen went with her cousins.

The next morning, Sunday morning, Skip took Grandma and Gretchen back east and H#2 left for a quick business trip. He'd be back Monday evening.

Monday around supper time he walked into the house looking furious.

He had an announcement to make:

"I don't like you."

"I don't trust you."

"I'm leaving."

Stunned, I told him I loved him. I was eternally grateful for all we had done together, from raising the boys, to the farm, to the joys we had shared.

Always speak your truth is my motto from the millrace.

He stormed upstairs, and I grabbed the car keys and drove to the Moffitt's. Years before, he awakened me in the middle of the night to say, "If anything ever happens to me, go to the Moffitt's. They'll take care of you." Something had clearly happened to him. Confused and devastated, I headed to the Moffitt's.

When I returned home Tuesday morning to get ready for work, he was gone. Madi was there. She looked a little shell shocked, herself, I thought. Madi and I didn't see him for days,-perhaps weeks. I don't remember. Everything was a blur. I went to work and sat and listened to actual searing pain and health crises and stories of abuse. It is hard to feel sorry for yourself with a broken heart and shattered dreams when you spend your days walking beside people in absolute agony.

One time when H#2 came back, he announced he was taking Madi to his sister's. He had rented an apartment which did not accept pets. "Bullshit, Madi is staying with one of us, and since you rented an apartment which does not accept pets, Madi is staying here with me." He didn't argue. He didn't fight for his "girl."

What kind of man deserts his dog? Leaving a wife is understandable. Madi was as close to a child as he ever had. She adored him. Madi somehow overheard and understood this conversation. From then on, when he would come into the house and call her to him, she would go, but the moment she could, she would come back and sit by me. Her allegiance changed completely.

H#2 said he was going to visit his younger sister in Connecticut for Christmas. Nick and Jen and I put up the massive, gorgeous Christmas tree in the family room. I can still see Nick high on a ladder stringing lights and hanging decorations. H#2's family came for Christmas dinner and we exchanged presents. Clearly, they didn't know what was going on with him either. They apparently thought his behavior was a temporary blip on the screen.

My dad had died June 5th and H#2 had left on December 6th. 1999 was not my easiest year. My dad's death happened within the natural order of things. He had been such a strong man of integrity and faith that I experienced an uncomplicated grief. If we have unsettled relationships, unexpressed feelings, broken promises, unresolved guilt or shame, unapologetic behavior in a relationship, grief becomes very complicated and very uneasy. My dad and I had our relationship house in order. Ever since the moment he died, I have felt him with me. I talk to him and thank him profusely for the lessons he taught me through the way he lived and the way he died: work hard, don't compromise your ethics or your honesty, find the humor in everything, and love generously.

H#2 abandoning ship was a shock I didn't see coming and a mystery I couldn't comprehend. We were happy. We had everything. We had plans and dreams.

It wasn't until I was cleaning out a desk drawer in the spring that things started falling into place. I happened upon the list of students who were in the class H#2 taught in October in Florida. One of the names on the list popped out at me. A woman who lived in Massachusetts. She was married. Then there was a receipt for a piece of gold jewelry. H#2 had talked both his Connecticut sister, for whom he bought jewelry, and me, for whom he also bought jewelry, to be contented with silver. The receipt in the drawer was for gold jewelry. The term "gold-digger" seemed appropriate. Six weeks after H#2 and the married student met, they apparently both ditched their former lives and concocted a new one. Wow. It was like a story one of my clients would bring to me.

H#2 cleaned everything out of the farm, sold all the equipment then sold the farm. I was called to an attorney's office to sign the deed of sale. They had the paper turned to the line for my signature. I signed. Then I turned the paper over to see to whom H#2 had sold our dream. It was a Land Development Company. I thought I was going to throw up.

One of the many things H#2 and I had agreed on was the sanctity of land. We loved driving and seeing the rolling hills and the big fields. Farms were sacred. We both hated seeing them cut into lots and sold for development. Now he had made me complicit in doing just such a thing and he, the man who had despised such behavior, had initiated it himself. Our beautiful big farm was not going to exist any longer. A few years later I had to see it for myself: the five-acre lots now hold houses, trailers, and a rag-tag of sheds and lean-tos for hunters.

I had felt, when he said he was leaving, like someone had come to me in the night with a large metal pincer to force open my chest and pull out my heart. In the morning, all that remained was an empty cavern where my warm heart had previously lived. Now, though, with the farm sold to a developer, I felt like the sun had stopped shining and all color had drained from the earth. It felt to me like an abomination. I was sick. I signed that paper; I had participated in it.

I stopped hearing from H#2's family. Apparently, they were finally privy to the new plan. Unbelievably to me, after Nick's wedding, not one of the three boys who had been his sons for sixteen years ever saw or heard from H#2 again. Sixteen years. Tossed away in six weeks. My friend Judy confessed she had always worried he would hurt me, maybe kill me. He did. Just not physically.

CONDO YEARS

As always in life, we hold fast to our mooring and venture into uncharted waters knowing we have the safety and peace of faith, hope and love. This time, the yin for the painful yang, was a tiny baby born December 28, 2000. I held fast to the hope and joy of that coming event all through the trials and tribulations of 2000.

"Hell hath no fury like a woman scorned," wrote Shakespeare. Mr. Shakespeare had apparently never dealt with a man who changed his mind, decided to dump his former wife and his entire former life, and expected his previously cooperative and loving wife to just roll over and play nice.

I was left by myself in a partially finished, huge house. Since H#2 had insisted on remodeling it, and I had trustingly but unwittingly gone along with the idea, I now had four garages and more than three thousand square feet of living space –most of it simply under roof with no drywall or finish work.

The massive structure no longer "fit" me, but I wanted to stay in the home I had lived in for twenty-five years. It was where I had raised my children, and I wanted to maintain their roots for them and me.

One estimate for making the house livable was $105,000. Clearly that was not happening on my $50,000/year salary. I was left holding a heavy bag of unfinished business which had never been mine but was now on my shoulders. The house wasn't even marketable. One real estate agent suggested a loss much greater than the rather small first mortgage and the rather large second mortgage which we had taken out for the addition.

Enter a miracle: a woman from the university heard I was getting divorced, bad news always travels fast, and came to ask if I was going to be selling. She had always loved my house, and although she was sorry for my loss, she'd be very interested in buying it. I named the price which was a bare-minimum break-even amount. "Deal," she said, shaking my hand. She agreed to have all the paperwork drawn up. How soon could I be out, she wanted to know.

I rented a storage unit and my sons became Three Men and a Truck, which one of them had, and we cleaned out that dear home with the three-story laundry chute and the odd but wonderful neighbors on the loveliest street in Akron. I had nowhere to go, of course, but another woman at work offered to rent me a room in her house. Agreeing to that was a desperately poor decision: she overcharged me and tried to control my time. But I was reeling and trying to find myself a safe harbor, a sanctuary.

Daughter-in-law, Jen, and Phil Hockwalt's wife, Jean, a real estate agent, helped immensely. After about thirty false starts, we found a development of new condos in downtown Akron, convenient to the University and my therapy practice site. I fell in love with the design of the condo. It had two-story windows on two walls of the open downstairs floor plan, a double garage, two downstairs bathrooms and two downstairs bedrooms and, for me, an upstairs bedroom and bathroom. I thought it was expensive, but I needed the cheerfulness and security it offered. I had to wait a few months for it to be finished, but it was worth the wait.

My own personal Three Men and a Truck returned to empty the storage unit and move me into my new condo. Perhaps now, with sunlight and new surroundings, I could unload some of my suffocating grief. It wasn't easy. But the event at the conclusion of 2000 was balm to my spirit and began filling the big hole in my heart.

It was just after Christmas and snowing like a bear when I walked into the front office to check out a client; the office staff was fairly twittering and twitching. "What?" I asked, but they wouldn't tell me until I saw the client off.

"YOUR'RE A GRANDMA!" they practically shouted. The baby was born. They wanted me to drop everything and rush to the hospital, but I had two more clients scheduled and figured if anyone ventured out in this weather, they must really need to talk. I'd leave for the hospital when we were sure no one else was coming to see me.

I drove north on Route 77 slowly and cautiously in that blizzard! I wanted to make sure I arrived in one piece.

Tiptoeing into the room, I found Jen, the new mama, asleep, and the new daddy, Nick, staring at a small bundle swaddled in a blanket. He motioned to me to sit in the chair and walked over and put this little darling in my arms. I barely got my coat off! I, too, just stared at the perfectly beautiful little face of Mikayla Rose.

He denies it, but I was wide awake and he was exhausted, so I'm going with my story. My third son said to me, "Be careful of her neck." I wanted to mention that somehow I had refrained all these years from wringing his, but, instead, I smiled and nodded. Wordlessly, he went back to his chair and promptly fell asleep.

That little imp in my arms pulled up her legs, snuggled into my neck, and made a small noise that sounded like a little "meow." We stayed like that until some nasty nurse came into the room, spied me, and said, starchily, "Visiting hours have been over for an hour."

"Oh," I said with all the innocence I could muster. Both parents were roused, and, after kissing and congratulating everyone, I tiptoed out as stealthily as I had entered.

Mickey, as we call her, changed many things for me. You know, it's fascinating. My Gram had eight grandchildren and I was far and away her "favorite" because she knew me the best. It was purely opportunistic. Gram and I were able to spend time together. We knew each other through conversations and games and the gift of hours in each other's company. I would go on to have eight grandchildren, also. Because I had the opportunity to babysit Mickey one day a week, and I grabbed the chance, and because I had a crib in the back bedroom and a bed beside it, and her parents allowed me to have their precious daughter overnight, she and I enjoyed endless, delightful hours from the first week on.

When Mickey was a tiny newborn, I spent at least one night a week on Nick and Jen's sofa. At about one or two a.m., her daddy would stagger out and say, "Special Delivery," and Mickey and I would go through the diaper/bottle routine and then I'd sit and hold her, waiting for the next time her tummy was rumbly. It was such a joy. The opportunities were extended to me, and I accepted every one of them.

I believe that's how it is with parents and grandparents and children. If there is a child with special needs, for example, that child requires more of your time and attention and devotion. That child becomes your favorite not because he or she is different, better, smarter, kinder or anything else. That child becomes your favorite because that is the child you know the best. Favorite is probably a poor choice of word, but the child with whom we are most familiar is a matter of geography, in-laws, daughters- or sons-in-law, her or his family patterns, and so many other things that have nothing to do with "preference" or "partiality" but just with the practicalities of life.

My middle son and his family didn't live in Akron, so I was not as familiar with his children. They lived in the same town as his wife's family, so it was her family with whom they spent the preponderance of time. My oldest son and his wife, when they were pregnant, came to the condo and I asked Andy to put the crib mattress in the highest position so I could reach the baby when she came stayed with me. I assumed they would want me to babysit. That privilege went to her family, as well. No animosity prevented closeness with that granddaughter, it was simply the way things happened. That only means that I don't know her very well, not that I love her any less.

I love them all. I know Mickey and her little brother, Nicholas, the best. It is all just a matter of opportunity and seizing the moments which are offered.

And then, to balance the joy of Mickey, there was a third great desertion in my life. First my dad's death, then H#2's abandonment, and then my boss, the psychiatrist, experienced a personal crisis which, when it was all sorted out, excluded me from his life and the lives of his three children with whom I had grown quite close. It was this psychiatrist/boss, a brilliant, intuitive doctor from whom I learned so much and with whom I had gone to China and later worked with for four years.

The psychiatrist was in a practice with another psychiatrist and a number of therapists. I was accommodated easily into this practice. After about a year an unfair, nasty rumor, which questioned his ethics, circulated about my psychiatrist friend, and he and I split from the larger practice to go out on our own. My daughter-in-law, Jen, joined us as our administrative staff and she was extraordinary. The three of us had a beautiful, easy relationship and she handled everything office-related.

After H#2 left, the psychiatrist started including me in events with his family and I began babysitting and playing with his children. It was balm for my spirit, as was the time spent with Mickey. Children, with their optimism and innocence, are the perfect medicine for an aching heart.

The psychiatrist and I were both musical and enjoyed all things theatrical. We started having parties and gatherings, suppers, potlucks, musical evenings, sing-a-longs, and both small and large group shindigs.

Then, in early 2002, the psychiatrist withdrew from our friendship. I questioned him. He was just in a difficult place, he explained. He needed me to be patient and steady. Of course, I could do that. That lack of personal connection continued for five months. All the while we worked together. Then he invited me to a breakfast meeting. What he had to tell me left me no choice but to leave our practice. I could no longer continue working with him.

I saw this as a third betrayal and abandonment. My father's death, H#2's desertion, and now a dear friend withholding facts about a situation which shattered the integrity on which any trusted association is grounded. I found a great therapist and started on anti-depressants. It was a dark night of the soul. They say the third time is the charm. The third time can also catapult you over the edge. Now, in addition to needing a new home, I needed a new job.

I contacted my first teacher at The University of Akron, Steve Perkins, the larger-than-life-person, remember? He met me for lunch at Wendy's and set up an interview for later that week. I was interviewed by Tari Riley, who was to become a trusted and dear friend, and Mike Smith, a totally intimidating guy who, unlike most of us therapists, worked with perpetrators instead of victims. I was hired.

In August of 2002 I started at Akron Family Institute, a practice at which I was to remain until November of 2014.

THE FAMILY AT AFI

At Akron Family Institute, Steve Perkins brought together a fine group of therapists with great educations and varied expertise. I felt like I had risen to Prime Time. I was given an office and a $600 allowance to furnish it as I liked. Since I already had most of the things I needed, I never did spend my entire allowance.

We had four administrative staff members who made life as easy for us as possible. We had schedules, mailboxes, 401K's, insurance and colleagues. It was heaven. I fell into AFI like a duck landing on a tranquil pond.

I began there about the same time Eddie, my middle son, was sent to Iraq. Here we go again with the yin and the yang of life. He had enlisted soon after 9/11. Eddie was a father of four children with a perfectly good job. But he was Eddie. His sense of right and wrong was indisputable and unrelenting. He had to do what his conscience told him to do.

He completed basic training and then headed for Fort Leonard Wood in Missouri. When he was graduating from boot camp, three of us, Eddie's wife and parents, flew from Cleveland to somewhere in

Missouri, which already felt like a foreign land to me. We-rented a car. Lisa insisted on driving. That was interesting, but H#1 and I were not about to cause additional strife. We had come to support our son, and quickly realized most of the soldiers had no family attending this ceremony. Of the group of 200 trainees, two received awards; one of them was Eddie.

Then, he was sent home for a few days prior to being shipped out to Iraq. Once again, I didn't think my heart could withstand the fear. Every night, I turned the fear and my son over to God. I never expected or asked for God to save his life. I asked for God to be with him and to be with each of us who loved him. I told God I trusted in the Divine Wisdom. Every night. For a year. Some version of the same releasing of my human control to the wiser divine control. THY WILL BE DONE. But it was so hard to say and do – to relinquish my will and my control –I had to repeat it every night and a hundred times in between.

I sent Eddie a television set which cost over a hundred dollars to ship, more than the price of the television itself. And since he had no way, and neither did his buddies, of playing video games or communicating with the folks back home, I sent him a computer. H#1 sent him money and all kinds of truly basic and necessary supplies. These soldiers were dispatched into this war zone with insufficient resources. It was appalling. Additionally appalling, Eddie told us about the cruelty of the weather, the climate, the living conditions of the people, the lack of sanitation, and the rampant disease.

While working on a truck motor, leaning over under the raised hood, another truck backed into Eddie, jarring him terribly and injuring his back. Then he developed trouble breathing. His lungs couldn't adapt to the sweltering days and frigid nights and he was life-flighted to Germany and, mercifully, sent home to Walter Reed. He had a long road to recovery, and for all this Eddie was granted 10% disability for the accompanying PTSD.

I had always understood what Gram meant when she said the greatest blessing of her life was that her two sons both came home safely from their enlistments in World War II. My gratitude for Eddie's safe-though-injured return was and is ongoing. I have never been unmindful that when Andy and Nick survive each day, it is also a blessing of the most generous proportions.

My personal dark night of the soul continued. I was humiliated to be a marriage and family therapist who was twice divorced. Steve Perkins solution: apply to become a Clinical Member of American Association for Marriage and Family Therapy -- AAMFT – which is quite a privilege. It is rare that someone with (only) a master's degree is admitted to this select group. Under Steve's direction, although it took two years, I jumped through all the hoops and became one of the elite. Steve was such a brilliant therapist. Take something you're humiliated by and elevate it so you cannot possibly be ashamed any longer. We don't so much solve the problem, which was unsolvable – I was twice-divorced--but we change the emphasis. I never forgot that therapy teaching.

Another issue I had in the early days after H#2 left was a resurfacing of the nightmares that began when H#1 left: I was physically afraid to be alone at night. Both because H#2 was gone and because of his behavior after he left, I was again having severe sleeping troubles. That was solved when I moved into the condo which was wired for a security system. The $39.00 monthly fee was my favorite bill! I set the alarm every time I left the condo, and set it at night before I climbed the stairs. All four condos in our little pod knew when one of our security alarms went off. Also, the phone rang almost immediately with the security company checking to make sure it was just an error and not an emergency. I loved that security system! And for the first five years in the condo, I had the company of the unwaveringly loyal Madi, who had become *my* German shepherd.

I stayed in touch with Kenny and Lena, and we're in touch to this day. H#2 told them the reason the farm was sold was because I didn't like it. However, when H#2 vanished from their lives and I stayed in touch, they doubted the truth of his explanation. As long as I was in Akron, Kenny and Lena and I met every other month or so for supper and mutual support. Like all of us, they, too, had their heart break when addiction took the life of one of their children. Nobody gets out unscathed.

Thanks to the robust demand for therapists and the reputation of my new practice, I was very busy at Akron Family Institute. I worked four long days and played with my darling Mickey the fifth day of the week. The exciting news was that Jen was pregnant again. In May of 2004, Mickey would have a sibling. The bad news was, that since Nick finished college and training and now had a great job, Jen would stay home with the two kids and I would not be needed for that one day a week. However, thanks to Jen's inclusion of me in their lives, while the cat (Nick) was away working, the four little mice (Jen, me and the two kids) would play and shop and hang out.

Nonetheless, weekends were long, and as I had when H#1 left, when H#2 left, I started writing again. When H#1 departed, I felt the need to write a romance novel, *Heart*, and create a fictional romance since I had been unable to create a romance in real life. This time, what came to me was not only entirely different, but, in fact, dark and sobering: *Only Her Naked Courage*. The story that began materializing was of a woman, a social worker; the heroine of the earlier *Heart* had been a teacher. My heroines changed profession as I did. Imagine that! This social worker was a single mother of two little girls and the book began with a fairytale romance. Then, perhaps metaphorically, the social worker, happily married and loving life, is kidnapped and tortured.

It occurred to me that I needed to design a roadmap of recovery from trauma. While twenty years before, I walked myself through recovering enough to still believe in romance, this time I was walking myself through recovering from having my sense of control and everything in which I had invested and believed stripped from me. Losing our personal control is, indeed, the definition of trauma – whether a tsunami, a crime, or a relationship. Powerlessness causes stress. Post-traumatic stress disorder is the group of symptoms which arise from stress reactions of the body and brain when one is traumatized by losing personal control.

Oh, good grief, you may be thinking: it was just a divorce. People get divorced every day. It's not a big deal. Perhaps it would seem so. One of the more poignant stories in *The Many Faces of*

PTSD, a book I would later write on trauma, concerns a young woman whose "trauma" was that her brother was a peeping Tom. No matter where she went in the house, he had peep holes and was able to see what she was doing. Of course, he didn't watch her all the time. She just never knew when he was watching and when he wasn't, in her bedroom, the bathroom, the kitchen. It was possible at any moment that she was under surveillance. He never touched her. He never verbally abused her. He kept her in a constant state of stress and paranoia. Their parents refused to believe her. He was the one assumed to be telling the truth, despite the peep holes she kept finding.

Trauma means different things to different people. The kidnapped social worker was the story my psyche unveiled for me. It was the story I wrote. I love that story. It's set in Durham, in my childhood home. Sara is the name of the social worker; her best friend is Karen, who, I imagined, lives on a farm, like my longtime girlhood friend Karen. The most fictional part of the story is that the hero, Sara's new husband, although he cannot understand what is happening, grows and changes. He takes the opportunity he is given, blooms where he's planted, alters his priorities and becomes a caring and devoted father to the little girls while Sara is missing and, later, recovering. The story was published in a most unusual way, but that is in the future. For these moments in the early 2000s, I was simply working on bringing it to life on the page.

We had lots of parties at the condo, thanks to the conniving of Christine, one of the therapists. She'd stir up interest and find a date that seemed to suit most of the therapists then announce, usually at a staff meeting: "We're going to have a party," on such and such a date, "and we'll have it at Susan's because she has the best space. Right, Susan?"

The condo was a great open space and I loved entertaining. My new home hosted family birthdays, complete with smashing piñatas in the garage, Akron Family parties, Mom's visits, Skip and Molly passing through on their travels, and family suppers with one son or another or multiples. Andy and I orchestrated a huge party for his wife whose birthday is the day after Cinco de Mayo. I enjoyed every minute of hosting each and every party.

Two delightful experiences from this period were two weddings, Skip's daughter Gretchen, marrying her John, and my Andy, marrying his Tiffany. Both were beautiful weddings and my mom was able to attend each. Gretchen and John would go on to have Toby, the ultimate list maker, who can tell you the top ten . . . anything. He is a funny kid. Andy and Tiff brought Morgan into our lives, a child with talents and interests that run all over the map and an insatiable appetite for House of Hunan Monkey Roll!

2008

The first eight years of being on my own passed in fits and starts. The grandest delight was time with Mickey and her now four-year-old brother, Nicholas. We called ourselves The Play Pals and invented games in which the kids had to jump on my bed, pretending to be dogs who performed amazing feats; a veterinary game in which the stuffed animals were brought to the vet, Mickey, with imaginary diseases; and a lion game in which Mickey, the mother lion, got to smack her brother, the baby lion, when he wandered too near the pretend creek. Then at night we'd gather pillows and blankets and sleep in a fort we made under the piano. It was our own private circus!

In addition to sleeping in tents under the piano and our indoor games, we had a repertoire of outside activities. We walked along the canal behind the condo, climbed rocks, and noticed schools of fish. The kids rode the old red trike my father had found along the roadside in Durham. Daddy had rehabbed it for my son, Andy, thirty years before Nicholas was born. Mickey would sit and steer, and Nicholas, standing on the back bumper, would cling to her for dear life.

Their older sister, Bree, joined us when she wasn't in school or with her other grandparents. Bree had another set of involved grandparents, so sometimes the kids went separate ways. We all enjoyed both options.

When we four were together, we had our special suppers: Bree and I had baked potatoes, peas and applesauce. Mickey and Nicholas had "Papa Plates," which consisted of a few rolled-up pieces of ham, a couple crackers, a piece or two of cheese, a few slices of fruit – apple or strawberry – and miniature marshmallows. Perhaps a bit of chocolate, too.

I don't think I've mentioned that when Mickey started to talk, she couldn't say the "g" sound for grandma. She began calling me, "papa." It stuck. Everyone started calling me papa, and many of Nick and Jen's friends simply knew me as Papa Susan.

My mom came to visit often, and I made many solitary trips to Allentown to spend time with her. My retired brother was the wonderful stability in her life, coming to see her, taking her to his family for all the celebrations and many of the just plain normal days, and watching over her and checking on her regularly by phone. I did the same, calling a couple times a week.

She was doing well. Her arthritis was a challenge and she took more and stronger arthritis medicine as well as more and more Xanax to sleep every night. She wrote letters and kept the checkbook for her neighbor, Ed, and became the eyes for her blind neighbor, Speed, who loved to make candy. He would come to her door with the ingredients and a pot, and she would combine the chocolate, sugar, milk, and vanilla and stir it on the stove until it came to the correct consistency, then he'd hurry home to pour it onto the tray he had prepared. They had a sweet friendship.

Speed, who had been a professional artist, was now blind and deaf. He struggled with depression. This life care center had apartments surrounding a central five-story atrium. Mom and her three widowed lady friends and Ed, for whom she wrote checks, and Speed, for whom she stirred candy, all lived on the fifth floor.

Outside each of their doors was a sturdy wooden banister which surrounded an open area from Floor One to the ceiling of Floor Five. It was on the top of the banister that Mom found Speed one day, ready to jump in hopes that the fall would kill him. She gently, but loudly, since he was deaf, talked him off the ledge. By the time he had put his feet on the floor again, she had help, but she had single-handedly resolved the crisis.

This lovely, introverted woman, who had always stood in the shadow of her exuberantly extraverted husband, blossomed in her eight and a half years of widowhood. She became the head of committees. She welcomed newcomers. She spent every Monday morning arranging flowers which churches delivered to Westminster Sunday afternoon so the dining room and common spaces might come alive with fresh bouquets. She watered them all week, too.

Mom also designed an exercise program for herself and climbed the five flights of stairs instead of taking the elevator. And my favorite story: each and every Wednesday she drove Mary, who lived on the third floor, to the liquor store so Mary could buy beer. (No beer was sold in Pennsylvania grocery stores in those days!) Then Mary would treat Mom to a sandwich at Burger King, and they'd sit and talk.

One of the things my mother most enjoyed in those last, lonely years, was balancing the checkbook. Miriam Hindenach Rau came from the mathematically gifted Hindenach family. She had been an elementary school teacher. Her gift for math became subservient to her gift of bringing security and comfort to children starting school. Teaching reading was what she was known for—a publisher of first grade reading books had begged her to stop teaching and work for them, teaching other teachers how to teach reading. She declined. She loved the children.

Being able to teach children to read is more unusual than being able to teach them to add or subtract. She, of course, did both, as well as teach them to enjoy being in school, raise their hands, wait their turns, and treat each other kindly. It is fascinating to me that my closest childhood friends, six of them, all had children whom Mrs. Rau taught in first grade. I wish my children had been so blessed.

(One sweet thing I learned about Mrs. Rau is that she had a few extra changes of clothes for first grade boys and girls in case they had "an accident" at school. No need to be embarrassed. She changed their clothes, and asked the parents to send them to school the next day in the clothes in which they'd come home. Meantime, she took their clothes home, washed them, and the next day, when they arrived in Mrs. Rau's clothes, they were simply changed back to their own clean clothes.)

Work at Akron Family continued to be encouraging, sustaining, and the source of my financial security. I was finally able to stop teaching at The University of Akron. I had been there thirty-five years, and it had been a rewarding experience. H#1 had been my boss most of that time, and he had been consistently willing to give me whatever schedule I needed. Of course, I had also accommodated his needs by teaching almost every undergraduate class for which he needed a teacher. And we were making sure our sons were always with a parent.

My friend Alice was an amazing support. She and her significant other, Bob, included me as often as they could, and being friends with the two of them, two wise, caring individuals, had helped me navigate the turbulent waters of single life, which I, then, and still, disliked.

Paula, the PhD who was my supervisor in grad school, was another rock in the churning waters of my new, single life. She and I walked together through her transitioning from therapist to teacher and my transitioning in the opposite direction – from teacher to therapist. We struggled together through the end of our marriages and rejoiced together at her bright and marvelous new beginning with a kind, loving man with whom she'd have two brilliant, funny, delightful children. We talked and shared from the depths of our souls. A soul friend is great solace.

On Christmas morning, 2007, our beautiful energizer bunny of a mother collapsed. She lived until Saturday, February 2, 2008. Skip or I were with her all of that time. Nick and Jen drove me to Allentown for my birthday, January 21st. Mom didn't even realize it was my birthday. She was already confined to bed and fading in and out.

Nick and Jen and I returned to Akron on Tues., January 22nd. On the 29th, Jen called me around 9 a.m. and said, "We have to go to Grandma right now." Within an hour we were on the road. Skip had been staying in mom's apartment and was exhausted. He left for a break when we arrived. By now Grandma was in the nursing home portion of Westminster Village. Because there was no other bed available, she was moved into the Alzheimer's Unit.

Jen and I sat with her all-day Wednesday, January 30th. The comic relief was beyond anything we could have made up. A resident who clearly belonged in the Alzheimer's Unit was confined in a huge white moving cage. This contraption was a sort of playpen with wheels but no floor which the person inside could sort of "steer." This confined woman kept coming into Mom's room demanding that we leave. My therapist skills were inadequate to the job. (I was, however, decidedly more patient than my brother when she shoved her way in the room. He demonstrated for Jen and me how to handle that mobile white cage!

Aides brought an exercise chart and insisted on tacking it on Mom's bulletin board so she could attend classes despite no longer being able to move from her bed. Although she had stopped eating, they brought her a tray for every meal, and were disheartened that nothing was touched. The Alzheimer's patient in the cage continued her visits.

Thursday morning when Jen and I got to Mom's room she was sitting on the side of the bed. This felt absolutely miraculous. She looked at us as though she couldn't get us into focus. She smiled, nonetheless, and seemed to know us, but it was as though we were fading in and out. She said, "I'm dying, aren't I?"

"Yes, mama," I answered through my tears. "Are you ready to go see Daddy?"

"He's here," Jen told her. "I can feel his presence. He's waiting for you to be ready to go with him."

She nodded her head. Then she said something really profound and wise. She left us with this sort of regrettable realization: "I always worried so much about what my hair looked like.

Mom sort of swayed, then, and we helped her lay back down. Those were the last words she spoke.

When she fell asleep, we walked across the street to the shopping plaza and bought her a beautiful new nightie. We washed it in the apartment, and then cut it straight up the back so it would cover her but not pull. We helped her into it, and sat with her from Thursday until Saturday evening.

Jen and I played Scrabble and rummy and talked so she could hear our voices and know we were there. I kept a hand on her arm or leg. A couple times she lifted her right arm and held her hand up in the air. "She's reaching for Grandad," we decided. She would hold her arm up for twenty minutes or so at a time.

Friday evening, I asked the hospice nurse if I should stay in the room with her that night. "If you'd like to be with her when she dies, it would be a good idea." I did.

The horror of that night was that we could never get ahead of her pain. It was early morning before my darling mother transitioned into a place where the pain could no longer reach her. The blessing of that night was that she had a nurse I had never seen before. His name was Dave, the name my mother always called my father, although his given name was David. This nurse/angel would gently touch her forehead and quietly and calmly say to her, "Miriam, It's Dave. I'm right here, and I have something for you to swallow to help with the pain."

Of all the nurses in all the world with all the names in the world, this gentle Dave who was there to minister to her must have been her greatest comfort.

The Alzheimer's resident in her clumsy white cage continued visiting.

Jen and I took turns going back to the apartment to shower or call Skip, or Nick, who called his brothers.

It was almost 5:30 Saturday evening, February 2, 2008, and Jen and I were once again playing Scrabble when Mom took a long deep breath and went still. I kissed her and told her she was the dearest mama anyone had ever had. Jen said, "We love you Grandma." Just like my mom. No fanfare, no drama. She just slipped, Jen and I know, into my dad's waiting arms.

It was Skip who wrote a moving tribute to our mom and delivered it at her Memorial Service:

MEMORY OF MOM
A LA DR. SEUSS

The earliest memory I have of my mother,

is shopping at Laubach's with Aunt Agnes, none other.

She had me in a harness and leash, you see,

I wasn't very big, not much past her knee.

The shopping it seemed like an event held weekly,

She didn't go about it all too meekly.

The World War II blackouts brought me quite a fright,

Dear Mother, she comforted me through the long night.

Just after the War there were hobos galore,

Seemed like there always was one at our door.

One such visit I will always remember,

It could have been June, July, or September.

She was doing the laundry when he came to the door,

He had a beard and looked scruffy, scared me to the core.

I was standing on a stool watching her do the wash,

Now don't you know, here comes the zinger,

Little Skip put his hand and arm in the ringer!

Mother handled the ringer event with such ease,

It was over and done in the time you could sneeze!

She put it in reverse and out came the arm,

She checked it over…no harm.

She sent me to school at Durham Elementary,

In those days you walked and needed no sentry.

In all kinds of weather, yes, uphill both ways,

I walked home for lunch in the earliest days.

Susan was aboard by now, don't you know,

Mother loved and nurtured, we continued to grow.

Mother worked so hard, I remember it well,

She did it with such grace, you sure couldn't tell.

I'd get up in the morning, at the desk she would sit,

Doing homework for Kutztown – science, math, and kids' lit.

She got a job teaching at a one-room school,

Grades 1 - 4, now isn't that cool?

Another event that now seems traumatic,

(No harm done if I'd only remained static.)

Boys were playing war, shooting BB guns at each other,

Not a good thing to do . . . Oh, Brother!

From behind a tree I stuck out my head,

In an instant in my eye, I had unwanted lead.

Scared to death, home I went,

My arrival could be called HELL-BENT.

As I came flying in the door,

Mother was vacuuming the living room floor.

"Mother, I think I've been shot in the eye."

She dropped the cleaner and, on the fly,

She bothered not to ask how, where, or why.

Now here my memory is a bit fuzzy,

I can't remember the order of events,

But happily this story is in past tense.

The hospital it was for three days on my back,

Mother was there to keep recovery on track.

Thankfully home with effects oh so nil,

A little bit of ointment and nary a pill.

A wonderful cook was our mother,

The peach cream pie, I preferred no other.

She would feed a houseful of family and friends,

She pulled out all the stops, her menu no ends.

Variety and flavor and quantity were there,

Yet she did it with grace and very little flair.

Alone on a mountain in Maine I reflect,

We all know from Mother there is no disconnect.

Miriam H. Rau, I write this today,

In hopes you can hear me and you're not far away.

With complete devotion, your son I remain,

Until sometime in the future we'll meet once again.

David M. Rau, Jr 2/3/2008

No eye was dry, including Skip's. It was a perfect tribute to the quiet, grace-filled mother we adored.

Gretchen, Skip's younger daughter, sat in front of me holding baby Tobias who was three and a half months old. I thought of my mother saying that when someone dies in a family, someone will just have had or will soon be having a baby in that same family.

Uncle Lee, her one living sibling, showed everyone the scar on his finger where Mom had nipped him with an axe eighty-some years before.

At the cemetery, Skip put his arm around me and said, "It's you and me, now, kid."

We requested in the obituary that in memory of Mom everyone donate a book or read a book, or, even better, read a book to a child.

We each sleep under quilts she made us and hear her voice in our heads.

It's surprising that in the dictionary when one searches for the word mother, the definition is not accompanied by her picture. She set the standard and the bar was very, very high.

One more comment about our mother which so set her apart, especially from those mothers who are as loving and nurturing as she was. Most of them seem to feel that their love entitles them to have strong and voiced opinions about the lives of their children. My brother and I can swear on a stack of Bibles, she NEVER once interfered in our lives, gave us opinions or prescriptions, or suggested courses of action.

When I was about to marry H#2, she said, "Susan. He is much younger than you are. This is fine now, but have you thought about how this might play out when you're 60?" I assured her I knew this man's heart and all would be well. Actually, I only made it to 56. And you know what? That woman never said, "I told you so." She was as heart-broken as I was that my trust had been violated.

My brother had no examples of her having any opinions about his choices or his life.

She raised us, and she let go. I wonder sometimes if my three sons think I'm disinterested because I try so hard to emulate her. I hope not.

PART FOUR

FROM MOORING TO MEMORY

No physical ties bind me to Durham and the millrace anymore. My brother and I were talking this week about "all of the family" being gone. We could no longer name the people who live in the houses we knew so well. The village of Durham looks as serene and well-tended as ever, but more polished. It looks like a postcard instead of like home.

My parent's duplex, which they bought for $20,000. in 1939, they sold for $180,000. around 1990. I can't imagine how much that solid, dear house would sell for today. I know I couldn't afford to buy it or to live in Durham.

And, so, for all of us, what we leave behind, what leaves us behind, what passes away and turns to ashes, all simply changes form. We cannot lose what created us, be it people or places or the vast variety of life's experiences. Sometimes I startle my brother when I come around the corner and he pauses to figure out if I'm the mother I have grown to look like or just that younger sister of his. Skip's hands have the same arthritic knuckles our dad had, and like our dad, he rubs his hands to try to relieve the stiffness. I emulate Aunt Agnes as a hostess, wave my hands like Aunt Ruth when I talk, work (for pay and by volunteering) like my father, and channel my mother when I need to be patient.

I am no longer physically moored to the millrace or to the white house on the hill that still looks down on that historic little stream. I no longer climb the uneven stone steps beside the original Durham Furnace. I can't burst through the dark cellar and land on one of Gram's black plastic covered chairs to enjoy a second supper.

And, yet, nothing, nothing, can detach or separate me from the millrace. I always will be the Rau girl from Durham. It's who I must be. It's the best of me.

Historic steps beside Durham Furnace. (photo: Martin Stemler, 2013)

PART FIVE

A SHORT HISTORY OF DURHAM

DAVE RAU'S "HISTORY OF DURHAM, PENNSYLVANIA"

Presented to the Durham Historical Society, November 27, 1988

Dave Rau at the podium.

Good evening: May I say that if you are finished listening to me before I finish speaking – raise your hand.

Durham Township was organized June 13, 1775, 213 years ago, and it is one of the smallest of the 29 townships in Bucks County. This township contains 6410 Acres-plus. According to records, this township had white settlers as early as 1682, and here it is 1988 and they are still settling in Durham Township.

Durham is principally watered by a fine stream that bears its name, and its tributaries, formed by two main branches in Springfield Township, and both from springs. One rises just west of Springtown and by some called Funk's creek, and the other is the southern part of the township and it is called "Cook's" creek. This name was formerly applied to the stream down to its mouth of the Delaware, but is now given to its southwest and main tributary. The earliest name given it was "Schook's Creek" and "Cook's" creek may be a corruption of it, as the origin of the latter cannot be traced. We are told that "Schook" is a Pennsylvania Dutch word that signifies "of a sudden" or "by fits and starts" which fitly expresses the sudden rise and fall of the stream. May I say that the geological theory is, that this valley was the bed of a river before the glacial period, and the Delaware had burst through the mountains at the Water Gap.

In the Village Center is the four-room school building with the eastern portion of the building being built in 1881 at a cost of $2728.33. The rooms added on the western side were built in 1928. If you note the western wall of this addition, you will see a re-alignment of the brick wall of this addition for the wall fell in while constructing due to a storm. The bell that was in the belfry has been removed and may now be seen in the entrance way at the Durham-Nockamixon Elementary School. This building and grounds were sold by the Palisades School District in September 1983 for $40,000. The purchases at that time gave Durham Township several acres for a ball-field and play-ground. This same property was recently sold with 2.42 acres for $275,000.

Let's go to the top of Durham Hill for a bit of religion. The first social, educational and religious impulse that came to this township was in 1727 when the Durham Furnace was built. In this year of 1727, we find Presbyterians worshipping here and we are told that the Presbytery of New Brunswick sent supplies to Durham as early as 1739 and that led to the organization of the Durham Presbyterian Church in 1742. In 1812 Mr. and Mrs. William Long conveyed an acre of ground to the trustees of the English Presbyterians, the German Reformed and the German Lutheran congregations at a cost of $30. In 1837 the old church building was too small and was torn down. That corner stone for the new church is a part of the Lutheran Church. In 1963 the creation of the Durham-Springtown Parish took place. Note the picture on the wall below the clock of the horse and buggy parade around Durham Church in 1912.

Now, to the adjoining cemetery which received its charter on the 15th day of September 1862. I hold here a copy of the charter which is 114 years old. An interesting note, found in this charter tells us that for digging, filling in, and sodding a grave 5' deep for a person over 12 years of age, the cost shall be $3. And for those under 12 years the cost shall be $2.

From the cemetery we go east to the Borough of Riegelsville where we will note that of the 44 tracts that made up Durham there were three of the tracts, #32, #33 and #36 that are now the Borough with a total of 641 acres. Of course, you will also note that the Borough has since that time annexed around three hundred acres from Durham Township in January 1969.

On to the Furnace School House built in 1855 and then it was destroyed by a fire in 1876. This was also a graded school with a second floor. The ground for this school was donated by Cooper and Hewitt and opened in 1877 at a cost of $1600. Exclusive of the porch which we are told cost around $100. the former Furnace School is now the home of Mr. and Mrs. William Free who reside on Stouts Valley Road between the former Red Bridge and Route 212. Records tell us that some of the teachers in this school house were: James Blackhouse, whose proficiency in math was extraordinary; John Ross, who later became a judge of the Supreme Court of Pennsylvania; Thomas McKeen, who later became President of Easton National Bank; and Richard Horner, who taught at a salary of seven shilling, six pence per day: $1.06.

As to the Walking Purchase, which had its first meeting of the Indians with the proprietaries to carry out the provisions of the treaty of 1686 ("where the metes and bounds were to be made definite") was held in the meadows of the same vicinity of this Furnace School and this was in the year of 1734 and then continued at Pennsbury and then on to Philadelphia. The walk started on the 22nd day of April 1735 and took nine days to complete. An old Indian trader named Wilson was in charge of the meetings.

Moving on to the intersection of Route 611 and Route 212 we find the Durham Cave which is one of the natural features of interest in Durham Township and is located on the north side of Durham Creek near its mouth but now, at this time, the cave is partially destroyed by the blasting away of the limestone rock. This cave is about 150' long averaging 12' in height and from 4' to 40' in width. As you enter, the floor descends with a fine spring partly covering the floor with water. A passage in about the middle of the cave led off to the right to a room about 8 x 12 which was called in olden times Queen Esther's Drawing Room which was named after an Indian woman. The Bucks County Conservancy has recently made an offer to secure this cave from the International Paper Company. I have been in touch with Linda Mead of the Conservancy and told her that the Board of Supervisors are interested that this cave be secured by the Conservancy and that the Board might be able to give some financial support in securing same. A tour of this cave might be possible at a later date and the Board will, through the Historical Society, keep the residents aware if this should happen.

Abraham Houpt says that the first Durham Boat about 66' in length was built on the river bank near the mouth of the Durham Creek by one Robert Durham who was the manager and engineer at the Durham Furnace. The boat was made nearly in the shape of an Indian canoe with its 6' beams and 3' in depth. It was supposedly propelled by setting poles, although sometimes oars were used. These boats after many years of hauling fell into disuse when the Delaware Division Canal was opened in 1832. As early as 1758 Durham Boats were used to transport flour from John Van Campens mill at Minisink to Philadelphia, and, of course, in the hauling of the pig iron produced at the furnace. This is one of the Pig Iron Moulds used at that time to harden the metal and make it possible to haul same. The last Durham Boat to leave Durham for Philadelphia was on March 6, 1867. Don't forget, that these same Durham Boats carried George Washington and his troops across the Delaware into New Jersey on Christmas night of 1776.

I have been unable to secure any information regarding the Catholic Church which was located on the right-hand corner of Route 212 facing the Delaware River. I well remember the church on this corner and feel that perhaps history of this church might be found in the Catholic Church in Haycock.

Leaving this intersection and going down Route 611 to the former Kutzler Garage, now the Ed Stibgen garage, we note, was the home of the Durham Post Office, known in those days as the Monroe Post Office, established in 1840 and the second oldest Post Office in the nation. Riegelsville Post Office opened in 1847. Durham's first Post Master was John H. Johnson.

Going from this location and proceeding up the hill to the area of the Cascade Lodge on the hill was the Monroe School House built in 1836. It is now occupied by Mr. and Mrs. Sidney Yates. The previous owners, a school teacher and a social worker, spent much time and money putting this building in living condition. Records tell us that this school house was built very much in the rough.

On Gallow's Hill Road we locate the former Rufe's School property with records telling us that it was purchased for the Lutheran and Reformed Congregations covering one acre and eight perches for 10 shillings, with the collections to purchase same coming from members of the congregations. The school was built in 1861 replacing a log school house built in 1802. This is now the home of Mr. and Mrs. Carl Ackerman and is located one block south of the intersection of Lehnenburg and Gallows Hill Road, it being the first house on the right.

Proceeding on north down Gallows Hill Road toward Route 212 and crossing same onto the Old Furnace Road we come to the Mansion House now known as the George Taylor Home which is the first home you will meet on Old Furnace Road and owned by George Ervin. Colonel George Taylor, one of the signers of The Declaration of Independence, was living in Durham when, on August 2, 1776, he affixed his signature on that immortal document. In 1755, at a time when he and Samuel Flowers were lessees of the Durham Works, they made Cannon shot for the Provincial Government, presumably for the French and Indian War. This is one of the shot that I am showing you and weighing a bit over six pounds. At a time when he signed this document, he was a member of the Continental Congress. Along with the production of shot, shell and cannon was also produced. Don't forget that the great chain that stretched across the Hudson at West Point to block the British from advancing up the river, was produced in Durham. The links of this chain each weighed 250 pounds.

Finally, let me say that Durham was slow in laying out it's roads because the river was close and travel took place on the river. However, in 1747 a road was laid out following the Indian Trail through Springfield and Richland townships over which pig iron was hauled to Sumneytown.

Various bill of sales, the original Secretary's tin box to carry papers and books in Durham Township, newspapers dated over 100 years ago, pictures of the engines that travelled over the Q & E Railroad through Durham, permits and deeds very old, are shown here for your interest.

P.S. I forgot to tell you to note the Bill advertising the Sauer Kraut Supper for 65 cents in which it states that if you don't like sauerkraut then you may have lima beans for the replacement.

(I, Susan Rau Stocker, Dave Rau's daughter, am sharing publicly this speech my dad gave. I would guess that the objects he describes as visual aids are all to be found in the Durham Township office or will be in the possession of the Durham Historical Society.)

Durham mill with what was later Melchior's store, left background.

ACKNOWLEDGEMENTS

This book is as much of a community effort as was growing up in Durham and features many of the same characters. Skip and Molly Rau read the first drafts; Skip remembered great details; Molly named the book. Lou Ann Anderson, Karen Melchior, and Suzanne and Marty Stemler all participated in some early "Durham" phone calls where we reminisced. I continued writing. I awakened one morning wondering if Suzanne would consider editing. She cautiously agreed. Everything changed. My writing kept revising itself to meet the standards and finesse of her editing. I seriously re-wrote. We worked together – two childhood friends in their seventies. Suzanne changed the way I thought about this project and myself as a writer. The book blossomed from some family tales about the ancestors and growing up in Durham during the 1950's, to a history of that time gone by and the way many of us survived and thrived because we had been well fed and watered early in life.

We had been taught we belonged and mattered; we had each other. Suzanne's husband, Marty, contributed some awesome photos. I asked my college roommate, Cathy Lindsay Biggs, an award-winning artist, if she'd do a cover for the book. She said, "No." I begged. She relented. She and her husband Bill drove to Durham and took more awesome photos. "I forgot how beautiful Durham is," Cathy reported. Bill figured out how to get the title of the book tucked into her perfectly depicted painting of Durham. Suzanne taught herself technical skills neither of us had imagined needing. My grandson Nicholas made house calls to provide computer savvy.

It takes a village. We are a village. I gratefully acknowledge my growing up village and our quite grown-up virtual village. Mooring at the Millrace is a personal memoir and a communal labor of love. We leaned on each other back when – and we still do.

ABOUT THE AUTHOR

Born into a family of story-tellers, Susan has spent her life reading and writing. As a college teacher and a mental health therapist, she tries to build bridges and strives to leave people in better shape than she found them. If you want some excellent writing, she suggests Richard Rohr or Gabor Mate'. If you want to feel you're at the kitchen table, talking things over, or listening to a story or two, join Susan. The coffee's on the house!

www.ingramcontent.com/pod-product-compliance
Lightning Source LLC
Chambersburg PA
CBHW071139130626
46553CB00004B/1444